OXFORD ENGLISH MONOGRAPHS

D0082032

LOUIS MACNEICE

THE POET IN HIS CONTEXTS

PETER McDONALD

CLARENDON PRESS · OXFORD

1991

Oxford University Press, Walton Street, Oxford OX2 6DP
Oxford New York Toronto
Delhi Bombay Calcutta Madras Karachi
Petaling Jaya Singapore Hong Kong Tokyo
Nairobi Dar es Salaam Cape Town
Melbourne Auckland
and associated companies in
Berlin Ibadan

Oxford is a trade mark of Oxford University Press

Published in the United States
by Oxford University Press, New York

British Library Cataloguing in Publication Data
McDonald, Peter
Louis MacNeice: the poet in his contexts.—
(Oxford English monographs).
1. Poetry in English. MacNeice, Louis, 1907–1963
I. Title
821.912
ISBN 0–19–811766–3

Library of Congress Cataloging in Publication Data
McDonald, Peter.
Louis MacNeice: the poet in his contexts / Peter McDonald.
p. cm.—(Oxford English monographs)
Includes bibliographical references (p.   ) and index.
1. MacNeice, Louis, 1907–1963—Criticism and interpretation.
I. Title. II. Series.
PR6025.A316Z79 1991   821'.912—dc20   90–7933
ISBN 0–19–811766–3

Typeset by Hope Services (Abingdon) Ltd
Printed and bound in
Great Britain by Biddles Ltd,
Guildford and King's Lynn

For my parents

Acknowledgements

For permission to quote from the *The Collected Poems of Louis MacNeice*, I am grateful to Faber and Faber Limited, and for permission to quote from poems and other writings of Louis MacNeice to David Higham Associates and the Estate of Louis MacNeice. In particular I wish to thank Mr Jon Stallworthy of Wolfson College, Oxford, who has given help and support beyond the call of duty for even the best of Literary Executors. I am grateful also for permission given to quote from various MacNeice papers held by the Bodleian Library, Oxford.

I have been fortunate in receiving a great deal of help from many people while writing this book. I am grateful to Dr John Kelly of St John's College, Oxford, for his copious encouragement while supervising the thesis on which this book is based; I wish to thank also Dr Roy Park and Dr Helen Cooper of University College, Oxford, Mrs Edna Longley of The Queen's University of Belfast, Professor Alan Heuser of McGill University, Montreal, Mr John Hilton, Sir Stephen Spender, and Professor Adolphe Haberer of the University of Lyon II, all of whom have given generously of their time and advice. Needless to say, I alone am responsible for my errors. It is my great regret that neither Hedli MacNeice nor Dan Davin lived to see the publication of this book: both were of considerable help at different stages of my work, and are remembered here with gratitude and affection.

My work on MacNeice began with the support of the Department of Education of Northern Ireland at University College, Oxford, was continued with the generous help of a Junior Research Fellowship at Christ Church, Oxford, and completed at Pembroke College, Cambridge. I am most grateful to all these institutions. Further invaluable support came from my wife Karen, and from Professor Patrick O'Brien and Mrs Cassy O'Brien of Oxford. My greatest debt is expressed in the dedication.

Contents

Author's Note

All quotations in the text from MacNeice's poetry are taken from *The Collected Poems of Louis MacNeice*, ed. E. R. Dodds (1966), unless indicated otherwise, when references will be found in the Notes.

References in the Notes to MacNeice's miscellaneous prose pieces have been expanded, where appropriate, to include the *Selected Literary Criticism of Louis MacNeice*, ed. Alan Heuser (Oxford, 1987) (cited as Heuser).

Place of publication is London, unless specified otherwise.

Introduction:
Canons and Contexts

ANY study of a fairly well-known modern poet which announces itself as contextual might well seem to be a cautious enough exercise, a filling-in of 'background' valuable mainly to the particular poet's admirers. That this is unlikely to be true in Louis MacNeice's case is neither the fault of the poet nor entirely the responsibility of his critics: to begin an examination of MacNeice in his contexts is to encounter, very quickly, the limitations and forceful orthodoxies of more than one critical canon. The suggestion that a critical re-evaluation of MacNeice is in order, and indeed that it has to some extent already begun, need not mean that the two principal canons within which the poet tends to be interpreted—that of the so-called 'Auden group' of 1930s poets, and that of Anglo-Irish literature—are necessarily invalid: what it does mean, however, is that their status and conditioning have to be examined, that their apparently discrete areas of 'context' have to be critically related to each other. It could be plausibly maintained that the difficulties from which Mac-Neice's reputation has always suffered have their origin in his poetic violation of certain canonical (and contextual) norms: a 1930s poet who insisted on his Irishness; an Irish-born poet who lived most of his life in England. In one case, he seems to threaten the critical elevation of Auden as a poet representative of both a generation and a time; in the other, he appears to undermine the stability of an orthodox notion of national 'identity'. Critics who have invested heavily in such canonical schemes have always attempted to put the poet into an evaluative contest, whether it is MacNeice versus Auden, or England versus Ireland. Few better examples could be found of the 'hidden agenda' of much apparently 'literary' criticism, whereby games of evaluation are played in order to strengthen what is in fact an extra-literary orthodoxy, whether the English myth of the 1930s, with all its built-in parabolic meaning for the relation between the artist and politics, or the Irish myth of Irishness, with its menacing, but ultimately empty, phantom of national 'identity'.

Studying Louis MacNeice in his contexts, then, must entail standing at a distance from those contexts and their assumptions. The trap which the dominant canons have set for MacNeice's readers is one of comparative evaluation, and this study refuses to place MacNeice in any poetic, or nationalistic, league tables. In her 1982 book *The Cave of Making*, Robyn Marsack concludes that 'If MacNeice is not in the company of Yeats and Eliot, among modern poets, his achievement is still considerable.'[1] This kind of formulation is almost guaranteed to leave the achievement unconsidered, and does not begin to bring the canonical structures of modern poetry into focus. All too often, MacNeice's poetry suffers under the canonically constrained codes of such evaluation.

In *History and Value* Frank Kermode writes that 'canons are complicit with power; and canons are useful in that they enable us to handle otherwise unmanageable historical deposits'.[2] Kermode's primary example, the literary image of a historical period we call the 1930s, exercises an abiding fascination in late twentieth-century Britain, but the 'historical deposits' which this image processes are perhaps not entirely what he supposes them to be. Despite his half-nostalgic return visits to the 'forgotten' proletarian fiction of the decade, Kermode accepts broadly the Auden-centred image which incorporates the so-called '1930s myth': this myth, which formed the backbone of Samuel Hynes's *The Auden Generation* (1976), had its origin in the decade itself, and its principal authors were highly active literati who transformed the failures of their own 1930s into a parable of the liberal dilemma in time of crisis. The Auden who is central to this myth is not the American poet of the 1940s, but the experimental radical of the early 1930s. MacNeice's place in the myth has to be a subordinate one: Kermode, like Hynes before him, must regard the poet primarily as the author of *Autumn Journal*, who must be put firmly behind Auden in the poetic rankings as a 'minor poet'.[3]

To be a 'minor' poet and to be an Irish poet is often the same thing for critics: W. B. Yeats is, on the face of it, an exception, though a surprising proportion of the Yeats industry seems to regard his 'major' status as transcending the still-continuing concerns of his

---

[1] Robyn Marsack, *The Cave of Making: The Poetry of Louis MacNeice* (Oxford, 1982), 151.
[2] Frank Kermode, *History and Value: The Clarendon Lectures and the Northcliffe Lectures 1987* (Oxford, 1988), 115.
[3] Ibid. 66.

nationality. If MacNeice is a minor poet, the 'major' poet, Auden, can be used to handle our 'historical deposits', so that, in Kermode's phrase, 'The canon, in predetermining value, shapes the past and makes it humanly available, accessibly modern.'[4] The Auden–MacNeice opposition, rather like the common eighteenth-century critical obligation to choose between Dryden and Pope, rests on a broad interpretation of the past, and a present orientation with regard to the future. In the case of the 1930s myth, Auden's development from the politically *engagé* to the politically disillusioned, from the urgent (if opaque) messages of *Poems* (1930) to the elegant resignation of 'September 1, 1939', functions as a parable of the irreconcilability of poetry and politics, keeping intact the liberal consciousness but questioning the notion of feasible individual action. By placing overtly political poems such as 'Spain 1937' at the heart of his reading of Auden, Kermode in fact strengthens the myth's paradigm of the 1930s, celebrating rather than, as is more common, ruefully deploring the ideological wild oats sown in a great poet's youth. MacNeice's scepticism about political commitment in the 1930s is, from this perspective, spoiling the fun; his continued scepticism about the motives for the post-1930s 'disillusion' of many artists has to be ignored (as have inconvenient details of Auden's actual, as opposed to mythic, 1930s career). Although Valentine Cunningham is more wary than Kermode of consigning MacNeice to a 'minor' classification, his encyclopaedic *British Writers of the Thirties* reads the decade as a slow communal discovery of the pervasiveness of original sin, seeming to demand from the writers the 'Peccavis' against which MacNeice set himself in 1941: 'And I have no intention of recanting my past. Recantation is becoming too fashionable; I am sorry to see so much self-flagellation, so many *Peccavis*, going on on the literary Left. We may not have done all we could in the Thirties, but we did do something.'[5]

If MacNeice was, from the myth's point of view, 'uncommitted' during the 1930s, he was unrepentant after the decade, and refused to allow the issues raised then to be dropped in favour of the safe haven of artistic integrity. In some senses, MacNeice continued to be a '1930s poet' until his death; like Auden, he understood that the crucial issues raised in the decade went beyond those of whether or

---

[4] Ibid. 117.
[5] MacNeice, 'The Tower that Once', *Folios of New Writing*, 3 (1941), repr. Heuser, pp. 123–4.

not to join the Communist party, and he understood also that they did not go away with 1939. Defining MacNeice as 'minor' is, in fact, a good way of making Auden into the poet the myth requires him to be, and this was probably put most honestly by Samuel Hynes when he wrote that the business of MacNeice criticism should be to explain why 'MacNeice is a good minor poet and Auden is a daunting major one'.[6]

Time has perhaps made such honesty less practicable, and Hynes has changed his critical position significantly. Reviewing MacNeice's *Selected Poems* in 1989, he switches contexts:

> For a time after his death his reputation sagged, perhaps because the myth of the Auden Gang was growing in the academies, and he had never really been a full-time gang member . . . But he seemed to have won no secure status in the poetic history of his own time, he didn't quite fit—as he never had.
>
> That this situation has altered in recent years is due in large measure to the way in which MacNeice has been adopted as an ancestor by the present generation of Northern Irish poets. . . . It seems entirely reasonable that the younger Irish poets, in their own urgent time, should look to him as a model of how to engage the history of the present moment, and yet remain a maker, as he did.[7]

Hynes's 'professional lachrymose Irishman' of *The Auden Generation*[8] 'didn't quite fit' as anything but the author of *Autumn Journal* or the heavily Audenesque play *Out of the Picture*; but the subsidiary role which MacNeice played in what Hynes saw as the five-act tragedy of the decade is no longer a sufficient excuse for a low evaluation of his poetry. The context which has made the difference, that of Ireland's recent 'urgent time', makes reading MacNeice within another canon possible, and clearly enables Hynes to praise the poet warmly, without the continual 'minor' implications of his earlier, Auden-centred readings. To 'engage the history of the present moment' is also, following Kermode's argument, the advantage of a literary canon; if MacNeice does not quite fit the bill in the 1930s canon, he is, as Hynes perceives, central to an Irish one.

However, the canon of Irish literature, being older than that of the

---

[6] Samuel Hynes, 'Auden and MacNeice', *Contemporary Literature*, 14/3 (1973), 383.

[7] Samuel Hynes, 'Like the Trees on Primrose Hill', *London Review of Books*, 2 Mar. 1989, pp. 6–7.

[8] Samuel Hynes, *The Auden Generation: Literature and Politics in England in the 1930s* (1976), 334.

'Auden generation', is less easy to see into than Hynes supposes. In this area, MacNeice has always sent the canonical compass bearings haywire, and, Northern Irish poets notwithstanding, appears to be doing so still. Referring to MacNeice in relation to 'Irish literature' is already problematic: might not 'Anglo-Irish literature' be more proper? Does this make MacNeice, then, a part of Anglo-Ireland rather than Ireland? Even at the basic level of naming the canon, there are huge unprocessed deposits of political disagreement and 'post-colonial' anxiety. Anthologies of Irish (or Anglo-Irish) poetry have always given MacNeice a grudging welcome, if they let him in at all: it was not until Paul Muldoon's *Faber Book of Contemporary Irish Poetry* (1986) that the poet figured in a substantial way, and even that must be balanced against Thomas Kinsella's *New Oxford Book of Irish Verse* (1986), from which he is effectively banished.

In recent years, Irish accounts of MacNeice when they have come at all, tend to make clear his physical separation from the country. Although he was certainly less of an exile than, say, Joyce or Beckett, his separation from Ireland is regarded by Seamus Deane as a vital conditioning factor in both the work and its value:

One of the most potent of Irish exiles was Louis MacNeice, who seems at first sight to represent in a particularly hesitant manner many of the dogged issues of provincialism and escape, commitment and evasion. . . . He loved Ireland, North and South, but could stand the oppressions and pettiness of neither one. Yet he did not make his mixed alienation and attachment the material of a defined or defining pose.[9]

At first sight, Deane's generosity is notable, praising MacNeice as 'the harbinger of a secular sensibility that retains a fondness for the sweet charms of myth but prefers the plainer, starker truths of poetry'.[10] Yet the qualities praised all point towards a particular kind of identity, one that is capable of simultaneous 'alienation and attachment' with regard to Ireland: implicit throughout is the motif of *division*, a characteristic easy to associate with Protestants and the North in general. Deane, even in his encomium for MacNeice, works within a theory that has pervaded Irish criticism since the Revival, that of a politically potent (and disastrous) dissociation of sensibility, producing minds torn between one country and another, rendered homeless. Of course, as Deane and others realize, artistic dissociation

---

[9] Seamus Deane, *A Short History of Irish Literature* (1986), 230.
[10] Ibid. 231.

between 'myth' and 'starker truths' is a condition of modernity, and is to be preferred to the consequences of the kind of unity forced into being in the work of Yeats; but this has more than just literary implications, and points towards the pluralism of a 'secular sensibility' on a national scale. Given this, it might reasonably be expected that MacNeice would move somewhere close to the centre of Deane's concerns, and those of other Field Day critics, but this does not happen. What prevents MacNeice's recognition here is the fact that his 'identity' and its 'division' are subject to unexamined critical and political prejudice: they are, from the Nationalist point of view, handicaps, the signs of a radical and historically rooted flaw which the poet shares with the Northern Protestants in general. In a lecture which he gave in 1985, John Wilson Foster spoke of a group of Irish critics whom he christened the 'New Partisans', the 'inheritors of a cultural identity and political stance pulling them one way, but academic practitioners of a discipline whose various imperatives and currencies pull them, by gravity of intellect, another way':[11] much Irish criticism of MacNeice over the years has served to bear out such an observation.

Few Irish critics would be naïve enough to see resistance to MacNeice's inclusion in the national canon as being on literary grounds alone, and Denis Donoghue writes on some of the real reasons for exclusion:

He had no interest in the Irish Literary Revival or the provocations which issued in it, he thought the attempt to revive the Irish language was daft—an error of judgement, in my view—and he deplored, as I do not, Ireland's neutrality in the war. Indeed, what disables MacNeice from consideration as a precursor is that his work touches Irish history and sentiment only occasionally and opportunistically. He wasn't sufficiently interested in what was going on.[12]

Donoghue's criticism is valuable, bringing to the surface some issues which make both MacNeice and his Irish context highly problematic

---

[11]　John Wilson Foster, 'The Critical Condition of Ulster', *The Honest Ulsterman*, 79 (1985), 39.
[12]　Denis Donoghue, rev. of Alan Heuser (ed.), *Selected Literary Criticism of Louis MacNeice*, in *London Review of Books*, 23 Apr. 1987, p. 19. See also subsequent correspondence of 21 May, 4 June, and 25 June, discussed in Tony Roche, 'A Reading of *Autumn Journal*: The Question of Louis MacNeice's Irishness', *Text and Context*, 3 (1988).

as parts of Irish history. However useful this kind of honesty may be, it remains ill-informed: MacNeice's 'interest' in Ireland was a deep and lasting one, in no sense either occasional or opportunistic, and critical work on the poet can make this clear. Yet, even when this has been done, the fact remains that MacNeice does see Irish history differently from Denis Donoghue: the real question is how far such legitimate disagreement can be incorporated within the terms of an Irish literary canon which will permit MacNeice to be a precursor for future poets in the country. Edna Longley's formulation, that Mac-Neice's poetry 'gives the poet a stake in the country and the country a stake in the poet',[13] suggests the need to face up to this kind of disagreement as being in the nature of Irish canonicity, where poetry plays a part in unfinished arguments, in dealing with 'otherwise unmanageable historical deposits'.

One contemporary Irish poet for whom MacNeice has undoubtedly functioned as a precursor of sorts is Paul Muldoon, and his poem '7, Middagh Street' concentrates many of the tensions of MacNeice's contexts, bringing the voices of 'Wystan' and 'Louis' together in a structure that continually refers back to Yeatsian precursor texts. One of the principal ideas refracted through Muldoon's poem is the notion that 'poetry makes nothing happen', an Auden stance (referring back to Yeats) which has taken on many layers of parabolic significance as part of the message encoded in the 1930s myth. Muldoon's 'Wystan' answers Yeats's 'Did that play of mind send out | Certain men the English shot?', with a brisk 'Certainly not', demanding instead: 'If Yeats had saved his pencil-lead | would certain men have stayed in bed?'[14] For the poem's 'Louis', on the other hand, it is another Yeatsian line which offers direction:

> In dreams begin responsibilities;
> it was on account of just such an allegory
> that Lorca
> was riddled with bullets
>
> and lay mouth-down
> in the fickle shadow of his own blood.
> As the drunken soldiers of the *Gypsy Ballads*
> started back for town

[13] Edna Longley, *Louis MacNeice: A Study* (1988), 34.
[14] Paul Muldoon, '7, Middagh Street', *Meeting the British* (1987), 39.

they heard him calling through the mist,
'When I die leave the balcony shutters open.'
For poetry *can* make things happen—
not only can, but *must*—[15]

The poem brings contexts into collision in an appropriate way for
MacNeice, seeing the poetry of the 1930s through an Irish lens, with
Salvador Dali transforming himself into 'O'Daly', and Lorca and
Auden brought into the same orbit as a 1937 *Belfast Newsletter*. The
only stable context within Muldoon's complex poem is in fact the
literary one of Yeats, as problematic as it is pervasive. In this sense,
the poem relocates MacNeice, as it does Auden, within a post-
Yeatsian context to which both Irish and English canons are sub-
ordinate. The anti-canonical pressures of '7, Middagh Street' are
those of contexts refusing to be held in check, 1980s Ireland colliding
with 1930s Britain. The implications of such a collision threaten
canonical stability.

The present study assumes that 'historical deposits' in Ireland have
to be managed more satisfactorily than the effective exclusion of
MacNeice from the canon of Irish literature—or his relegation to
'minor' status within that canon—will allow. It is with that assumption
in mind that it makes an attempt to trace some of the complexities of
the Irish context. In doing this, however, the other dominant context,
that of the English 1930s, cannot be set aside; in fact, the reasons
why MacNeice 'doesn't fit' into one context help to explain his
failure to fit into the other. The critical truism, which has done the
poet more harm than good over the years, that MacNeice is too
English for the Irish and too Irish for the English, fails to register the
anti-canonical forces within MacNeice's work, leaving both canons
secure in their own notions of context, with the poet granted at best a
resident alien status in both.

A more usual angle of approach for a critical study of a poet is that
of the 'internal' logic of development shown by his work. In Mac-
Neice's case, this is certainly important, but it would be unwise to
regard the 'private' side of MacNeice as in some way separable from
the tangled issues of context. Ultimately, the 'internal' context of the
poet's imagination feeds on both 'Irish' and 'English' aspects of his
life; not only this, but, as the poet realized, the apparently personal
context does shed light on more 'public' areas, whether in Irish or

---

[15] Paul Muldoon, '7, Middagh Street', *Meeting the British* (1987), 59.

1930s issues. This study takes a course through MacNeice's career which follows, broadly chronologically, the development of his poetic imagination; but it does not seal off this course from the other contextual problems which the poet raises—in Ireland or in England. This reading of MacNeice will assume that the canons in relation to which his work is often read are all liable to be *changed* by his writing, that the '1930s myth', as much as Irish 'identity', becomes something different once it accommodates his poetry in full. Such an accommodation is, of course, beyond the reach of a single critic, let alone a single book: but the beginnings of a rereading of MacNeice, in the light of Irish poetry, 1930s poetry, and British poetry after Yeats, have in fact been evident for some time, and it will be the aim of this study to provide at least some of the material necessary for them to be pursued further, allowing contextual analysis to complicate the workings of the 'literary' canons which tend to condition our approaches to modern poetry in general.

I
Poems (1935)

I<small>T</small> was MacNeice himself who asserted that 'the best English poets have been those most successfully determined by their context', going on to claim that (in 1935) 'The English context is now more congenial to poets than it has been for a long time.' While this alone is enough to suggest that isolating the poet from the literary/political milieu of England in the 1930s is something of a distortion, it must be qualified by what MacNeice wrote earlier in the same essay, that 'the generalisations so often offered by poets themselves we must accept only as dramatic; they are not scientific rules but are merely a moment in the context of the poet's life and work, just as one character in a play can give the lie to another character'.[1] These two contexts—of historical situation and personal artistic history—are bound together closely in MacNeice's work, and neither, taken alone, will account for that work satisfactorily. The danger in trying to combine the two, however, is that the simplification of compromise may take over from the complication which MacNeice's juxtaposition of the historical and the dramatic implies. It would be unwise, therefore, to expect the bringing-together of what could be termed external and internal contexts of MacNeice's writing to contribute to a hierarchical reading of modern poetry. Whether or not Mac-Neice was, as Anthony Thwaite maintains, 'one of the best poets of the century',[2] the game of putting the poet into a league table should be made more difficult by proper contextual study. In the study of Yeats that represents MacNeice's most deeply considered meditation on the issues of that decade, he insisted on the need to refer poetry back, not only to the life of the poet but to the external conditioning factors of the life around him. The assertion that 'This intimate connection between a poem, its author's life and the wider life beyond the author . . . establishes certain conditions for the truth,

---

[1] MacNeice, 'Poetry To-Day', in G. Grigson (ed.), *The Arts To-Day* (1935), 31, 28 (repr. Heuser, pp. 14, 12–13).
[2] Anthony Thwaite, *TLS*, 14 Jan. 1983, p. 28.

and therefore for the value, of poetry',[3] cannot be simplified into a translation of personal experience into public expression; to do so is to lose the complexity, and creative difficulty, behind MacNeice's 'intimate connection'.

It is necessary to set MacNeice's *Poems* of 1935 in the context of the mid-1930s and to try to establish the role played by that volume in the literary world of the time. This raises questions about aspects of 1930s writing and areas of literary dispute in England during the decade, from which certain themes in MacNeice's poetry may be seen to derive, and to which they, in their turn, contribute. It is often observed that *Poems*, published in the autumn of 1935, marked something of a poetic début for MacNeice, appearing at a time when Auden, Spender, and Day-Lewis were already established names in the literary world. Although MacNeice's poems had been appearing in the right places (such as the *Criterion* and *New Verse*) since the early 1930s, and the volume *Blind Fireworks* had been published by Gollancz in 1929, *Poems* might well be seen as a début of sorts, and one that had considerable impact on the writers and critics of the time. The extent to which the publication of *Poems* tended to be seen as a turning-point for contemporary poetry has generally been forgotten by later writers on MacNeice, or on the 1930s, in their concern to make of him either an artist of substantial imaginative autonomy or something of a lesser Auden. Yet the ease with which, after 1935, MacNeice was established as one of the most important poets of his generation suggests that the contemporary reaction to *Poems* is of direct relevance to any attempt to understand the poet's conception of his own role in the 1930s (which is important all through his career), as well as the position which he did in fact occupy.

By 1935 the change in poetry signalled by the success of Auden and the other poets in *New Signatures* and *New Country* was irreversible. In critical terms, the orthodoxy had shifted decisively to the left. As Samuel Hynes puts it: 'At this time, midway through the thirties, young critics take it as given that political content is un-avoidable for the serious writer.'[4] Yet the initial excitement created

[3] MacNeice, *The Poetry of W. B. Yeats* (1941, repr. 1967), 29.
[4] Samuel Hynes, *The Auden Generation* (1976) 161. Books like John Sparrow's *Sense and Poetry* or Ivor Brown's *I Commit to the Flames* (both 1934) were the last full-scale assaults on the new orthodoxy from the literary critics—the severest review of *Poems* came from the traditionalist *Poetry Review*.

by a new literary movement was beginning to show signs of diminish-
ing by 1935. As political pressures increased from a growing number
of left-wing critics (some of them, like Edgell Rickword and Randall
Swingler, incisive and subtle), writing started to exchange a dynamic
conception of its relation to political change for a more defensive,
almost apologetic, sense of its own independence. Michael Roberts,
who in 1933 had introduced *New Country* by announcing that 'it is
for us to prepare the way for an English Lenin',[5] was insisting by
1935 that 'A poet is essentially a bad party man.'[6] At the same time,
investigation of alternatives to, or developments from, the new
orthodoxy was beginning: David Gascoyne's important *A Short
Survey of Surrealism* of 1935 was the first serious attempt to intro-
duce surrealist principles to the English literary scene, and the New
Burlington Exhibition of surrealist art, which was to attract over
20,000 visitors, was less than a year away. After 1935 the literary
climate did not favour the emergence of new 'political' poets (as the
fates of Charles Madge or Rex Warner testify); the eagerness of the
younger British surrealist writers to win ideological approval from
the left does suggest that 'political' in this context might well be
interpreted in terms of literary stylistics, perhaps even as referring to
the kind of writing to be found in *New Country*. On the dust-jacket
of MacNeice's *Poems*, Faber and Faber announced the arrival of a
writer who, while he had been a contemporary of Auden at Oxford,
was also 'The most original Irish poet of his generation, dour
without sentimentality, intensely serious without political enthusiasm.'
This rather odd description represents an opportune distancing of
MacNeice from what was seen as the *New Country* school of
committed political writing (he had not in fact appeared in either
that anthology or its 1932 predecessor, *New Signatures*). As an
Irishman, he could be presented as somewhat remote from the
insistent Englishness of Auden or Day-Lewis, while the publishers'
disavowal of political commitment, mildly anticipating Yeats's later
description of MacNeice as 'anti-communist',[7] pre-empted ideo-
logically prescriptive criticism without giving up the claim to con-
temporary relevance. What justification the book itself offered for

---

[5] Michael Roberts (ed.), *New Country* (1933), 11.
[6] Michael Roberts, 'Poetry and Propaganda' (from the *London Mercury*, 31/183
(Jan. 1935), repr. in *Selected Poems and Prose*, ed. F. Grubb (Manchester, 1980), 98.
[7] *The Oxford Book of Modern Verse*, ed. W. B. Yeats (1936), p. xxxvii.

this critical reaction was largely along the lines offered by the publishers' blurb.

At first the description of *Poems* as in some way apolitical seems a distortion in view of the gloomy satire of a number of the pieces it contains; in 1935, however, works such as Auden's *The Dance of Death* (1933) or Spender's *Vienna* (1934) were the recent examples of politically committed writing against which a new volume might be measured, while Spender's *The Destructive Element*, also published in 1935, or Day-Lewis's *A Hope for Poetry* (1934) represented substantial pressure for the adoption by poets of explicitly political subject-matter. Of course, by 1935 Auden, Spender, and others were already beginning to turn away, however subtly, from their own political prescriptions; the timing of MacNeice's *Poems* was fortuitous, offering some measure of relief from the insistent messages delivered over the past couple of years by poets and critics alike concerning the necessity of political directives in verse. The volume was to become something of a foil for ideologically prescriptive criticism. Geoffrey Grigson's ranking of MacNeice as 'next in importance to Auden in spite of politicians in criticism who can only see merit under immediate flag-poles',[8] reflects the post-1935 change of mood which *Poems* to some extent encouraged and from which it also benefited. Dilys Powell, whose book on contemporary poetry, *Descent from Parnassus*, had appeared in 1934 without mentioning MacNeice in its sympathetic account of the Auden group, noted with some relief that *Poems* 'has, strange to say, no political allegiances',[9] an observation developed to the point of distortion in John Lehmann's identification of 'poets of a highly distinctive talent of the Auden generation, such as Louis MacNeice, all of whom carefully avoid any political subject'.[10] A more sensible distinction was made by Michael Roberts when he wrote of *Poems*: 'It is didactic poetry, but it is not simply political.'[11] This interpretation, corresponding to the publishers' 'intensely serious without political enthusiasm', suggests a poetic middle way which Powell's review also identified and attempted to place in relation to recent literary history:

[8] Geoffrey Grigson, 'A Letter from England', *Poetry* (Chicago), 69/2 (Nov. 1936), 103.
[9] Dilys Powell. 'Disillusion Again', the *London Mercury*, 32/192 (Oct. 1935), 603.
[10] John Lehmann, 'Some Revolutionary Trends in English Poetry: 1930–1935', *International Literature*, 4 (Moscow, Apr. 1936), 81–2.
[11] Michael Roberts, rev. of *Poems*, in the *Listener*, 9 Oct. 1935, Supplement p. xii.

Readers of poetry had no sooner accustomed themselves to the mood of disillusion in the 'twenties than they were asked to accept the Auden–Day–Lewis–Spender 'change of heart'. Mr. MacNeice brings us back to disillusion, but a less tormented disillusion than that of Mr. Eliot's waste land period: disillusion with resignation. He does not look for even the most difficult way of escape . . .[12]

This image of MacNeice, as almost post-political in literary terms, tended to make him the third element in a chronological sequence that could be expressed roughly as Eliot–Auden–MacNeice. The notion of an end to the search for a 'way of escape' was beginning to define the position of the contemporary poet for critics, and perhaps also for the poets themselves. The implications of this, as they affected MacNeice himself and some of his contemporaries, are parts of the process by which notions of history become themselves aspects of the creative impulse in poetry.

A review by Rayner Heppenstall paid *Poems* some backhanded compliments which are of relevance to these larger perspectives. Heppenstall looked back to 'The Waste-Land bubble' and 'The New Country bubble' as fashionable movements which 'swelled to enormous size and then burst', leaving behind 'small drops of an exceedingly valuable fluid'. He went on to force the metaphor still further:

And Mr. MacNeice, an acute analyst, has been able to extract formulae for the virtuous properties. . . . This is not to call him anything so simple as an imitator, of course . . . No, he comes at the end of a very complicated dual phase of experience and is simply in the fortunate position of being able to bring it to its limit of possible perfection.[13]

The intention here, as the author was later to acknowledge, was to accuse MacNeice of 'a new Georgianism',[14] a poetic opportunism thriving upon the fluctuations of literary fashion. Allowing for the personal motives which may have been behind this,[15] the line of poetic succession is the same as that used by altogether more sympathetic critics. Roberts, for example, was to place MacNeice midway between the two poles of modern poetry represented by

[12] Powell, 'Disillusion Again', p. 603.
[13] Rayner Heppenstall, rev. of *Poems*, in the *New English Weekly*, 3 Oct. 1935, p. 416.
[14] Rayner Heppenstall, *Portrait of the Artist as a Professional Man* (1969), 96.
[15] Heppenstall's own *First Poems* had also appeared in 1935, attracting much less attention than MacNeice's volume. There is also an element of anti-Grigson feeling in the review, as subsequent correspondence in the *New English Weekly* made clear.

Eliot, Muir, and Read (the 'Waste-Land bubble', in fact) on the one hand, and Auden, Spender, and Day-Lewis (the poets of *New Country*) on the other.[16] The reviewer for *Scrutiny* (a journal with little patience for the Auden group) also set MacNeice apart as 'far more pleasing than many better-known contemporary poets', because of his 'great virtue of being unaffected which, especially in view of the attitude he takes, is a definite achievement'.[17] MacNeice's position as the exponent of a newly developing kind of poetry, learning from and reinforcing certain aspects of both the modernist aesthetics of decay and the early 1930s eye for contemporary significance, received its clearest expression in Day-Lewis's 1936 postscript to a new edition of *A Hope for Poetry*, in which *Poems* was referred to as 'the most interesting of the poetical work produced in the last two years', part of 'a new element in contemporary verse':

It may prove, as may the 'new Country' trend, to be nothing more than a localised and temporary disturbance of the general progress of poetry. But to my mind it is of more significance . . . This element is a reaction from the recent preoccupation of poets with social justice . . . a return to the ideals of poetic integrity and artistic individualism: a setting out again in the direction of 'pure' poetry.[18]

This sits uncomfortably with MacNeice's 'plea for *impure* poetry' of 1938,[19] and suggests how far the reception of *Poems* diverged from the ideas which the poet himself was developing at the time. The terminology used by Day-Lewis here leaves the issue of MacNeice's actual relation to 'the "new Country" trend' ambiguous: the 'return' may represent either a gain in strength or mere regression, while a term like 'artistic individualism' would have been seen in left-wing quarters as incompatible with 'poetic integrity'. Nevertheless, it is clear that, in 1935 and immediately afterwards, MacNeice's position, whether seen as 'a new Georgianism' or 'a return to the ideals of poetic integrity and artistic individualism', was regarded as one of direct rather than marginal importance to the contemporary poetic world.

---

[16] Michael Roberts, 'Aspects of English Poetry: 1932–1937', *Poetry* (Chicago), 49/4 (Jan. 1937), 211.

[17] F. Chapman, rev. of *Poems*, in *Scrutiny*, 4/3 (Dec. 1935), 300.

[18] Cecil Day-Lewis, 'Postscript 1936' to the 2nd edn. of *A Hope for Poetry* (Oxford, 1936), 80.

[19] MacNeice, *Modern Poetry: A Personal Essay* (Oxford, 1938), [v].

These issues are of importance with regard to more than just the history of MacNeice's critical standing. *Poems* is a volume intensely aware of its own contexts, and it needs to be read partly in relation to them as an implicit critique and development of the aesthetics of much early 1930s poetry; for this the contemporary reaction offers valuable guidance. One significant area is indicated by Day-Lewis's observation that MacNeice, 'Like all the present-day young writers . . . feels the need to withdraw on to some terra firma from the bewildering flux of modern life', and his contention that, 'unlike most of them, he does not intend or believe this vantage point to be also a starting point toward any new continent of thought and action.'[20] In 1935, while Auden was writing of the need to 'Make action urgent and its nature clear',[21] MacNeice, in this account, was fostering a kind of ornamental paralysis. The point is by now a familiar one in criticism of 1930s writing—it was put concisely in Spender's admission in 1938 that 'The poet is always to some extent a frustrated man of action'[22]—but it is this kind of division between art and action, or private and public concerns, which tends to be misapplied in relation to MacNeice's work of the period. The beginnings of this may be seen in Day-Lewis's assumption that *Poems* searches for a 'terra firma' or 'vantage point' on which to settle; in this case, occupation of the poetic high ground may presumably be identified with 'artistic individualism' in its divorce from social action. The ideas of a stable perspective and dynamic art are linked in the poetry of the first half of the 1930s, whether in Auden's apparently panoptic hawk's-eye perspectives or in Day-Lewis's and Spender's insistently mechanistic imagery, and MacNeice does in fact take them up in *Poems* as elements capable of manipulation both within individual pieces and in the structure of the volume as a whole.

Some indication of the extent of MacNeice's awareness of the problems of 'individualism' and the relation of aesthetics to 'action' in 1935 is offered by his review of Spender's *The Destructive Element*, a book largely concerned with just these issues:

The individualist is an atom thinking about himself (Thank God I am not as other men); the communist, too often, is an atom having ecstasies of self-

---

[20] Day-Lewis, *A Hope for Poetry*, p. 82.
[21] W. H. Auden, 'August for the people . . .', repr. in *The English Auden*, ed. Edward Mendelson (1977), 157.
[22] Stephen Spender, *Fact*, 20 (Nov. 1938), 75.

denial (Thank God I am one in a crowd); and this too is attitudinizing. It is essential to get rid of this atomist conception of personality, which psychology has undermined from below and which true communism ignores from above. The ego as an indestructible substrate is as obsolete as the old philosophical conception of 'substance'. Yeats has recognised this in insisting that there are no hard and fast, no private minds. Communism in the truer sense is an effort to think, and to think into action, human society as an organism (*not* a machine, which is too static a metaphor).[23]

It is clear from this that MacNeice was attempting to take up the theoretical middle ground which Spender's dramatization of the issues had tried to ignore. Yet the attempt to define a *via media* should not be mistaken for mere neutrality; the bite of this passage, like that of *Poems*, comes from its radical questioning of the possibility of any privileged and secure perspectives. In using Yeats's 'Anima Mundi' to show that 'there are no hard and fast, no private minds', MacNeice touches on an area of ideological debate which runs through *Poems*. 'An effort to think, and to think into action', depends here on abandoning the isolation of the individual mind; in *Poems*, this entails undermining the notion of a 'terra firma' or 'vantage-point'—that is, rejecting the fixed, panoptic gaze of Marxist analysis along with the entrenched positions of bourgeois liberalism. This does not necessarily imply 'a setting out again in the direction of "pure" poetry': such purity is, in fact, the antithesis of the principle behind much of *Poems*. The Communist critic R. D. Charques expressed a common view of the artist's privileged position as one 'which alone possesses a charm against insecurity and want', and in which 'They toil not neither do they spin; but they produce works of "pure" art.'[24] The purity of an artistic perspective is here seen as merely an adjunct to the secure and isolating padding of social and economic factors. As the retrospective account in *The Strings are False* suggests, MacNeice's position as a university lecturer in Birmingham in the early 1930s fitted him well for this kind of artistic purity, but the repeated metaphors there of hothouses and glass tanks, the knowledge that 'we were living on an island' and that 'I wanted to smash the aquarium',[25] argues against any kind of

[23] MacNeice, the *Listener*, 8 May 1935, Supplement p. xiv (repr. Heuser, p. 6).
[24] R. D. Charques, *Contemporary Literature and Social Revolution* (n.d. [1933]), 53.
[25] MacNeice, *The Strings Are False: An Unfinished Autobiography* (1965), 133, 146.

poetic individualism, however 'pure' its products. It is this which lies behind the various strategies employed in *Poems* to subvert 'the islanded hour' ('Ode').

If Day-Lewis's remark is, then, in some sense misplaced, Dilys Powell's observation that 'He does not look for even the most difficult way of escape', comes closer to the technique of *Poems*. The phrase echoes the 'escape' of 'The Individualist Speaks', a poem in which the contention that 'I will escape, with my dog, on the far side of the Fair', is the only refuge from the images of dissolution and destruction. As often in *Poems*, the speaking voice is employed dramatically to undercut its own position, describing a strongly Audenesque landscape against which 'the Individualist' sets both himself and 'the Fair'. The first stanza's assumption that 'We cannot remember enemies in this valley' is developed into the perspective of any *New Country* prophet:

> But to us urchins playing with paint and filth
> A prophet scanning the road on the hither hills
> Might utter the old warning of the old sin
> —Avenging youth threatening an old war.

The poem forces together the long perspective of the prophet with garish close-up, 'Drunk with steam-organs, thigh-rub and cream-soda', reminiscent of the kaleidoscopic jumble of images in *Blind Fireworks*, earlier associated by MacNeice with what he once called 'the high Metaphysicke of the Fair'.[26] In the last stanza, the panoptic prophecy contracts into the Individualist's myopic range, with the 'Avenging youth' 'Crawling down like lava or termites': however cold the initial perspective, there is nothing abstract about the activities of 'You who scale off masks and smash the purple lights'. Beyond the fact that it takes him 'on the far side of the Fair', nothing is known about the Individualist's way of escape; he seems to be left deeper in isolation, with a dog and 'the ego as an indestructible substrate'. It is the poem rather than the speaker which has succeeded in breaking down this 'substrate', bringing the coloured lights of the Fair up against the elevated 'scanning' of the prophet.

A poem like 'The Individualist Speaks' is plainly in certain senses 'political'; to tackle the subject of individualism at all was to engage in ideological debate in the 1930s. The left-wing consensus was

[26] MacNeice, to John Hilton, summer/autumn 1930, Hilton papers, Bod. Lib., fo. 44^r.

always that, as Alick West was to write: 'The social order which individualism unconsciously asserts . . . is the social order of capitalism',[27] and the artistic consequences of this attitude were later put clearly by Spender: 'The isolated individualist may imagine that he escapes from his environment. . . . It is not true. He cannot escape from his own consciousness: and consciousness is never completely isolated. He cannot reject every impression of his senses: and every impression is imperceptibly coloured with the time in which he lives.'[28] What for Spender is mere self-castigation, turns for MacNeice into a poetic, and implicitly dramatic, resource. 'The Individualist Speaks' provides a perfect example of a speaker who 'cannot escape from his own consciousness', and the idea of thwarted escape into individualistic privacy recurs in the volume's opening eclogues and poems such as 'Wolves' or 'Turf-Stacks'. In all of these, 'the pretence of individuality' ('An Eclogue for Christmas') spectates on its own obsolescence with passivity; in 'Trapeze' (a generally weak poem, later dropped), the signs of disaster are present, and are in some degree understood ('the moon | Limps on a crutch whose ferrule taps to us | Doom (if rightly we decodify)'—the brackets adding self-conscious cleverness to the Yeatsian symbolism). Yet the speaker of this poem, too, merely waits for disaster to happen:

> Still we are happy even if our nerves
> Twitch now and again as the grasses do.
> We know that we only live on sufferance
> And that however well this star-seat serves
> Our purpose as trapezists for this once,
> In any case the rope is wearing through.[29]

If this were simply satire on a sophisticated and affected bourgeois pessimism, a great deal of the force of *Poems*, which comes from more than satire alone, would be dissipated. The individualist, whether he is to be found inside or outside the self, cannot be dismissed by MacNeice as merely an enemy to be resisted. Just as Auden made room for 'escape-art' alongside the altogether more

---

[27] Alick West, *Crisis and Criticism* (1937), 5.
[28] Stephen Spender, *Forward from Liberalism* (1937), 26–7. But see Valentine Cunningham, *British Writers of the Thirties* (Oxford, 1987), 214, on the decade's tendency towards 'a kind of apotheosis of Romanticist individualism in a literature of self-regard'.
[29] MacNeice, *Poems* (1935), 55.

moral 'parable-art',[30] so the idea of individualism, however culpable
under certain conditions, might at least be seen as preserving the
concept of the individual in the face of totalitarian demands for
the conformity of 'one in a crowd' (as in the review of Spender) or the
fascist conformity to patterns, the struggle 'to re-establish a vital
connexion between the individual and the race' for which Eliot was
calling in 1934.[31] The problem, then, is to define and give voice to the
individual without either the wilful blindness of individualism or the
cypher-making generalizations of dogma. A parallel could be drawn
with MacNeice's retrospective distinction between the 'Ivory' and
'Brazen Towers' of the 1930s, the first of which 'represents isolation
from men in general', while the second, 'of political dogma', 're-
presents isolation from men as individuals . . . and also from oneself
as an individual'.[32] If *Poems* does not look for any ways of escape, it
is because such escape-routes are seen as themselves isolating the
individual from both public and private realities.

It is in the light of such concerns that the group of eclogues at the
beginning of *Poems* should be read. In these pieces, written between
1933 and 1934,[33] MacNeice's manipulation of different voices has
allowed critics to infer the poet's own neutrality somewhere above
the debate which they see taking place in the poems. A. T. Tolley's
assumption that 'the dialogue form permits the poet to play off
contrary points of view, while remaining in uncertainty himself',[34]
or Robyn Marsack's reference to 'a genuinely dialectical structure'
used by MacNeice 'without requiring a resolution',[35] suggest that
the eclogues are partly exercises in inconclusion, their modish image-
displays leading to nowhere but the poet's own 'uncertainty'. How-
ever, these poems, and the position in *Poems* which they occupy, are
of central importance to MacNeice's writing and its contextual
orientation in the mid-1930s; it is possible to see in them the crux of
an aesthetic and ideological debate which MacNeice was conducting

[30] W. H. Auden, 'Psychology and Art To-Day', in Grigson (ed.), *The Arts To-Day*,
p. 20.

[31] T. S. Eliot, *After Strange Gods: A Primer of Modern Heresy* (1934), 48.

[32] MacNeice, 'The Poet in England Today', the *New Republic*, 25 Mar. 1940,
p. 412 (repr. Heuser, p. 114).

[33] MacNeice, 'An Eclogue for Christmas' (Dec. 1933); 'Valediction' (Jan. 1934)
(originally printed as 'Valediction: An eclogue', in *Life and Letters*, 10/54 (June
1934), 352–4); 'Eclogue by a Five-Barred Gate' (May 1934).

[34] A. T. Tolley, *The Poetry of the Thirties* (1975), 184.

[35] Robyn Marsack, *The Cave of Making: The Poetry of Louis MacNeice* (Oxford,
1982), 25.

at this time both with himself and with contemporary writing. Yet the notion of 'debate' has proved treacherous for critics of the eclogues, and the modes and function of the dialectic involved have generally been misunderstood. If MacNeice had, in fact, so very little to say in these poems and merely a novel way of saying it, then the contemporary reaction outlined above over-read them and the rest of the volume: but it is at least possible that the significance of the eclogues in the 1930s went further than merely an exquisitely cultured cynicism, as subsequent criticism has implied.

It is perhaps necessary to stress that 'dialectic', from Plato onwards, cannot be without direction, a rhetorical trick for getting nowhere;[36] if there is a sense in which the eclogues embody only a very slight progression of ideas, and seem to be without specific conclusions, then criticizing them in terms of 'dialectic', a word whose Marxist associations MacNeice distrusted, may be inappropriate. In any case, it is easy to confuse this 'dialectic' with drama, and so forget the significance of the eclogue form in the first place. A reading of these poems as debate that has been stage-managed so as to be without resolution sets MacNeice, as stage-manager, on precisely that 'terra firma' somewhere above 'the bewildering flux of modern life' mentioned by Day-Lewis. However, a great many of the poet's contemporary critics saw him as carefully avoiding this position. The eclogue, as MacNeice would have understood the term, was not concerned primarily with debate; certainly the 'singing match', a contest between the set pieces of two shepherd-poets, is a prominent feature of Theocritus' *Idylls* or Virgil's *Eclogues*, but this device is in no sense a part of any larger, dialectically achieved meaning. In Theocritus, the eclogue form is often a framing device for separate poems, with 'dramatic' elements playing only a small part. In this respect, the two shepherds of 'Eclogue by a Five-Barred Gate' are properly 'of the Theocritean breed', eager for the singing match which 'Death' finally arranges and, ironically for them, resolves. The harmony of such a resolution is one of negation, Death opening his 'gate the façade of an image' on to a place where 'There is no life as there is no land'. The dismissal of the notion of any viable land for

---

[36] Cf. MacNeice's comment of 1931: 'Plato's achievement was that he dramatised philosophy. Not in that he makes his characters jolly and chatty but in that the dialectical method of his Socrates allows ideas to "run their course". A static idea is dead; the ideas in Plato when they stop running are not dead, they have merely handed on the torch.' (The *Oxford Outlook*, 11/55 (June 1931), 146.)

the shepherds is closely linked with the poem's self-regarding ironies
of form. Whereas, in Theocritus, the formal structure of the idyll
contains and, to that extent, reconciles the competing songs, Mac-
Neice's poem keeps turning in on itself, whether by stressing the
artificiality of the pastoral conventions themselves (Death for the
shepherds is both 'Thanatos in Greek, the accent proparoxytone',
and 'Same as took Alice White the time her had her third'), or by
Death's self-conscious orchestration of the proceedings, constantly
pointing out the limitation of the genre and, in particular, of the kind
of 'poetry' it embodies. In some ways, this may be identified with the
more modish aspects of the *New Country* writing, 'the half-truth
that poetry is *about* something, is communication':[37]

> Poetry you think is only the surface vanity,
> The painted nails, the hips narrowed by fashion,
> The hooks and eyes of words; but it is not that only,
> And it is not only the curer sitting by the wayside,
> Phials on his trestle, his palms grown thin as wafers
> With blessing the anonymous heads;
> And poetry is not only the bridging of two-banked rivers.

The 'curer' here alludes perhaps to Auden's insistence in the early
1930s on the therapeutic role of the artist as healer or 'Truly Strong
Man'. In so far as Death himself in the eclogue epitomizes the idea of
a 'river without a further bank', he undermines the concept of poetry
as purely referential, a means of direct and unequivocal communication
which would be, in Stephen Spender's phrase, 'complementary to
action'.[38] Yet the apparently negative force which Death represents
is not, in poetic terms, absolute: in the same way that 'If Nil is a word
it can't be nil',[39] Death, by offering limits beyond which the shepherds'
poetry cannot penetrate, destabilizes that poetry and begins to edge
it towards something else.

Before staging the eclogue's singing match, Death harangues the
shepherds with his insistence upon time—the urgent need to act
'with Here and Now for your anvil', with the reminder that 'no clock
whatever, while winding or running down, | Makes any difference to
time'. This serves also as an intimation of the formlessness shadowing
the artifice of the singing-match itself, the shepherds' dreams which

---

[37] *The Poetry of W. B. Yeats*, p. 17.
[38] Stephen Spender, 'Poetry and Revolution', in Roberts (ed.), *New Country*, p. 63.
[39] *The Strings are False*, p. 109.

will not 'wear' as reality, just as 'Water appears tower only in well'. The dreams themselves bring the shepherds up against the limits of their own stable, self-justifying art, the first to 'that face I knew to be God', the awareness of the other discovered inside the self, and the second to the point of real communication—sexual and non-verbal —with the other as it exists outside the self. Reaching these points of contact, the shepherds are ready to enter Death's 'no land'; in touching the formless and uncontrollable, whether of time or reality outside the self, they inherit homelessness, and the eclogue itself thus ends in an inversion of the Theocritean harmony of shared victory.

The notion of home, or homelessness, runs through the three eclogues that stand at the beginning of *Poems*, and returns forcefully in the volume's last piece, 'Ode', in which 'nothing is more proud than humbly to accept | And without soaring or swerving win by ignoring | The endlessly curving sea and so come to one's home'. 'An Eclogue for Christmas' and 'Valediction' are both poems of displacement, the first openly 'public' in its frame of reference, and the second ostensibly 'private'. 'An Eclogue for Christmas', which is again static in terms of dialectic, uses the voices of a city- and a country-dweller, following Virgil's Eclogue I, to produce a poem to which, as Terence Brown has written, 'any of the left-wing verse of the period would supply analogues', 'informed with fashionable apocalyptic tones'.[40] Yet the eclogue goes further than its status as either 'an amoeban pastoral on a Virgilian model'[41] or as a mid-1930s Party poem might suggest, undermining the comforts offered by both models. Where Virgil allows one speaker to continue in rural comfort while the other complains 'nos patriae finis et dulcia linquimus arua',[42] MacNeice offers hope for neither speaker's habitation. The bluntly labelled 'B', MacNeice's equivalent of Virgil's contented Tityrus, can provide the urban fugitive with no more advice than that 'It is better to die *in situ* as I shall, | One place is as bad as another'. Both the speakers, in effect, spend the poem presenting images for the same imminent catastrophe, finally sharing the same 'What will happen . . .' tropes that recall the prophetic strain common in the early 1930s. The question, at any rate, accords with those being asked by Auden ('Here am I, here are you: | But what does it mean?

[40] Terence Brown, *Louis MacNeice: Sceptical Vision* (Dublin, 1975), 51, 50.
[41] Graham Hough, 'MacNeice and Auden', *Critical Quarterly*, 9/1 (Spring 1967), 12.
[42] Virgil, Eclogue I. 3: 'We are leaving the borders and sweet fields of our home'.

What are we going to do?'),[43] but the answer twists the more
orthodox prophecies of the time:

> What will happen will happen; the whore and the buffoon
> Will come off best; no dreamers, they cannot lose their dream
> And are at least likely to be reinstated in the new regime.

This is to take things one step too far in terms of the Marxist view of
historical progression; it is in fact a side-stepping of history as
interpreted by the left in favour of time, a less specifically directed
force that is not finally susceptible to utopian prediction. The thrust
of the whole poem is away from historical understanding towards
the flux of time and 'ephemeral things'. MacNeice's speakers bypass
the point reached by Virgil's dispossessed Meliboeus and his 'carmina
nulla canam'[44] by shifting their emphasis from the symptoms of
catastrophe to the minute details of experience, relishing that 'pretence
of individuality' which they acknowledge as part of 'The old idealist
lie'. Prophecy is undercut without being contradicted in the final
lines of the poem. An acceptance of the ephemeral as a source of
paradoxical stability is used strategically by MacNeice as a means of
questioning the fixed historical perspective which prophecy in 1930s
poetry generally implies. However, the price of using flux against
historical patterns is the realization that, by the same token, indi-
vidualism and the idea that 'What we think we can', also exist
against a formless and inhospitable chaos of time; 'the ego as an
indestructible substrate' has to go into oblivion along with history.
This is the dispossession which overshadows the 'ephemeral things'
at the end of the poem, and both speakers are aware throughout of
just this obsolescence; unlike the first-person voice in 'The Indi-
vidualist Speaks', they harbour no illusions as to the possibility of
escape from the temporal flux of which historical decay is itself a
symptom. Again, the poem works towards an understanding of the
meaning of displacement, of the fact that 'My country will not yield
you any sanctuary', which is taken up in *Poems* as a principal theme.

   The degree to which an awareness of, even an obsession with, time
is a corollary of the three eclogues' displacement is taken up in the
series of shorter poems which forms the core of the volume: it is in

---

[43] W. H. Auden, 'It's no use raising a shout . . .', *The English Auden*, p. 42. First
published in 2nd edn. of Auden's *Poems* in 1933, the same year as the composition of
MacNeice's eclogue.
[44] Virgil, Eclogue I. 77: 'I will sing no more songs'.

'Valediction', however, that MacNeice makes his most direct con-
nection between place and the problem of time. The poem's status as
an eclogue, supported by its original subtitle,[45] may parallel those
eclogues of Virgil or Theocritus in which only one speaker is indic-
ated:[46] this has some bearing on the way in which the voice used by
MacNeice in 'Valediction' should be interpreted. If the classical solo
eclogue is taken as being more of an extended set piece on a clearly
defined theme than a personal 'expression' of the poet, it may be
worth looking twice at the 'personal' aspects of 'Valediction' which
seem to cry out for a largely biographical interpretation. Behind the
poem's outspoken stridency, it is possible to make out the shadow of
its classical antecedents in the measured enlargement upon an initial
theme through its practical consequences for the speaker: the 'voice'
is employed not so much to express feelings, as to perform an act, in
this case one of exorcism. Of course, the personal causes and
implications of that act are of undiminished importance in Mac-
Neice's development, but an interpretation of 'Valediction' cannot
afford to ignore the place occupied by the poem in the volume as a
whole, providing, like the other two eclogues, an extreme position
which shorter lyrics will examine from different angles; in this
respect, its bringing-together of time, place, and history is crucial.

In its first appearance, 'Valediction' was divided into four sections,
bringing to the surface four distinct movements within the poem's
protracted ritual of exorcism. The first section, ending with acts of
violence hardening into 'Dumb talismans', relies on an impressionistic
and deliberately confused presentation of violence—the 'seals' heads'
of the second line influence the 'taken by the limp fins | And slung
like a dead seal in a boghole', to blur the lines somewhere between
metaphor and simile, with a subject that is itself indeterminate. From
the initial shock the apparently more satirical aspect of this section
develops:

> Park your car in the city of Dublin, see Sackville Street
> Without the sandbags in the old photos, meet
> The statues of the patriots, history never dies,
> At any rate in Ireland,

---

[45] See n. 33 above. MacNeice also refers to the poem as an 'Eclogue on Ireland' in a
letter to Blunt of 1934 (quoted in W. T. McKinnon, *Apollo's Blended Dream* (1971),
23).
[46] For 'solo eclogues', see e.g. Theocritus, Idyll III, Virgil, Eclogues II, IV, VI, X.

The shifting images of terror here petrify into the design and finality
of 'history', at once barren and powerful—the statues are alive in
that they can still destroy, but dead in so far as they are incapable of
change. A long second section, continuing to 'drug-dull fatalism',
picks up the mock tour-guide tone, and introduces the particular and
personal past as part of the poem's speaking voice ('I cannot deny my
past to which my self is wed'). In allowing this voice to identify and
articulate its past, MacNeice also allows it a degree of that freedom
which Ireland seems to deny here: Belfast, for example, extends the
unchanging petrifaction of 'the statues of the patriots' to a whole city
'devout and profane and hard': time is part of a nightmare stasis
which the speaking voice breaks in its distinction between present
and past, and its setting-out of its heritage as a kind of balance sheet
('Set that against your water-shafted air', 'pay for the trick beauty of
a prism | In drug-dull fatalism'). The attempt to 'tot up my factors' is
in itself a gesture towards a certain objectivity which, like Joyce's
identification of 'paralysis' in *Dubliners*, relies upon distancing the
speaker from his subject. The formal act of separation between these
two elements is attempted in 'Valediction' 's third section, beginning
with the determination to 'exorcise my blood', and ending with the
assertion that 'You cannot change a response by giving it a new
name'. However, the act of exorcism remains equivocal to a degree:
as Edna Longley has pointed out, it is significant that 'Even *in*
extremis*—*'Farewell my country, and in perpetuum'—MacNeice
attaches the possessive pronoun to Ireland.'[47] The speaking voice, in
separating itself from the land which 'will remain as it was', has to
imply its own capacity for individuality and change, but cannot quite
'undo its thread' by giving it the new name of a tourist-like objectivity.
What Robyn Marsack sees as MacNeice's successful attempt 'to
immunize himself, preserve himself in detachment',[48] is undermined
further by the final section of 'Valediction', in which the speaking
voice comes back to its land in the role of apostate. The first lines of
this last movement, 'Fountain of green and blue curling in the wind | I
must go east and stay', are already in the voice of self-conscious
nostalgia, though Ireland is in fact no more capable of being turned

[47] Edna Longley, 'Louis MacNeice: "The Walls are Flowing"', in G. Dawe and
E. Longley (eds.), *Across a Roaring Hill: The Protestant Imagination in Modern
Ireland* (Belfast, 1985), 105.
[48] Marsack, *The Case of Making*, p. 11.

into simply a subject for poetry than it is of becoming purely the raw material for tourism; in proving its freedom, the speaking voice finds its course laid down already:

> But being ordinary too I must in course discuss
> What we mean to Ireland or Ireland to us;
> I have to observe milestone and curio
> The beaten buried gold of an old king's bravado,
> Falsetto antiquities, I have to gesture,
> Take part in, or renounce, each imposture;

The repeated expressions of obligation here ('I must', 'I have to') are parts of the conditioning which runs under the whole poem, and threatens its step-by-step separation of present and past, voice and country, so that in the end the difference between having to 'take part in, or renounce' is marginal—it is the obligation itself which counts and which the final resignation of farewell cannot lessen through outright rejection.

It would be unwise to pigeon-hole the poem into a relatively self-contained 'Irish' compartment within MacNeice's work. Rather, 'Valediction' functions within *Poems* as a kind of *exemplum* for the difficulties encountered in untangling past and present within a voice that aspires to individuality. This difficulty is compounded by the extent to which the voice is dispossessed, its willed exile mirroring the homelessness of the two eclogues which are printed immediately before and after the poem. In the shorter pieces in *Poems*, these concerns reappear in direct or indirect contrast: 'Valediction' is complemented directly by the differing perspectives of 'Train to Dublin' and 'Belfast', just as the themes and imagery of 'An Eclogue for Christmas' are taken up by 'Birmingham' and 'Trapeze'. The petrifaction of a time that seems rather to nullify than bring about change recurs throughout *Poems*: Simeon with 'nothing to be seen | But a stone posture' ('Cuckoo'); Perseus 'Carrying a stone death', Time 'shown with a stone face' ('August'); 'we who have always been haunted by the fear of becoming stone' ('The Glacier'); or the 'hours of stone | Long rows of granite sphinxes looking on' ('Mayfly') —all suggest the barrenness of the 'evil time' of the volume's first line. However, another theme of the first three eclogues of *Poems*, time in its aspect of flux, is also developed through the shorter poems. As in 'An Eclogue for Christmas', this is time as change that cannot be controlled by either the individual or the abstract patterns of history, but is caught in the minute details of experience: 'the faces balanced in the toppling wave' ('Train to Dublin'); 'A turning page of shrine and sound' ('Morning Sun'); or the world 'Incorrigibly plural' ('Snow'). These two aspects of time, as stasis and flux, are in no sense balanced in *Poems*, where images of stone face the 'dance above the dazzling wave' ('Mayfly'); it is in their opposition, remaining unresolved, that the volume makes its most original contribution to 1930s poetics.

In *Poems*, an understanding of time as stasis or flux, stone or sea, becomes explicitly a matter of perspective. In 'August', for example, it is 'the mind, by nature stagey', which imposes a frame 'Tomb-like around each little world of a day', and can therefore remove time from the process of immediate experience into artful personification, 'shown with a stone face'. The poem's final stanza, however, effects an abrupt volte-face:

> But all this is a dilettante's lie,
> Time's face is not stone nor still his wings;
> Our mind, being dead, wishes to have time die
> For we, being ghosts, cannot catch hold of things.

As often in the volume, the writer's recollection of himself as in some senses a conditioned observer undercuts the poem's ostensible assumptions. Similarly, the two speakers in 'An Eclogue for Christmas' acknowledge that their 'role as individual man' is in certain ways a pretence, part of their inability to prevent disaster. The notion of conditioned responses was itself a commonplace of the *New Country* writing, understood as the recognition of socially inculcated distortion which poetry could replace with 'objectivity' (though 'a kind of objectivity achieved *from the inside*', as Montagu Slater warned in 1935[49]). MacNeice is distinctive in acknowledging a deeper form of conditioning within poetry itself, which takes place not in any surface coding of ideology, but in the very act of accommodating flux to pattern. This has implications both for MacNeice's poems themselves and for the part played by his volume in the 1930s debate on the nature and function of art within society.

Time, in its two aspects of stasis and flux, had political implications in 1935, and its prominence in *Poems* reflects a general poetic preoccupation which had been building since the early 1930s. Time,

---

[49] Montague Slater, rev. of Stephen Spender, *Vienna*, in *Left Review*, 1/5 (Feb. 1935), 187.

in David Gascoyne's 'Morning Dissertation' of 1933, 'like an urgent finger moves across the chart', and is followed by the warning: 'Time is not yours alone, | You are but one dot on the complex diagram'.[50] This idea of time as a force greater than any individual is often identified by the writers with the concept of history central to a Marxist analysis of the contemporary crises: Auden could invoke (though with the equivocation of a mixed metaphor) 'history, that never sleeps or dies, | And, held one moment, burns the hand', or a 'possible dream' that would come 'out of the Future into actual History', as active forces within and outside poems.[51] Another example of history as an element of poetics is provided by a series of prose poems in John Lehmann's *The Noise of History* (1934), in which past, present, and future exist in a direct and easily interpreted relationship, where 'They are irrevocably past, our reveries among the island willows, as the wind-rustled pages of the open book beside us'; all present-tense observation is in this way essentially symptomatic—'A dog howls in a side-street, and silence falls on a group talking at the corner . . . A pencil drops from the hand of a writer, as a loud knocking at his door begins.'[52] MacNeice, in making use of this symptomatic present tense throughout *Poems*, implicitly alludes to the poetics of history, but the doomed perspectives of 'Trapeze', or the 'newsboys crying war' of 'Aubade', are set against a background of flux in which historical modes of interpretation begin to lose their validity, as in 'An April Manifesto':

> Sharp sun-strop, surface-gloss, and momentary caprice
> These are what we cherish
> Caring not if the bridges and the embankments
> Of past and future perish and cease;

This purposefully irresponsible voice, often employed in *Poems*, disallows the settled perspective of history: far from regarding time as the force of progression towards an inevitable culmination, MacNeice's conception of flux undermines historical patterns and, with them, the idea of finality itself, putting up resistance to any kind of conclusion. The deep unease with regard to the ending of poems,

[50] David Gascoyne, 'Morning Dissertation', repr. in *Collected Poems*, ed. R. Skelton (1965), 5.
[51] Auden, 'August for the people . . .' (1935), 'O Love, the interest itself . . .' (1932), repr. in *The English Auden*, pp. 157, 119.
[52] John Lehmann, 'No Retreat' and 'Writing', in *The Noise of History* (1934), 40, 54.

and the closure of the problems they raise, is felt throughout *Poems*, and bears a direct relationship to the use of the poetic 'voice' in that volume. It is this tension which dictates that the opposition between time as stasis and time as flux cannot reach a resolution, and prevents MacNeice from sharing in the *New Country* objectivity of history.

The short poem 'To a Communist', like the more famous 'Snow', can be considered as part of the conflict in *Poems* between flux and stasis, in this case with explicitly political implications. The imagery of snow is itself midway between that of fixity and fluidity, petrifaction and water, elsewhere prevalent:

> Your thoughts make shape like snow; in one night only
> The gawky earth grows breasts,
> Snow's unity engrosses
> Particular pettiness of stones and grasses.

As water with the temporary property of solidity, snow gives form to landscape with its 'particular pettiness', but returns to fluidity with the passing of time ('The poise is perfect, but maintained | For one day only'). Snow here is almost a symbol for the patterning of history, which is not negated but redefined by developing the initial imagery. The poem does not deny the 'shape' made by the Communist analysis, any more than the speakers in 'An Eclogue for Christmas' deny the left-wing diagnosis of bourgeois society in decline, but the permanence of that 'shape' is put into question. 'Snow' operates by celebrating the particular, suspending flux in the perception of individuality, a world 'crazier and more of it than we think'. Particularity may be seen here as a gesture against flux without lapsing into the petrifaction of stasis; for the moment of the poem, if only for that moment, individuality is value. Taken together, 'To a Communist' and 'Snow' provide moments of equilibrium between history, the individual, and the passing of time that are rare in *Poems*, though they are gestured towards again in the final piece, 'Ode'; but these poems' conclusions, in their recognition of flux and plurality, are also in some sense *in*conclusions, denying the possibility of any entirely finished state. A poise 'maintained | For one day only' already hints at the more volatile treatments of 'the dilettante's lie' elsewhere in the volume that cannot be brought under control by imagery alone.

Although its position, thematic content, and range of imagery make it in some ways the culmination of *Poems*, 'Ode' also represents an attempt to disown closed and finalized systems and leave behind a legacy that is open to change and, in that measure, unfinished. In trying to find 'a sufficient sample, the exact and framed | Balance of definite masses, the islanded hour', the poem is caught between its formal status as a poetic set piece (recalling the 'custom' and 'ceremony' of Yeats's 'A Prayer for my Daughter'), and the rejection of 'any code' in favour of 'The marriage of Cause and Effect, Form and Content'. MacNeice's poem, like Yeats's, struggles to accommodate and understand its own symbols: 'the islanded hour', another juxtaposition of solidity and fluidity, cannot finally maintain the balance between time and identity which its mixing of images suggests; just as Yeats's 'murderous innocence of the sea' and 'green laurel | Rooted in one dear perpetual place' force their poet towards a reinterpretation of both symbols.[53] The sea in 'Ode', associated early in the poem with the threateningly formless and uncontrollable, puts the individual in danger from both society and the abstractions of the conscious self. The concern with building a home, implicit throughout *Poems* and explicitly present in the eclogues, returns in response to these internal and external threats:

> I would pray for that island; mob mania in the air,
> I cannot assume their easy bravery
> Drugged with a slogan, chewing the old lie
> That parallel lines will meet at infinity;
> As I walk on the shore of the regular and rounded sea
> I would pray off from my son the love of that infinite
> Which is too greedy and too obvious; let his Absolute
> Like any four-walled house be put up decently.

But establishing 'one dear perpetual place' in 'Ode' is not made possible simply by balancing the images of fixity and flux, land and sea, in some kind of poetic equation. The sea here has to be perceived in terms of visual limits, as a symbol of the necessity of perceptual limitation in holding back the temptations of an abstract infinity; yet this is a 'horizon | Not to swim to but to see', in that its relation to reality may be lost under its symbolic function. In the sections of the poem dealing with his specific wishes for his son, MacNeice uses the sea as a metaphor for time almost too effortlessly (the 'sham soul',

[53] W. B. Yeats, 'A Prayer for my Daughter', in *The Poems*, ed. R. J. Finneran (1984), 188–90. Cf. also Yeats's first line: 'Once more the storm is howling...', with MacNeice's opening 'wind blowing from Bournville'.

for example, is 'the cask bobbing empty | On leaden waves, the
veneer the years crack'); it is when the relation between the evidence
of the senses and its symbolic representations is called into question
that the isolated building of the self in 'Ode' begins to be destabilized:

> Coral azalea and scarlet rhododendron
> Syringa and pink horse-chestnut and laburnum
> Solid as temples, niched with the song of birds,
> Widen the eyes and nostrils, demand homage of words.
> And we have to turn from them,
> Compose ourselves, fit out an ethic:

The flux of lived experience undermines the construction of an
islanded, and isolated, identity. The question, 'Have I anything to
hand my son', is now answered by 'Only so far, so far as I can find,
symbols', but these are no longer examples of decorous limitation,
and instead impinge directly upon the individual and his independence.
In developing these new symbols—a fly on a window, an aeroplane
in June—MacNeice moves the poem closer to the characteristic
1930s idiom, the sounds in past experience being transformed in the
present into portents of future catastrophe. In what is perhaps an
allusion back to 'An Eclogue for Christmas', the individual suffers
the consequences of his own isolation:

> The town-dweller like a rabbit in a greengrocer's
> Who was innocent and integral once
> Now, red with slit guts, hangs by the heels
> Hangs by the heels gut-open against the fog
> Between two spires that are not conscious of him.

To be 'innocent and integral', then, is not enough; the individual is
not impervious to time. The poet has here to accept the necessity of a
non-integral attitude, in which it is impossible to 'draw up any code'.
The sea, which has been the crucial image in 'Ode', can no longer
function as a poetic prop; the poet's dream of 'the both real and ideal
| Breakers of ocean' is part of the 'drug' which has to be renounced at
the end of the poem. The legacy cannot, then, be finalized, and the
sea cannot be reduced intellectually to a metaphor to cap an argu-
ment; 'Ode' tries to enact the impossibility of coming 'to one's peace
while the yellow waves are roaring', and brings *Poems* to a close by
questioning the implications of conscious endings.

In 1933 Stephen Spender asserted that 'If a poem is not complete in itself and if its contents spill over into our world of confused emotions, then it is a bad poem.'[54] That poems should be embodiments of good order, should say what they mean, was one axiom of 1930s poetics that survived changes in specific political options; MacNeice's use of flux as an element of poetry, however, tends to subvert this assumption. The hail of sensory images to which this leads is more than just poetic bravura: Conrad Aiken's complaint, 'And so, in we go; and out we come; and it is only then that we find how little of all this has stuck to us',[55] fails to perceive the relationship between MacNeice's use of shifting imagery and the theme of time threatening the finalities of history, the limitations of individualism, and the smaller finalities of poems. In a volume in which many poems feed into each other, so that thematic concerns evolve and are continually modified by different pieces, it must be the *process* of the poetry rather than its separate conclusions which is important. The reader of *Poems*, as well as its author, finds the central concerns such as time and historical catastrophe, identity and individualism, incapable of final definition or solution; rather, both poet and audience have to put themselves in the position of 'a boy | Who chases a winged bird', in the terms of the epigraph,[56] and understand the value and function of instability as an element of broader coherence.

This would seem to beg important questions as to MacNeice's 'voice' in the collection. It is worth recalling the poet's references in 1935 to two contexts for writing, the social, 'English context', and that of 'the poet's life and work' which is regarded as essentially dramatic; in *Poems*, the second of these bears more directly on the first than the apparent disparity between the two in MacNeice's essay for *The Arts To-Day* might suggest. In a manuscript note among John Hilton's papers which seems to have accompanied *Poems*, MacNeice discussed 'lyrics' in terms of their 'dramatic' character:

People tend to think of short poems as 'lyrics' as something very personal. This does not apply to mine any more than to many other poems. I should rather they were thought of as *dramatic*. This will preclude two mistakes.

(a) You will not look for any message, creed or theory of life in these poems.

[54] Spender, 'Poetry and Revolution', p. 62.
[55] Conrad Aiken, 'MacNeice, Louis' (1941), in *A Reviewer's ABC* (New York, 1958), 286.
[56] In MacNeice's translation, *The Agamemnon of Aeschylus* (1936), 26.

(b) You will not draw any wrong conclusions from the preponderance of gloomy ones.[57]

This is not primarily evasive, a way of disowning poems, but it is an attempt to claim the integrity of artifice, the fact that 'commitment', as understood in the mid-1930s, is in some ways an extra-literary consideration. This does not mean that the 'external' context may be discounted, but proposes that there should be a more subtle relation between this and the poems than the abstractions of 'commitment' or 'position' tend to allow:

If a man writes 'tragedies' one knows what to expect and one does not accuse him of melancholia. Macbeth is speaking as Macbeth and not as (the whole) Shakespeare. But when it comes to 'lyrics' people seem to think that anything the poet writes is the 'expression' of the whole poet. This is bosh. The lyric is the expression of it maybe, a particular moment, or else a particular facet in a man's outlook. Different parts of him want or believe different, or even opposite, things. Which parts shall have the most say depends largely on external circumstances. (cf reigns of Queens Elizabeth & Anne.)

While this seems to accord well with the patterns of unfinished development in *Poems*, in both the longer and the shorter pieces, the question of the openness of the 'lyric' voice and its particular relevance to 'external circumstances' did not concern MacNeice alone. In 1934 Day-Lewis was complaining that 'the lyric is the form of poetry, more than any other, within which the poet is answerable to nothing but its own laws and the experience of his senses', and argued that in the contemporary world, 'the lyric irresponsibility of the artist is hard to achieve'.[58] The equation of irresponsibility with 'the experience of the senses' clearly suggests the point at which MacNeice's approach has to diverge from the *New Country* orthodoxy proposed by Day-Lewis. MacNeice's 'lyric' voice embodies precisely that 'irresponsibility' which troubles Day-Lewis, and the poems enact the recognition that ideological stability is alien to an imagination open to the apparently random contradictions of experience and belief.[59] By incorporating this principle in a full volume, *Poems* offered a recognition of division which was to prove exemplary for

---

[57] Hilton papers, fos. 85[r], 86[r].   [58] Day-Lewis, *A Hope for Poetry*, p. 67.

[59] The desire to pin MacNeice down to a 'position' did not die with the 1930s, especially as regards his attitudes towards Ireland. In the MS note, he continues (fo. 86[r]): 'To take a concrete instance—"Valediction" is not of course the sum of what I think about Ireland. It is only the way my thought follows my feeling at certain moments.' (Bod. Lib., MS Don., c. 153.)

the work of Spender, and even Auden, later in the decade: and that recognition, often seen as political (or culpably apolitical), was certainly more original in 1935 than a quasi-Marxist acceptance of 'necessity' as the major conditioning factor in a 'responsible' poetic voice.

If *Poems* is, then, designedly unstable and resistant to finalities, its distance from the *New Country* writing, often judged to be especially important by reviewers, may be seen as a matter of development rather than wholesale divergence. MacNeice took certain aspects of the new poetry—its admission of 'unpoetic' imagery and subject-matter, its sense of urgency and stress on the present ('It is now or never, the hour of the knife, | The break with the past'[60]—and pushed them further, the symptomatic details of the present becoming aspects of a more profoundly threatening flux, hostile to all of the abstractions by which it might be contained. As contemporary reactions suggest, this could be construed as either literary opportunism or as a political gesture, in so far as it could suggest a divergence from the Marxist ideology thought to be common to the *New Country* writers. However, MacNeice's preoccupation with flux must also be traced back to the writings of his earlier years, when its associations for the poet were far from political. That concerns which had always been native to his imagination should have put him in a position of considerable influence in 1935 was certainly fortunate for Mac-Neice; writing that he 'has neither the passion for "justice" ' of Spender, nor 'the intense scientific, analytical interest in historical development' of Auden,[61] John Lehmann identified (albeit negatively) MacNeice's significance for the other writers of his generation as his resistance to abstractions, whether of 'pity' or 'history'. For Mac-Neice, both history and the individual are compromised by time and flux, just as the separate pieces in *Poems* are compromised by each other. After *Poems*, the search for a 'vantage-point' that could function as a 'starting-point' for action became less intense among the 1930s poets, and hawk's-eye perspectives over history started to give way to an understanding of the divisions in the self at a time of crisis.

Without some understanding of the originality of *Poems* at the time of its publication, estimates of MacNeice's standing as a '1930s

[60] Cecil Day-Lewis, *The Magnetic Mountain* (1933), Poem 25 in *Collected Poems 1929–1933* (1938), 139.
[61] John Lehmann, *New Writing in Europe* (Harmondsworth, 1940), 116.

poet' are uncertain; in his work from 1935 until *Autumn Journal*
(1939), which will be examined in Chapter 3, the poet wrote from
the centre of a clearly defined literary movement—before *Poems* he
was on its periphery. In gaining admission, MacNeice undermined
the first, optimistic *New Country* phase of 1930s writing: Death's
announcement in 'Eclogue by a Five-Barred Gate' that 'There is no
life as there is no land', chimed on one level with Richard Rees's
observation that 'This new country is not a very lively place.'[62]
MacNeice offered no stable and defined alternative, however, other
than the cold comfort of time, change, and flux. Whatever the
literary or political implications of this in the mid-1930s, MacNeice
had always found himself forced to come to terms with an imagination
that remained stubbornly homeless.

[62] In a marginal note to John Middleton Murry's copy of *New Country* (see Robin
Waterfield Ltd., Sales Catalogue 66, Item 523). Rees had been editor of the *Adelphi*
since 1930.

Epitaphs for Louis: Early Writings

WHEN it is read in the literary context of the mid-1930s, MacNeice's *Poems* begins to seem something of a public document. Yet the central images and ideas of the volume—of time, flux, petrifaction, and stasis, which in 1935 took on topical associations—have their origin in distinctly private areas of the poet's thought. The process of literary development towards *Poems* has a bearing on MacNeice's development away from that volume. In order to bring the lines of continuity in the work into focus, it is necessary to start early, with the kind of writing that is often forgotten as 'juvenilia'. No poet would ever wish to be judged on his earliest work; given that, the actual significance of juvenilia varies considerably from writer to writer. If some poets prefer such work to be given a quiet burial, there are others who find youthful productions, and mistakes, serviceable in the context of their mature careers. MacNeice belongs to this second category: the poetry of his early years, though for the most part dropped from the collected editions, has distinct relevance for his writings from the 1930s onwards. Indeed, MacNeice gave public burials to his early work with some regularity in his personal and discursive critical essays. The reasons for this have largely failed to engage the poet's critics, but the juvenilia has enough inherent value to be of interest beyond the small circle of MacNeice's scholars; this largely forgotten body of work casts a revealing light on the experience of the poetic '1930s generation', the first 'modern' poets in England whose encounter with Modernism was, to use Eliot's phrase for his generation's reading of Shelley, 'an affair of adolescence'.[1]

The seventeen poems which make up the 'Juvenilia' section of MacNeice's *Collected Poems*, edited by E. R. Dodds in 1966 and still in print, tell a great deal less than the whole story of the poet's development. Besides the considerable number of poems printed in the *Marlburian* from 1924 to 1926, MacNeice's work appeared in

---

[1] T. S. Eliot, *The Use of Poetry and the Use of Criticism* (1933), 89.

many Oxford publications between 1926 and 1930, while a substantial volume of his poetry, entitled *Blind Fireworks*, was published by Gollancz in 1929.[2] In addition to the published work, some manuscript material survives which gives a fuller picture of MacNeice's development, particularly in his last year at school, when, along with friends such as Anthony Blunt, he was patching together an eclectic and eccentric approach to life and art. The responsibility for the slimness of the 'Juvenilia' section of the *Collected Poems* does not lie with Dodds, but with MacNeice himself, whose selection from his early poetry, made for the *Collected Poems 1925–1948* (1949), was repeated by his posthumous editor. There is, however, one significant difference between the 1949 and the 1966 *Collected Poems*. In the earlier text, MacNeice decided to position the 'Juvenilia' after an opening group of longer poems from the 1930s, and before a group of shorter lyrics from his volume *Poems*; Dodds restored the early work to a chronological position at the beginning of the volume. In 1949 MacNeice had implied by his positioning of the early poems that they might be read more profitably in the context of his 1930s work, and might in their turn offer sidelights on his poetry of that period. For this reason, the selection itself is more than usually careful. However, it is worth looking beyond the perspectives offered by MacNeice himself, and in order to do this, more material has to be considered than simply the work which the poet chose to preserve.

MacNeice spends more time talking about his early writings than many of his critics do. Both *Modern Poetry* (1938) and *The Strings Are False* (written 1940–1) devote considerable space to early poems and intellectual development, while later articles such as 'Experiences with Images' (1949) or 'When I Was Twenty-One' (1961) treat the early writing in some detail.[3] But no writer's perspectives on his own past work are ever uncoloured by his literary concerns at the time of the recollection; in *Modern Poetry*, MacNeice's declaration that in the 1920s 'I attempted to dope my mind and see what would come

[2] C. M. Armitage and Neil Clark, *A Bibliography of the Works of Louis MacNeice* (1973, 2nd edn. 1974), give an incomplete list of uncollected juvenilia; a selection of school poems appeared in the Michaelmas 1975 issue of the *Marlburian*, edited with notes by MacNeice's friend, John Hilton.

[3] MacNeice, 'Experiences with Images' (*Orpheus*, 2 (1949)), repr. in *Selected Literary Criticism of Louis MacNeice*, ed. Alan Heuser (Oxford, 1987); 'When I Was Twenty-One', *The Saturday Book* 21, ed. J. Hadfield (1961), 230–9.

out of it',[4] recalls the determination to 'put away this drug' of 'Ode', and brings the early writing into line with a reading of literature as concerned primarily with 'communication', a key MacNeice term of the 1930s. Yet in recalling his early work, MacNeice tended to shift the emphasis from poetry itself to the psychological state which produced it; in this respect, he was engaged in something of a misreading, or at least a distortion, of his juvenilia. Similarly, MacNeice's attribution of 'what I now think an excessive preoccupation in my earlier verse with things dazzling, high-coloured, quick-moving, hedonistic or up-to-date',[5] to a reaction against the circumstances of his childhood in the rectory at Carrickfergus allows its psychological slant to obscure other important elements. The line between personal, obsessive brooding and bravura intellectual display, which the later MacNeice invites his readers to see in the early writing, is in fact much more difficult to discern there than the retrospective accounts suggest.

As in a great deal of MacNeice's writing, personally rooted tensions and obsessions are important elements of the early poems. One untitled piece, published in the *Marlburian* in 1924,[6] presents its nightmare imagery with a particular directness:

> The ways are green and gorgons creep
> In and out among the hay—
> Rotten hay, sunken hay;
> And the creatures of the bay
> Mourn a dismal roundelay
> To their accompanist the deep.
> In my dreams that flit and flow,
> Flit and flow, flow and flit,
> I cannot help but think of it,
> When I am dead that I shall sit
> Crumbling, crumbling, bit by bit,
> Where the yellow gorgons go.

The 'yellow gorgons' who inhabit a conventionally pastoral landscape are parts of MacNeice's own remembered imaginative landscape. In all of his work, the childhood scene of Carrickfergus is associated with images of petrifaction; the gorgons in this very early poem are in MacNeice's work to stay. Recalling the surroundings of his child-

---

[4] MacNeice, *Modern Poetry: A Personal Essay* (1938), 61.
[5] 'Experiences with Images', p. 160.
[6] The *Marlburian*, 59/855 (20 Nov. 1924), 160.

hood and their influence upon his writing in 'Experiences with Images', MacNeice remembered the sea as 'something alien, foreboding, dangerous, and only very rarely blue'; here, the 'early stratum of experiences which persists in one's work just as it persists in one's dreams', also includes 'the very small, very green hedged fields of Northern Ireland', and 'my father's medium-sized lush garden with a cemetery beyond the hawthorn hedge'.[7] Far from being a green world of remembered innocence, this scene often represents a place of danger and fear in MacNeice's poetry.

If one aspect of the young MacNeice's poetry is rooted in the nightmare imagery of his early childhood, another is altogether more artificial and self-consciously sophisticated. It is this premature and dandified intellectualism which the poet himself later deprecated, and which still does much to stand in the way of the poetry, all too often ruining the more acute and individual aspects of the poems themselves. Towards the end of his time at Marlborough, MacNeice was both a brooding and nightmare-haunted adolescent, and a self-possessed aesthete and wit. Above all, there—as at Oxford—he was determinedly 'modern', gathering and displaying the most attractive elements of a distinctively up-to-date intellectual stance. The structure of the school year accentuated the difference between the aesthetic ambience of his Marlborough set and the sterner, more troubling surroundings of his home life in Ulster. Modernity was, in an important sense, a way of escape from the 'yellow gorgons' of nightmares with their disabling gaze. The artist's pose, the inclination towards the world of what MacNeice called 'Romance' throughout his early writings, was also a gesture of defiance. It is not enough to describe many of the early poses adopted by the poet as aspects of a pervasive affectation; they are parts of a deliberate, almost aggressive decision to be 'difficult', a refusal of, and sometimes a confrontation with, an unhappy past.

MacNeice certainly took his 'difficulty' seriously; indeed, for him, as for Auden, also born in 1907, modernity in thought implied intellectual difficulty. However, the kind of difficulty encountered in Auden's post-1927 poetry, which has been seen by Edward Mendelson as 'an extreme extension of modernist ideas',[8] cannot be dissociated from the kaleidoscopic jumble of mythological and personal imagery which MacNeice was to employ in *Blind Fireworks*. If MacNeice

[7] 'Experiences with Images', pp. 158–9.
[8] Edward Mendelson, *Early Auden* (1981), 11.

was slower than Auden in arriving at the style which would serve as a basis for his 1930s writing, he was remarkably quick in finding the themes, images, and even forms which would be at the core of his later work.[9] MacNeice's recollection that he had, before leaving Marlborough, 'become interested in being fashionably modern',[10] means to imply the superficiality of certain of his tastes at that time; this modernity entailed a belief in what MacNeice referred to then as 'Significant Form', an idea derived from the writings of Clive Bell by way of Anthony Blunt. The notion is made to seem simply whimsical and adolescent by MacNeice in his later accounts, but its implications were not quite so limited as 'that People were of minor importance compared with Things'.[11] In however crude a form, the idea was part of a more general modernist awareness of art as partly self-referential, in some ways hermetic and autotelic. In an early Marlborough formulation of his ideas, Blunt had written:

The difficulty is to decide what is the most essential and intrinsic quality of a natural object. To do this it is necessary to imagine it isolated from all external and human connections, and to determine what is left. Take the example of a boat: imagine it completely isolated from all human connections. What remains? What but significant form?[12]

The artistic puritanism of this goes several steps further than Pound's description of the vortex which 'purges [the external scene] of all save the essential or dominant or dramatic qualities, and it emerges like the external original'.[13] By 1926 Blunt was announcing that 'the imitative part of a painting has no aesthetic value', and that the artist 'is at liberty to use nature exactly as much or as little as he pleases'.[14] The young MacNeice spoke along very similar lines, claiming in 1925 that 'Facts are the foundation of everything but for most people

---

[9] In terms of early publication history, MacNeice was somewhat ahead of Auden. The latter sent off his first MS volume of poems to T. S. Eliot at Faber and Gwyer in June 1927, when it was rejected; his *Poems* was hand-printed by Stephen Spender in the autumn of 1928; before November of that year, MacNeice had sent the MS of *Blind Fireworks* to Gollancz. It is possible that Auden also sent his poems to Gollancz, following MacNeice, during 1929, only to have them rejected (see Mendelson, *Early Auden*, p. 32 n.).

[10] *Modern Poetry*, p. 51.

[11] 'When I Was Twenty-One', p. 236.

[12] Anthony Blunt, 'Some Aspects of Modern Art', the *Heretick*, 1 (Mar. 1924), 11.

[13] Ezra Pound, 'Affirmations' (1915), repr. in *Selected Prose 1909–1965*, ed. W. Cookson (1973), 375.

[14] Anthony Blunt, 'De Cubismo', the *Marlburian*, 61/870 (23 June 1926), 88.

they have to be touched up to mean anything.'[15] In the same year, speaking in a debate in favour of Sir Jacob Epstein's then controversial panel *Rima* (1925), he 'pointed out that art is not merely imitative, as is generally believed . . . The panel expresses the noble rather than the petty side of nature, a result achieved largely by the recovery of the qualities of primitive art.'[16] Less thoroughgoing than Blunt, Mac-Neice shared his assumptions in believing that 'Primitive art is superior to developed, in that it has the essential qualities more clearly shewn': 'distortion' was justified, since 'if it is not allowed most good art goes'.[17] Blunt too had asserted that 'All artists have distorted and the only distinction that can be made is one of degree.'[18] There is an obvious conflict here between sophistication and primitivism, which Blunt was able in some degree to resolve through his interpretation of Cubism, but which MacNeice found more difficult to handle in literary terms. For him, of course, the 'primitive' levels of experience were no mere abstractions, leading back as they did to early memories of the Carrickfergus rectory, a brother suffering from the condition recognized now as Down's syndrome, and a mother who left mysteriously for hospital and died when MacNeice was aged 7. Having been fed on a diet of rather reductivist Modernism as the means of a desirable sophistication, MacNeice seized upon its sanctioned primitivism as an excuse for what he called 'Romance', 'the stuff of personal dreams made sufficiently impersonal to be palatable to others than oneself'.[19]

This division of allegiance, between what was 'either stark and realistic or precious and remote',[20] shows in MacNeice's schoolboy writing, where a prematurely jaded modernity combines with a flamboyant mixture of mythological references. In the poetry, two distinct elements may be seen: a habitual association of myth with images drawn from the experience of early childhood; and a reluctant acceptance of both modernity and art itself as inevitable impoverishments of the imaginative scope of mythic antiquity and infancy alike. MacNeice devoured Robert Graves's *Poetic Unreason*, and followed its contention that 'Since the nursery is the one place where there is an audience not too sophisticated to appreciate ancient myths and

---

[15] MacNeice, paper of 1925, quoted in *Modern Poetry*, p. 53.
[16] Report of debate, the *Marlburian*, 60/864 (19 Nov. 1925), 136.
[17] Ibid. 137.
[18] Blunt, 'De Cubismo', p. 88.
[19] 1925 paper, *Modern Poetry*, p. 98.
[20] MacNeice, *The Strings Are False: An Unfinished Autobiography* (1965), 98.

so-called nonsense rhymes of greater or lesser antiquity, it happens
that when we remember a dream, or write a poem in which we
afterwards discover this emotional mode we say we are making a
regression to childhood.[21] The personae often adopted by MacNeice
in these early poems, however, tend to be preoccupied with their own
obsolescence rather than with the privileges inherent in their nursery-
mythic perspectives. In one poem of 1925, the speaker complains
that 'I am left to tell my beads | In this gaud-faded old band-stand |
Where I alone have no sweet sleep.'[22] The conflict between the
rationalism of the modern world and the ingredients of romance
could easily be dramatized into one between philistinism and art: in a
sonnet of 1925/6, 'The dark empoppied gypsy's daisy chain | Stretches
across the barge-begrimed canal', and leads back from the present
with its 'plump workhouse' to a mythic heart, 'To find a Queen upon
the Sphinx's knee | Weaving a lotus wreath of Why's and How's'.[23]
This could be compared with a short prose piece of 1924, where the
world is 'so glutted with knowledge of the "hows" and "whys" of
things, so determined to put everything in its right place as in a well-
oiled engine, that it is becoming itself an engine—and a poor one at
that.'[24] This relocation of the origins of rationality within the realm
of myth is a characteristically crude retort to empiricism, but Mac-
Neice was capable of still more direct confrontations. In another
sonnet of 1925/6, he dropped the mythological element in favour of
direct satire of 'Common Sense':

> Yes! Insulate your souls in cotton wool
> Like real good fellows; prime yourselves with beef
> And sentimental novels and a sheaf
> Of popular songs. Go on, enact John Bull,
> Bear round the bowler hat and gaily pull
> The purse strings of men's brains, beyond belief
> Forced blind, forced dumb, forced brutish & forced deaf.—[25]

MacNeice's desire 'to outrage the Boy in the Street'[26] leads him
finally to identify the hostile audience with the murderers of Socrates,

---

[21] Robert Graves, *Poetic Unreason and Other Studies* (1925), 126.

[22] MacNeice, 'Cradle Song', the *Marlburian*, 60/864 (19 Nov. 1925), 150.

[23] MacNeice, 'And the Spirit Returns . . .', ibid. 61/866 (17 Feb. 1926), 17.

[24] MacNeice, 'The Story of The "Great Triobol Clan" as Created by Mr. Schinabel',
ibid. 59/854 (23 Oct. 1924), 135.

[25] Contained in MS notebook of 1925–6, given by John Hilton to E. R. Dodds as
MacNeice's literary executor in 1964, and at present deposited in the Bodleian
Library (cited hereafter as 1925/6 notebook). The poem is found on fo. [26]ᵛ.

[26] *The Strings Are False*, p. 97.

but the sonnet is revealing for the lack of substance in the young man's ideas which the removal of the customary mythological paraphernalia lays bare. Like Thersites, a prominent member of the MacNeice pantheon at this time, the writer entertains scorn for its own sake. MacNeice was evidently aware of the limitations of such an attitude, and was thus all the more keen on finding a way, through romance, to an art unpolluted, as he saw it, by 'external' connections, close to the significance of significant form. The poet tried to make his early attempts at writing into vehicles for, or assemblages of, what might be styled significant myth; but the fact that ' "significant", on any analysis, ought to mean significant or something outside itself',[27] became more troublesome as the writing gained in assurance and began to recognize an impasse in the second-hand Modernism by which it had been influenced.

Despite MacNeice's implication, in *Modern Poetry*, that 'Literature had become miles removed from life' because his personal life was 'so inadequate to my emotional demands that I fled toward euphuism on the one hand and a dream world on the other',[28] the actual representation of romance in his juvenilia always leads back to the world from which it attempts to escape: it is always, in a sense, defeated as an impulse. In *Third Time*, a short play that was probably written in 1925,[29] a character called 'Romantic Temperament' elaborates upon his identity and foresees his own end:·

I am Merlin. I am Apuleius. I am the Wizard in the Bystreets and the Enchanter in the Side-Alleys. I was born in a cave of the Atlantic, I was reared on the crests of the rocks; I was fed on the sound of piping, Pan and the pennywhistle; I whirl round the bowl of the world on my hairy mat of imagination. . . . I shall die, I the wind, the fire, the foam, on a palliasse in a cottage with cigarette ends on the floor and the window pane stuck up with candle-grease.

As often with MacNeice, the Romantic Temperament's lineage here suggests a Celtic twilight gone to seed; the dandified 'Pan and the pennywhistle' end up in the unromantic poverty which they have never really transcended. In the play itself, these claims go unregarded by the central character whom Romantic Temperament is trying to influence. In claiming access to a romantic heritage (for which a degree of Irishness came in handy), MacNeice always emphasized his

---

[27] *Modern Poetry*, p. 60. [28] Ibid. 52–3.
[29] 1925/6 notebook, fos. [15]ᵛ–[16]ʳ.

own belatedness; in one poem, a Norseman and a Gael, who have
lost 'power', 'gods', and 'home', pass their knowledge on to the poet:

> Then they raised a lament by the Western Sea
> And set the seagulls keening;
> The song they sang is sense to me
> Though for you it may have no meaning.[30]

MacNeice's schoolboy writing is remarkably reluctant to expand
upon what this 'sense' may be, other than a basic refutation of
rationalism and a recourse to myth.

A distancing of the persona from the romantic pursuit may be felt
in one important piece of 1926, entitled 'Sentimentality'.[31] Here, the
lover of romance is presented in the third person as an 'old grey
dotard straddling times abyss' who searches through a cupboard full
of mythic props. The poem, extant in manuscript, is reproduced here
in its entirety:

Sentimentality

> Mona Lisa among yellow roses
> Ever blows her faint peach blossom kiss:
> The old grey dotard straddling times abyss
> Feeds his quick soul on those pressed kisses: posies
> And sentimental spiders ~~drape him round~~
> With love-letters inscribed in their drab thread
> Sing, Old Cat by the Fire, thy hardihead
> Grasp sugar pennies & scrap paper pound.
> Have you not a cupboard full of mysteries,
> Diadems wrought of long-surrendered hearts
> And all the riotous jams of animal marts
> And all the preserved fruits of histories?
> Do not the ~~bottles~~ stand like marble towers
> Of cold, imperial, variegated shine?
> Are these not dusty bottles of good wine
> Mellowed by many melodramatic hours?
> He goes to the cupboard, that old man:
> The cupboard behind her tapestry fan

---

[30] MacNeice, 'The Hope of the Present', the *Marlburian*, 60/861 (24 June 1925),
71.
[31] 1925/6 notebook, fos. [16]ʳ–[17]ʳ. This is a pencil draft, often smudged, which
MacNeice has partially revised. The poet's revisions are incorporated into the present
text, except in l. 13, where 'bottles' is replaced by an indecipherable word. The reading
'mockery' in l. 34 is uncertain.

I search, for who knows what lies hid
In Pharaoh's dusky pyramid.
Souls will rise like a pack of cards,
Scented with nard and spikenard,
Bright as leopard and camelopard
And all the constellate of pards.
Hearts will flaunt like lampshades bright
(And the wizards will light the lamps again.)
We will see the guitars of Aramaine
And the old toys of the infant night
The phoenix feathers, the mitred Popes
In open coffins on mothfull shelves;
The stamp albums stuck full of elves
The postcard albums of cracked hopes.
And the autograph album vellum-gilt
And the names of mockery chessboard kings
And Guinevere imaginings:
And ladies who flutter & knights who tilt;
That heap of gramophone records too,
Black crinkled halos of old tales,
More mournful than the north wind wails
When he comes the South to woo.
With a grating sound the key unlocks
The cupboard grained like chickenpox
Out flops the wan old pendulous air.
What has the old man found in there?
Found after many centuries
Found of his silken mysteries?
He has found nothing. The cupboard is bare.

'Sentimentality' is almost a compendium of images used habitually throughout MacNeice's juvenilia, but seen here in less of a gaily coloured light. Besides the devaluing of childhood memories into 'old toys of the infant night', the elements of romance are presented as 'preserved fruits of histories' and wine in 'dusty bottles', while the poem's bathetic ending further intensifies the atmosphere of sterility and decay. It is a reductive poem, an enumeration of aspects of romance myth, from 'Pharaoh's dusky pyramid' to 'Guinevere imaginings', which finally signify nothing other than their own dead antiquity. The poet's position, despite the third-person distancing, is uncertain, or even, at the end of the poem, potentially redundant. The poem's only escape from the sentimentality of its title is the rough bathos of the ending, which is obviously unsatisfactory as a basis for development in other directions.

The solution of this problem was already implied in some of the early poems, and perhaps even in the sinister atmosphere of 'Sentimentality' itself. In MacNeice's schoolboy verse, as well as the poetry of *Blind Fireworks* and after, the plethora of mythological allusion functions as a kind of deferral of direct imaginative access: that is, access is generally implied to be possible rather than actually made. This deferral is recognized as such by the poet, who can control, to use the most economic terms, different configurations of signifiers without there having to be any definite signified. While this is perfectly justified within the terms of what MacNeice understood by significant form, the poet does not in fact regard the significant as non-existent, or even entirely as irrelevant, but rather as lost. It is this attitude which leads to the blunt impasse encountered in poems such as 'Sentimentality', and it prompts MacNeice to make use of an alternative mythic frame of reference. His 1925 claim, reproduced in *Modern Poetry*, that 'My earliest memory is one of memories and they were melancholy',[32] is one of the poet's many mythopoeic darkenings of personal history, and suggests the direction in which he attempted to develop Graves's sanctioning of 'nonsense' and the nursery. In 'Spring' (1926), the figures of Pythagoras and Adonis are set alongside images of modernity—a mowing-machine and a petrol-pump. The effect is disconcertingly incongruous:

> But the mowing-machine upon the lawn is calling
> With whirring chirp her welcome to Adonis—
> (Yet they cannot stop the clock to keep Adonis;
> From the felt roof the drops of time are falling).[33]

Adonis, in falling victim to the time dispensed by Pythagoras, enters the worlds both of 'modern' imagery and of the poet's own history. In the paper he wrote in 1925 attacking 'common sense', MacNeice had made the mowing-machine one of the elements in a personal memory store of interacting symbols:

When I was little I lived in a perpetual chiaroscuro; noises ticked themselves into other noises, the cracks in the ceiling slid into faces and the marble markings on the mantelpiece became an epic with a hundred plots. Mowing-machines reappeared in dreams to chase me; they lived in the hen-house;

---

[32] 1925 paper, *Modern Poetry*, p. 54.
[33] MacNeice, 'Spring', the *Marlburian*, 61/868 (29 Mar. 1926), 53.

without drums were beating and soldiers marched about, very stiff and wooden and red.[34]

'Spring' brings together the mowing-machines and Adonis to explore the point at which 'Memory cannot go back' and 'fades into myth'.[35] By locating the significance of the mowing-machine firmly in memory, as an image of inescapable pursuit, MacNeice is able covertly to fuse the victim-figure of Adonis with his own remembered nightmares, associating both with the inevitable victory of time. The poet's adaptation of his own memories into a shifting and rich pattern of myths enables him to sidestep the problem of a mythic vocabulary in which multiple deferrals of the signified effectively close off the field of reference; if this 'lost' signified is to be found anywhere, it is in the imagination's transformations of personal experience. This habit was to persist long after Marlborough and Oxford—in the mythic co-ordinates of *Autumn Sequel* (1954), for instance, or in MacNeice's application of his ideas of parable to the late poetry. The (mistaken) conception of MacNeice as a slice-of-life 1930s realist dogged him throughout his career, but his insistence on poetry's relation to myth in fact goes back much further than the procedures of *Autumn Sequel*, beginning in the early poetry.

Once at Oxford, MacNeice's pronounced self-consciousness in writing started to give way to self-confidence; the external trappings of modernity seemed to him to be satisfactory camouflage for the more raw and painful areas of his own experience. A belief in form as a guarantee of impersonality, which was always to some degree to remain with MacNeice, began at Marlborough in the development away from 'significant' myth and romance. Any belief in 'blind inspiration' was qualified by a need for form; in a poem of 1926, MacNeice wrote of how 'Aganippe's stream | Is somewhat strong for most unless diluted', and continued:

> One needs the power to realise one's dream
> To reign the divine madness Plato bruited;
> The inspiration-mongers are confuted
> If they deny the miller to the stream.[36]

---

[34] Quoted in *Modern Poetry*, p. 55.

[35] *The Strings Are False*, p. 36.

[36] Sonnet entitled 'Moral', possibly intended as a coda to MacNeice's 1926 entry for a school poetry prize on the theme of 'Inspiration', among Hilton papers, Bod. Lib., fo. 88ʳ.

'Realise' here, which has been substituted in the manuscript for 'express', perhaps indicates the literariness of MacNeice's notions of reality at this time. Yet the insistence upon formal qualities itself brought the poem back to the difficulty of significant form and self-defining systems. Writing to Blunt just before going up to Oxford, MacNeice could declare that 'I don't believe in pure form, I don't believe in pure anything. Anything pure is an abstraction.'[37] At Oxford, composing the poems which were included in *Blind Fireworks*, MacNeice worked elements of private symbolism into a mythology which was kept both fluid and personally anchored; in one sense, this left what the poet called the 'earlier stratum' of his instinctive images 'the most uncovered', but the poems were also 'in spite of that the most artificial or literary'.[38] However, MacNeice tended to take that very artificiality to imply the genuineness of the material it contained: 'You are, to start with, irretrievably artificial when you set pen to paper, when you select, when you limit a book by beginning or end.'[39] This inclination to see the very act of writing as distinct from some pre-existent essence or idea was resisted by the poet, but an awareness of form as a defence against what might otherwise defy control did remain, and may be felt in the problems and tensions of formal closure in some of MacNeice's later writing. In *Blind Fireworks*, the artificiality is highly pronounced because it is also, in some ways, desperate.

A reviewer of the anthology *Oxford Poetry 1929* saw in MacNeice 'a double self . . . trying to play the censor on the threshold of the unconscious';[40] this is perhaps the impression which the poetry of MacNeice's Oxford years is intended to create. Certainly, the foreword to *Blind Fireworks* emphasizes the individuality of the 'esoteric mythology'[41] upon which the poems are founded, and the recurrence of the same symbols in a number of different poems tends to suggest the presence of personal obsessions without making them explicit. 'Child's Terror',[42] which MacNeice dismissed in *Modern Poetry* on account of its Sitwellian opening, is in fact one of the most direct of

---

[37] MacNeice to Blunt, 25 Sept. 1926, quoted in William T. McKinnon, *Apollo's Blended Dream: A Study of the Poetry of Louis MacNeice* (1971), 95–6.

[38] 'Experiences with Images', p. 161.

[39] From a paper by MacNeice, 'We Are the Old', written in 1930, quoted in *Modern Poetry*, p. 71.

[40] M. C. D'Arcy, the *Oxford Outlook*, 10/50 (Nov. 1929), 380.

[41] Foreword to *Blind Fireworks* (1929), 5.

[42] MacNeice, 'Child's Terror', *Blind Fireworks*, pp. 9–11.

these poems, cast in the mode of first-person recollection, though suffering somewhat from occasional rococo decoration. The memory of a broken swing in a park beside a cemetery (a version of 'my father's medium-sized lush garden with a cemetery beyond the hawthorn hedge') opens up into nightmare:

> I fell into a nightmare down suddenly
> Into a hole without a bottom. Music
> Died above my head, died in silence.

MacNeice seems to retreat from the directness of this at once into more artful composition:

> Mute is the lute and the flute and the drum
> And the trumpet dumb; and I have lost my swing
> That I thought would climb the sky. But now falling,
> Dropping plumb, listening to silence . . .

This is a typical instance of artificiality being made to function as an attempt at impersonality, though in fact the effect of the clumsy internal rhymes and repeated assonances is to suggest only inept evasion. Where the poem is stronger, however, is in its use of images as intensifying elements; snow turns into the marble of tombs, and clocks tick menacingly, leading to the final lines:

> Nurse, nurse, drive away the nightmare,
> Turn a light on my snowy counterpane,
> Tell me it is linen, it is not rock,
> Only tell me I am alive again,
> And the pampas grass will raise plume aloft again—
> And stop the clock, nurse, stop the clock.

The images of time, sleep, and petrifaction are already fully formed into what would be their characteristic expressions in MacNeice's work, foreshadowing such poems of the 1930s as 'Perseus' (1934) or 'August' (1935), in which the fear of stasis refers to more than private obsession. The poem is explicit in its use of personal symbolism without becoming thereby obscure, though the same could not be said for some of the other pieces in the volume. The amalgamated casts of classical and Norse mythologies who populate *Blind Fireworks* are approached by the poet in a manner that is not merely post-Frazer, but consciously post-Eliot in its assimilation of legend, having learned from the schoolboy experiments to deal with the interrelated sign systems of mythological reference as modes of deferral rather than simply ornament. In order to approach the imaginative core of the writing, whether it was 'personal' or anything else, MacNeice regarded the artificial, deferring mode as the only one still possible: 'we who are sailing between Scepticism & Stupidity as in a nightmare never make headway, but are caught in this narrow strait for ever, with the alternative prospects of eternal deafness with stoppers of cotton wool or else a little music & foamsplashed nudity & foamsplashed bones thereafter. As for Odysseus he had a head for business . . .'.[43] Self-consciousness, a recognition of artifice as strategy, lies behind MacNeice's undergraduate writing: critics have been too quick to dismiss his 'head for business' in this respect, one which was never really to desert him, however greatly his particular aims were to change.

At this point the degree of divergence between Auden and Mac-Neice is interesting. Auden had recourse to various images linked closely to his personal background and childhood memories, but these were beginning to preclude for him the use of already-formed symbolic systems. In a notebook entry of 1929, he wrote: 'While Yeats is right that poetry in the past has been symbolic, I think we are reaching the point in the development of the mind where symbols are becoming obsolete in poetry, as the true mind, or non-communistic self does not think in this way. This does not invalidate [its] use in past poetry, but it does invalidate it in modern poetry.'[44] This suggests a poetry that is based psychologically upon 'the true mind' in its capacity as an individual phenomenon, and is therefore concerned with individuality as opposed to any 'Anima Mundi'. Mac-Neice was at this time just as sceptical about the possibility of tapping a reservoir of common subconscious knowledge through myth, but this did not, initially at any rate, push him towards discarding mythological or symbolic systems altogether. MacNeice's much later combinations of history and myth within the individual mind were for him vindications of the direction, if not the actual execution, of his undergraduate instincts:

However deep one's ignorance, historically, of the Decline of the West, it has been since World War 1 something that must hit one in the marrow at adolescence; anyhow Waste Lands are not only community phenomena,

[43] From fragmentary minutes of a paper, 'The Policeman', read by MacNeice in Corpus Christi College in Jan. 1929, Hilton papers, fo. 81ʳ.
[44] Quoted in Mendelson, *Early Auden*, p. 11.

there must be one somewhere in each individual just as everyone contains in himself those places which Spenser described as the Cave of Despair, the House of Busyrane, and, thank God, the Gardens of Adonis.[45]

In other words, to centre symbols upon the individual is not necessarily to deprive them of their value in a wider context. For the MacNeice of *Blind Fireworks*, of course, this was a much more tentative proposition, partly because of the difficulty in reconciling access to symbols of personal relevance with the artificiality inherent in their poetic expression.

'Summer Remembered', a short prose poem of 1927,[46] is a good example of some of the difficulties which MacNeice experienced in his artificial representation of the personal. This short meditation sets the first-person voice in a passive relation to its surroundings, the imagery anticipating strikingly later poems such as 'Ode' or 'Hidden Ice':

Summer Remembered

The dimly gaudy drums of summer thumping in the distance and noises rising hazily like sea-drowned bells. The scent of mown grass lulled and lullabied and lapped me in a cradle, eiderdown'd with mottled blue. I could see nothing but the clouds lifting, sinking, drifting over the sky. A tap dripped music on the thirsty silence. The flies answered with their distant music, virelays and yawns and roundelays. The sun had shot me through and through with arrows, Sebastian fallen on his back. When I shut my eyes I retired behind heavy curtains into a chapel; incense hung about and there was a laver of water flecked with rays from a stained glass window. The cool, marble saints were nodding, drowsing, were dozing; the candle flames were sloping, drooping, were sleeping. Then again the drums of summer like red-hot-poker flowers beating on parchment. The sun was stretching down dog-like to lick Sebastian's wounds with a hot and hairy tongue. A lawn-mower droning, a butterfly flapping, a wheel-barrow trundling. The tap was dripping again like peaches or strawberries. If I were lying beneath a fruit tree the juices would be dripping on my lips. Coolness would pervade me like the vans of shadow, dissolve me like a pearl in wine. When I pressed my eyelids peacocks came with constellated tails. It was too hot to move; they had hardened in their moulds. So I lay all afternoon, and the sun yawned on his cushioned chariot behind the foaming horses, whose feet were shod with sparks. So all afternoon I lay encrusted in sunlight, taut on my blazing wheel that cycled through the blue. The jagged blue of the sky bit me like a toothed

---

[45] 'When I Was Twenty-One', p. 237.

[46] MacNeice, 'Summer Remembered', the *Oxford University Review*, 3/5 (24 Feb. 1927), 144.

collar. The fruit had shrivelled on the trees, the watertap was silent, only the drums of summer kept up their stupid beating while the butterflies were fainting. I lay all afternoon.

If the sun is for MacNeice one of the 'great symbols of routine',[47] and Sebastian its victim ('The sun was stretching down dog-like to lick Sebastian's wounds'), the retreat back into the self prompts images that are equally sinister: the self's complete passivity brings MacNeice back to the images of obsolescence that had haunted some of his schoolboy verse. The aspects of the natural world in the garden have 'hardened in their moulds', and the self is 'encrusted in sunlight', while 'The jagged blue of the sky bit me like a toothed collar'. The attempt to 'remember' summer entails the internalization of descriptive metaphors to the point where they are parts of a disabling stasis, leaving no room in which the self can move freely. The alternative to this process is to pin down metaphorical usage to direct correspondence (the correspondences in 'Summer Remembered' run out of control): one of MacNeice's relatively few attempts at this is a poem of 1928, 'En Avant: A Poem Suggested by Marco Polo',[48] in which the poet follows drily Eliot's 'objective correlative' formula with imagery taken second-hand from Eliot himself. An emperor's funeral procession, its horsemen 'Dead upon dead horses | With lances at rest and cakes in wallets', is set in juxtaposition to a contemporary street scene where 'buses | Pass full of passengers', 'Wooden upon seats of wood, | With pipe in mouth and coppers in pockets'. A third stanza ends the poem by bringing the two scenes together:

> Foot in stirrups, clutch releasing,
> Horse procession, bus procession,
> Mummy-head, wooden head,
> Never ceasing, never ceasing,
> All dead, dead.

As the two images move syntactically towards identification, the poem gutters into complete negation: neither scene has added anything to the other. The poem is worth noting, all the same, as a very early version of the death-bound journey by bus or by train which would feature so successfully in late poems such as 'Figure of Eight' or 'Charon': indeed, one of MacNeice's most common images was to be that of the passenger waiting for the future (in 'Corner Seat' or the

[47] *Modern Poetry*, p. 176.
[48] MacNeice, 'En Avant', the *University News*, 1/4 (10 Nov. 1928), 124.

last canto of *Autumn Sequel*, for example). 'En Avant''s failure
suggests that MacNeice's deliberate mythological indiscipline in
many of the *Blind Fireworks* poems was part of a strategy that left
little room for direct metaphorical or symbolic correspondence. 'En
Avant' and 'Summer Remembered' illustrate two poles of MacNeice's
early writing, the first allowing metaphor to correspond with 'subject'
so closely as effectively to obliterate it, and the second internalizing
metaphor to the point of obliterating any 'subject' outside a self-
crippling imagination. Between an artistic Scylla and Charybdis of
this kind, the 'head for business' of an Odysseus was clearly necessary.

The strategy of *Blind Fireworks* might be outlined as an attempt to
construct a modernist 'myth-kitty' and then watch it explode, or, in
the poet's own terms, to stage a series of explosive displays which 'go
quickly through their antics against an important background, and
fall and go out quickly'.[49] MacNeice's later attitude towards the
book, as an adolescent work 'full of mythological tags, half-digested
new ideas and conceits put in for the hell of it',[50] leaves unclear what
might have been meant (however mistakenly) by this 'important
background', concentrating on the firework display rather than on
the surrounding element to which he had originally drawn his
audience's attention. MacNeice intended his poetry to convey a
sense of the personal areas of tension behind it, and to draw attention
to the forces by which it is undermined, or against which it struggles.
Time, which appears in various guises, is more than just a fruitful
source of 'poetic' melancholy or a good subject for stylized personi-
fication: the 'dotard Time' who 'Hobbles on a crooked stick', or
Pythagoras, whose stone beard wags 'Like a clock's pendulum', are
artificial representations of the same force that ends the nightmarish
poem 'A Cataract Conceived as the March of Corpses' (*Blind
Fireworks*):

And the beat of the bells on the horses' heads and the undertaker's laughter,
And the murmur that will lose its strength and blur at last to quietness,
And afterwards the minute heard descending, never ending heard,
And then the minute after and the minute after the minute after.[51]

Throughout the book, images of death and decay are associated with
the progression of time. MacNeice's way of countering the stasis of

---

[49] Foreword to *Blind Fireworks*, p. 6.
[50] 'Experiences with Images', p. 160.
[51] Repr. as 'River in Spate', in *Collected Poems*, ed. E. R. Dodds (1966), 6.

poems like 'En Avant' was to distinguish patterns in flux—'pattern is value and a *static* pattern dies on you'.[52] Yet the attempt to 'impose exactitude on the flux of the moment'[53] already implied its own final impossibility in the face of time, with its endless successions of minutes-after always outrunning the artificial frames and limits of poetry. The time metaphors of *Blind Fireworks* are deliberate deferrals of direct reference to the element in which the poems exist but which cannot be pinned down with any exactitude. The awareness, or rather fear, of this is perhaps the 'important background' which survives the displays given by the poems themselves.

The most ambitious poems in *Blind Fireworks* (which also, in some senses, are the ones which misfire most seriously) are the last two, 'Adam's Legacy' and 'Twilight of the Gods',[54] in which Mac-Neice forces together a great many otherwise disparate mythological motifs. The poems attempt to delineate mythic beginnings and endings of time. Adam inaugurates human history with the Fall, and his legacy is seen as a rolling wheel that 'opens gates that clang again too soon'. The wheel becomes a 'pain-spoked legacy', and the individual, in a sideways shift of myth, becomes Ixion:

> I straddle my wheel, and we move steadily onward,
> And as I grow the fettering pain grows more
> And the reeling wheel spins out a wake of history,

The poem reduces this 'wake of history' to images half-witnessed by the slumbering Adam in a cave reminiscent of Plato's, where 'shadows creep and crawl over all the cavern wall, | And one can hear the pendulum go to and fro till cockcrow'. The poem ends with Adam and all of the dead waiting for history's end, though 'The trump of doom is still deferred': instead of the cock that 'crew harshly out of the sepulchre', all that is offered is the question, 'have you heard the mocking bird?' Reality is kept at several removes in this poem— literally the Pindaric 'dream of a shadow'—with history's momentum breaking the stasis only as a wheel, bound to repetition by its own circularity; the often irritating jingle of internal rhymes seems to complement this. 'Twilight of the Gods' provides an ending for such

---

[52] *The Strings Are False*, p. 127.

[53] MacNeice, rev. of *The Enormous Room* by E. E. Cummings, in *The Oxford Outlook*, 10/47 (Nov. 1928), 173.

[54] MacNeice, 'Adam's Legacy', *Blind Fireworks*, pp. 74–6; 'Twilight of the Gods', ibid. 77–80.

cycles, but again purely in the terms of an amalgam of myth which has few points of contact with ideas outside the motifs themselves. However, the theme of obsolescence, to which MacNeice had been drawn in his schoolboy images of tarnished romance, when combined with mythological versions of Apocalypse such as those in the Norse stories, provided an attractive way of ending *Blind Fireworks*. Time here, as Pythagoras, is killed by a 'stone child' rising from apparent death under water:

> Stone he seems to-night turned beneath blue water:
> No hair will stir, no feature alter,
> Except when the wind sends a fond ripple over,
> Shrouding the dead whom the marble waters cover.

Again, the image is one which was to stay with MacNeice, occurring in his 1946 radio play *The Dark Tower*, where Roland's mother bears a 'child of stone' upon her death-bed.[55] The gorgon's stare is never far away in *Blind Fireworks*. In 'Twilight of the Gods' the end of time comes from the sea—water is identified ambiguously with both life and death throughout the book, and is also, following Heraclitus, a symbol itself of flux—at the hands of that which had apparently been petrified, rendered static, by time. The poem makes use of its overlapping myths, which MacNeice later criticized as the product of 'junkshop minds',[56] to create an impression of the point at which myth gives way to its own obsolescence, to that which it cannot adequately encompass or express. If the use of mythological allusion is considered as a mode of deferral, it is here that the acknowledgement of its artificiality is necessary, and the 'important background' starts to come forward. 'Twilight of the Gods' ends in a white-out of snow, imposing a dead uniformity, 'Covering this and that and the other thing, | Anything, everything, all things covering'. With the projected ending of time, differentiation and perception end also; again, the poem does not really conclude, but ends in an impasse, without suggesting adequately any relation between its symbols and their referents. *Blind Fireworks* itself, then, finishes with the conclusion of its conglomeration of myths, but once this goes, nothing remains other than an awareness of time as under-mining the constructed patterns and finalities of myth and poetry alike.

[55] MacNeice, *The Dark Tower and Other Radio Scripts* (1947), 60.
[56] 'Experiences with Images', p. 161.

Blind Fireworks, as a modernist text of sorts, elevates the ephemeral and exemplifies it all too accurately; the self-consciousness of its use of mythological metaphor as deferral of reality entails a general retreat from reality into system which its rather precious ironies are insufficient to reverse. MacNeice avoids direct reference or metaphorical correspondence in order to protect the integrity of the 'self' hidden beneath the poetry which is, to all intents and purposes, hermetically sealed off from the forces beyond its control. In the 1930s, MacNeice was to revise this strategy in favour of preservation of the self through its very capacity to refer, to communicate with others and so keep safe the 'consciousness of himself as a man, not consciousness of himself as a poet'.[57] Yet the self 'as a man' cannot, strictly speaking, exist in the medium of writing, as MacNeice implied in 1940, in his qualification of 'the half-truth that poetry is *about* something, is communication'.[58] Like significant form, significant myth was futile without something to signify; even so, as MacNeice's later work shows, belief in at least the possibility of such signification was never quite abandoned.

In 1929, the year that *Blind Fireworks* was published, MacNeice's poetry was moving in more than one direction: as often, personal obsessions made for stronger work than intellectual preoccupations did. By now, the poet could make particularly powerful use of nightmare imagery, as, for example, in a piece contributed to *Oxford Poetry 1929*:

Laburnum (May 1929)

Laburnum gaily weeping
Well expresses us
Whose laughter tinkles downward.
Yellow crowns and dresses and bland insignia
Will not stem our waterfall, will not keep
Old Tom Time from peeping through our branches.

A hundred and one times the bell tolls,
Our souls are gay in yellow and green
With little mockery bells at ankles
Jingling under the motley sun,

---

[57] *Modern Poetry*, p. 1.
[58] MacNeice, *The Poetry of W. B. Yeats* (1941, repr. 1967), 15.

Unseen the cold bell murders them,
A hundred and one times he damns our souls
Concludes our carnival
With a smack of the metal lip at a hundred-and-one.

Here it is we who are blinded and not him,
Peeping Tom has the best of it these days
And when the clown has laughed himself to nothing
And the shadowy ground has drunk his yellow tears,
The next act appears, to merit the praise
Of damned disillusioned impeccable connoisseurs
Whose monocle supplies a cleverly just horizon—
The skeleton of the beautiful clacks in the wind
His leprosy-blighted pods, fingers of poisoned death.[59]

The gaily coloured images here are covering other habitual night-mare symbols, notably 'the cold bell', which recurs often in MacNeice (compare 'Homage to Clichés', for example). 'Laburnum' shows how acute was the young poet's sense of the clash between surface and core, 'beauty' and death. The 'damned disillusioned impeccable connoisseurs' are forerunners of the doomed class in 'An Eclogue for Christmas' (1933), though their moral redundancy has not yet acquired its political overtones.

One of MacNeice's last poems to be written recognizably in the *Blind Fireworks* mould is 'Neurospastoumenos', also from 1929.[60] The poem's epigraph and title are taken from the Greek of Marcus Aurelius: 'An empty pageant; a stage play; flocks of sheep, herds of cattle; a tussle of spearmen; a bone flung among a pack of curs; a crust tossed into a pond of fish; ants, loaded and labouring; mice, scared and scampering; puppets, jerking on their strings—that is life.'[61] The Greek word νευροσπαστουμενα is used by Marcus Aurelius to mean being jerked on a string, and refers to all the creatures of the passage: MacNeice changes the form to the singular, thus leaving open whether it is the poem or the poet who is being thus manipulated. This long poem is essentially a revision and expansion of pieces like 'Adam's Legacy' or 'Twilight of the Gods', giving a 'rough draft of history' from creation to dissolution with various mythological 'puppets' as its characters. It is more successful than the earlier

[59] MacNeice, 'Laburnum (May 1929)', *Oxford Poetry 1929* (Oxford, 1929), 29.
[60] MacNeice, 'Neurospastoumenos', the *Oxford Outlook*, 10/51 (Feb. 1930), 421–9.
[61] Marcus Aurelius, *Meditations*, trans. M. Staniforth (Harmondsworth, 1964), 105. (MacNeice quotes in the Greek.)

poems, however, in its ironic measure of detachment from this puppet-world, and the recognition that 'The philosopher in the stalls is also pulled by strings'. The emphasis shifts away from rococo decoration to philosophical scepticism, and symbols used in earlier poems return more clearly realized: where 'Time on his camel passes down the steppes of sand' in 'Twilight of the Gods', the desert sand is used more simply here as an image of oblivion, a function which it would perform again in MacNeice's wartime poetry, notably 'Jehu'. The sea also is clarified and stripped of extraneous symbolism to become an element resisting the patternings of imagination, a manifestation of the principle of flux: 'We regard | The sea intently but the sea intently | Regards not us'. Here the language becomes explicitly metaphysical:

> Regards not us the One but plays at being Many,
> Regards not us the Point but dreams of three dimensions,
> Regards not us the Absolute.

Anticipating 'Ode', where the sea plays an equally complex role, this begins to destabilize the observing subject, so reducing the autonomy of the self behind the poem. Similarly, when Adam, who has found his toy puppets of human history in Pandora's box, finds himself 'Banned from his theatre':

> Stood he a stylite spitting into the stars
> And set out then to face at last reality
> Without paint, gilt gingerbread, foreign gewgaws.

The stylite alone facing a blank reality (again, an image that was to remain with MacNeice, in poems such as 'Stylite' or 'Spring Cleaning'), is, like the annihilating sand and the sea, resistant to metaphor, an emblem of the dissolution of the mythological world. Unlike the rather precious 'snowflakes of Nirvana' in 'Twilight of the Gods', the poem's ending forms a conclusion that directs attention to verbal elements rather than pictorial ones ('The world is round | The day is over | And the daily round, | . . . All | The round world is over.'). The ending is a word-game, mirroring the games played with Adam in the poem that also have to be brought to an end.

   Another poem from 1929 shows a lighter touch than the *Blind Fireworks* material, though there is a serious level beneath its ironic surface:

Epitaph for Louis

The fire's profanity
Tickled him,
The candle's whimsicality
Amused him
Till, life having abused him,
Death came and pickled him.

Born of a Bryant and May's pentecost
Having put on the cone-cap of a dunce
(Which, strange to say, never seemed absurd to him)
He began to glut his burning soul on beeswax
(Louis was a candle once.)
That he was eating his own flesh
Never once occurred to him.
Louis was a candle once.

Peddling his vocabulary
Muttering, vexed
With this world, guttering
Into the next
In a white flux he dipped
His dunce-cap under
And slipped in a fit
To the crypt of it,
It was no wonder
    Obiit.[62]

Two common elements of MacNeice's imagery are put to work here: the candle, which in 'Candles' (1927, printed in *Blind Fireworks* and retained thereafter) is seen as a figure in a shroud, standing at the foot of the 'grave-bed', and the 'grave-bed' itself, the recurring image of the 'crypt' waiting to receive the poet. The whimsicality of 'Epitaph for Louis' is tinged with nightmare; like a great deal of the early poetry, its ironies are learned from others (here in particular from Eliot), but its tensions are distinctively MacNeice's own.

The problem of MacNeice's early indebtedness to philosophical ideas, or the lack of it, is necessarily involved here. W. T. McKinnon has formulated the poet's position on the various issues raised, implicitly or explicitly, by the early writing as a 'decided love–hate attitude towards the absolute', maintained 'from his Oxford days to the very end', so that 'While his logical reason and his unbelief both

---

[62] MacNeice, 'Epitaph for Louis', *Sir Galahad*, 1/1 (21 Feb. 1929), 9.

yearned for an absolute, his common sense and his highly developed individualistic inclination to revolt cried equally loudly to him to deny an absolute—or, at least, any absolute that was either transcendental or in any way resembled a static idea.'[63] Seizing upon the hints dropped readily by MacNeice in his later retrospective accounts of his youth, this creates a 'position' which, at best, clarifies only a very little of the early work itself. The poet's claim that 'Metaphysics for me was not something cold and abstract; it was an account of reality, but an artistic account, not a scientific one',[64] should perhaps make one wary of any formulations, even those of the 'love–hate attitude'. However, it is true to say that the writing registers a certain dissatisfaction with idealist theories, whilst acknowledging the emotional pull on the ego which Idealism may exert. Using the philosophical language drawn from this Idealism, dominant in Oxford in MacNeice's time,[65] falsifies issues central to the early work by playing down the poet's own, rather cavalier attitude towards them. Part of the rationale of 'standing Plato on his head to insist that Appearance was more real than what he would have called reality',[66] was to demonstrate the value and integrity of the purely individual.

By the end of his university career, if not before, MacNeice had grown hostile to all forms of aesthetic abstraction, and had begun to regard art as that which theory could not encompass. In his article 'Our God Bogus' of 1929, he returned to the idea of significant form in order to dismiss it on just such grounds:

Theory begins by pointing out something which is unessential to art. We bow the head and eliminate that element (e.g., narrative content of a picture or metrical form of a poem); our art is now possibly one-sided, but still runs the risk of being art. But theory if it goes forward bravely will ban the other side also, and if the artist is still obedient he will eliminate this residue of the unessential and his art is now nothing.[67]

This anticipates the 'impure poetry' of the 1930s, but reaches that position by way of reaction to the theory and artistic consequences of a version of Modernism. MacNeice habitually associated a reaction from Modernism with the impurity of injections of unliterary 'reality'

---

[63] McKinnon, *Apollo's Blended Dream*, p. 44.
[64] *The Strings Are False*, p. 119.
[65] E. F. Carritt, a don at University College, was an Oxford proponent of the Italian idealists Gentile and Croce: his *Philosophies of Beauty* appeared in 1931.
[66] 'When I Was Twenty-One', p. 236.
[67] MacNeice, 'Our God Bogus', *Sir Galahad*, 1/2 (14 May 1929), 3.

and 'healthy vulgarity'.[68] It was exactly this which he found lacking in Laura Riding, remarking 'How refreshing to turn from her sophistication to e.g. Mr. Auden (however bragging or bogus his nigger-cum-Lenin-cum-gearbox virility).'[69] Yet the poet did not himself abandon 'sophistication' in favour of 'vulgarity' quite so neatly as the account in *Modern Poetry* might suggest: *Poems* (1935), for example, relies in some respects upon the heightened awareness of flux, artificiality, and closure which MacNeice developed in his earlier work, and his later writing returns to the experiments in the relation between self and myth by which *Blind Fireworks* had been dominated. The uneasiness of MacNeice's common sense increases after the 1930s (though it was hardly negligible then), and in this respect especially, the early work's 'sophistication' is relevant; as he wrote of Yeats in 1927: 'While scientists picked the carcass of matter and found no soul beneath the ribs, Mr. Yeats with a borrowed, antiquated marsh-light of magic followed the *Anima Mundi*. We, of course, do not believe in magic, see only a blind staircase that gapes on the night.'[70] Like the stairs in his schoolboy play *Third Time*, that 'end in a cul-de-sac' and have 'no door at the top—only a window', a 'blind end' in MacNeice's imagery is not always what it seems: there is always the chance of 'light | Before him as through a window | That opens on to a garden' ('The Wall', *Solstices* (1961)).

The two elements that contributed most to the failure of much of MacNeice's early writing were to prove abiding stimuli as well as problems; firstly, in handling myth, the self as the centre of coherence, and its difficulty in 'controlling', 'ordering', and 'giving a shape and significance' (in Eliot's terms[71]) to an almost arbitrary system, constituted a block; secondly, the awareness of time as a subversive element in writing and theory alike, along with the personal fears and obsessions linked to this, served to subvert the stability of any self in MacNeice's poetry. With the 1930s, questions of individuality and time were translated into ideological issues by the left; MacNeice had been preoccupied with such problems from an early stage,

[68] Preface to *Modern Poetry*, p. 1.
[69] MacNeice, rev. of *Life of the Dead* by Laura Riding, in *New Verse*, 6 (Dec. 1933), 19.
[70] MacNeice, rev. of *Autobiographies* by W. B. Yeats, in *The Cherwell*, 29 Jan. 1927, p. 28.
[71] T. S. Eliot, 'Ulysses, Order, and Myth' (1923), repr. in *Selected Prose of T. S. Eliot*, ed. F. Kermode (1975), 77.

nor was he to leave them behind him when their political implications became vieux jeu. Past and future, which are co-ordinates for a great deal of 1930s poetry, are threateningly unfixed points in MacNeice's early writing. In 'Sleep' (1932), the 'dull titanic thuds | In time's graveyard' suggest both burials of the days that have passed and 'those unburied because they had not been, | Lean impossible corpses'. Time here runs out of imaginative control:

> the knowing that it was all
> Going, flowing in a flux, nothing fixt, firm,
> No term, limit, end to the vomit of time—[72]

To measure oneself in terms of flux is to lose any stability of identity, whereas to fix oneself with relation to the past (or the future) often suggests for MacNeice images of petrifaction or sterility, as in 'Circe' with 'Something of glass about her, of dead water'. This comes close to the tensions involved in reconciling time and history which MacNeice was to feel later in the 1930s but its personal application came first, and was to be more enduring. The pursuit of the self in 'Circe' ends with a recognition of distance and intangibility:

> Be brave, my ego, look into your glass
> And realise that that never-to-be-touched
> Vision is your mistress.

Similarly, Devlin Urquart's dream in *Roundabout Way* shows him 'his own life's lady', whom he chases 'round a clump of yews' (the cemetery again) only to find that 'She was beautiful and white but only a stone statue'.[73] 'Time's graveyard' is never far off in Mac-Neice's attempts to fix a stable self in his work, while instability and flux are also threatening elements busy in the poems.

It is a pity that critical treatment of MacNeice's early writing seems to have come little further than an Oxford satire of 1928, which referred to 'The sensuous nonsense of that man MacNeice', 'with his perverse facility in song'[74]—and even that was written to satirize the critic rather than his subject. Much that was to prove vitally important in his later work is present in MacNeice's juvenilia, and much also that helps to make sense of the particular attitudes adopted by the poet in the 1930s. If *Poems* (1935) is something of a

---

[72] MacNeice, 'Sleep', *This Quarter* (Paris), June 1932, p. 610.
[73] MacNeice (*pseud.* Louis Malone), *Roundabout Way* (1932), 13.
[74] From the poem 'Mr. Denzil Batchelor in Shabbington Wood' by 'H. C. H.' [Christopher Holme], the *University News*, 1/8 (8 Dec. 1928), 266.

manifesto for MacNeice's 'flux', its use of time as a counter to history also develops the ideas inherent in his early writing and reading. MacNeice's 'time' was not an idea of time only, but it did see in the present tense the undoing of all imposed coherences, including those of abstract ideas. For MacNeice, poetry always deconstructs philosophy: in 1934 he looked back in this spirit on his admired figures of the late 1920s, writing that 'Gentile's Eternal Present makes an excellent foil to the Platonic Ideas: it would be impressive to uncover a latent Gentile within Plato and Aristotle themselves.'[75] Time, the threatening present, is the mainspring of even the most stilted and artificial of MacNeice's juvenilia; in the 1930s and particularly after 1935, it was threatening in a more obvious sense, and the line between text and context, preserved so carefully by the schoolboy and undergraduate of the 1920s, seemed to be in the process of vanishing altogether.

[75] MacNeice, rev. of *The Domain of Selfhood* by R. V. Feldman, the *Criterion*, 14/54 (Oct. 1934), 162.

3
The Falling Castle: 1936–1939

HOWEVER inconvenient for literary historians, MacNeice's relation to the rest of the poets of the 1930s was hardly straightforward. *Poems*, written during the years when the drive towards 'committed' poetry was at its strongest, seemed in 1935 something of an aggressively neutral book; MacNeice's writing of 1936–9, and in particular *Autumn Journal*, was his most obviously 'political' work of the decade, at a time when Auden, Spender, and even Day-Lewis were edging away from the public contexts of their poetry. Samuel Hynes has shown that, by 1936, 'the tide of political literature was ebbing', even going so far as to claim that by then 'a return to the main stream of modernism had begun'.[1] It is as though MacNeice, in both the first and second halves of the decade, was moving decidedly against the tide. Of course, the term 'political' begs a number of questions: that MacNeice's work in *The Earth Compels* and *Autumn Journal* is not propaganda, or even card-carrying *New Country* writing, is clear enough—in terms of actual political 'commitment', MacNeice was no nearer Marxist orthodoxy in 1936 than he had been before (indeed, he was possibly even further away). Yet his poetry in the late 1930s was more committed than ever to the exploration of, and engagement with, its public contexts, to the programme made explicit in *Modern Poetry*: 'The poet does not give you a full and accurate picture of the world nor a full and accurate picture of himself, but he gives you an amalgam which, if successful, represents truthfully his own relation to the world.'[2] It is clear that neither world nor self can be discarded here, though at the same time the exclusive claims of both are resisted. *Autumn Journal* represents MacNeice's most successful, and ambitious, 'amalgam' along these lines, and because of this it is, in 1930s terms, the most 'political' of his works. Certainly, the poet could go no further in this particular direction, and his aesthetics after 1939 were to change significantly,

---

[1] Samuel Hynes, *The Auden Generation: Literature and Politics in England in the 1930s* (1976), 205, 206.
[2] MacNeice, *Modern Poetry: A Personal Essay* (Oxford, 1938), 198.

but his poetry of the late 1930s represents a pushing to the extreme of the idea (or, as he later called it, the 'half-truth') that 'poetry is *about* something, is communication', against a background of mounting international crisis.[3] The differences between Auden's 'September 1, 1939' or 'In Memory of W. B. Yeats', or Spender's *The Still Centre*, and *Autumn Journal* are principally those between a retreat from, and an engagement with, the volatile stuff of 'history'. Instead of consigning contemporary events to 'the desert of the dark' where 'All the dogs of Europe bark', or admitting with Spender that 'Even while he is writing about the little portion of reality which is part of his experience, the poet may be conscious of a different reality outside',[4] MacNeice's long poem refuses to distinguish clearly between inside and outside, private and public, just as it avoids the status of the fixed and settled statement—'It is in the nature of this poem to be neither final nor balanced' (introductory note). MacNeice's poetry of 1936–9 tackles issues that are constantly present in his work—the relation between self and other, coherence and flux, expression and time—but in ways that reflect particularly the concerns of the time, poetic or otherwise. Questions of individuality, responsibility, history, and time are to the fore in this poetry. The present chapter will attempt to set MacNeice in the context of such issues, and to place them within the larger context of his work as a whole.

In *Poems*, MacNeice had used the idea of the present tense as a manifestation of uncontrollable temporal flux in ways that undermined familiar *New Country* patterns of 'historical' coherence. The previous chapter traced the poet's preoccupation with time back to some of his very early work, and proposed that the idea of the present tense represented a crucial artistic stimulus for MacNeice as well as a personal anxiety. In the late 1930s these concerns became absolutely central to MacNeice's work—and the present tense more urgent and subversive than ever before. Yeats's shrewd estimate of the 1930s poets in his 1936 *Oxford Book of Modern Verse* is relevant here: Yeats observed that 'the contemplation of suffering has compelled them to seek beyond the flux something unchanging, inviolate, that country where no ghost haunts, no beloved lures because it has neither past nor future'.[5] Actually finding such a country, as Yeats knew, was a different matter. Auden's 'Spain 1937' sets present crisis

---

[3] MacNeice, *The Poetry of W. B. Yeats* (1941, repr. 1967), 15.
[4] Stephen Spender, *The Still Centre* (1939), 10.
[5] *The Oxford Book of Modern Verse*, ed. W. B. Yeats (1936), p. xxxvii.

between clear perspectives of past and future—'history', in fact—
but with less than complete success:

> The stars are dead; the animals will not look:
> We are left alone with our day, and the time is short and
>   History to the defeated
> May say alas but cannot help or pardon.[6]

What presses down upon Auden's poem at its close is not history but
time, working against the concluding statement of a logically con-
structed argument. The audible hurrying of 'and the time is short
and', jars with the confident poise of the final two lines; one effect of
this is to seal off the lines *as an ending*, the point at which the poem
stops and the form of history has to be imposed on the formlessness
of time. In so far as 'Spain' says one thing and does another, Auden's
disquiet is akin to the anxiety noted by Stan Smith, that 'To enter
history is to be recruited from volatile freedom to the defined and
finished, quite literally conscripted from speech to print.'[7] This kind
of difficulty is tackled directly by MacNeice, but whereas, in *Poems*
and before, his work emphasized the volatility of 'flux', his writing
later in the 1930s acknowledged more openly the desire for coherence,
for history as well as time. Even then, MacNeice realized that history
would still be trumped by time, in the same way as the self's
coherence could be disrupted by the other outside it. In *Autumn
Journal* II, the poet admits that 'I must leave my bed and face the
music':

> As all the others do who with a grin
>   Shake off sleep like a dog and hurry to desk or engine
> And the fear of life goes out as they clock in
>   And history is reasserted.
> Spider, spider, your irony is true;
>   Who am I—or I—to demand oblivion?
> I must go out tomorrow as the others do
>   And build the falling castle;
> Which has never fallen, thanks
>   Not to any formula, red tape or institution,
> Not to any creeds or banks,
>   But to the human animal's endless courage.

---

[6] W. H. Auden, 'Spain 1937', repr. in *The English Auden: Poems, Essays and Dramatic Writings 1927–1939*, ed. Edward Mendelson (1977), 212.
[7] Stan Smith, *Inviolable Voice: History and Twentieth-Century Poetry* (Dublin, 1982), 133.

MacNeice's question, 'Who am I—or I—to demand oblivion?'—so far removed from the somewhat cavalier manifestos of flux to be found in *Poems*—brings to the surface the disruption in the self that had been induced by events in the late 1930s, where self and other, private and public concerns were drawn into the conflict between coherence and chaos, history and time. Building the falling castle was, for MacNeice, part of the refusal to retreat into individualism or to take refuge in a present tense 'where no ghost haunts'.

In this respect, MacNeice was not so orthodox a 1930s poet as some critics have supposed. In 1937 he insisted that Auden and Spender 'are themselves escaping at the same time as they are preaching parables';[8] and he praised the later Yeats's apparent renunciation of 'the imagination that neither desires nor hates, because it has done with time'.[9] It may seem odd, in view of his later preoccupations, that MacNeice should be the least concerned with parable of all the 1930s poets, but his distancing himself from the forms of 'parable-art' proposed by Auden can be explained by the 'escape-art' with which he insisted on linking it, despite Auden's apparent separation of the two forms.[10] The need to confront the material of writing directly, and with what MacNeice called 'honesty' to the condition of the observing self, effectively precluded the possibility of parable art of the kind that Samuel Hynes saw as central to the writing of the decade. However, this does not leave MacNeice as simply the 'charming Irish classicist with upper-class tastes and a gift for making melancholy poems' that Hynes calls him.[11] On the contrary, MacNeice's directness, although it entailed a great degree of autobiographical reference (as in *Modern Poetry*), also allowed the poet to work within an aesthetic of the unfinished analogous to the inconclusions of personal history. It is a biographer's task to decide whether MacNeice's fragments of autobiography are any more accurate factually than Yeats's, but the personal content of his 1930s work fulfils a rather similar purpose to that of the older poet: that is, it brings the finalities of poems into the context of the

---

[8]   MacNeice, 'Subject in Modern Poetry', in *Essays and Studies 1936* (1937), 149, repr. in Heuser, p. 65.

[9]   Ibid. 150 (quoting W. B. Yeats, *Essays and Introductions* (1961), 163).

[10]   See W. H. Auden, 'Psychology and Art To-Day' (1935): 'There must always be two kinds of art, escape-art, for man needs escape as he needs food and deep sleep, and parable-art, that art which shall teach man to unlearn hatred and learn love.' (Repr. in *The English Auden*, pp. 341–2.)

[11]   Hynes, *The Auden Generation*, p. 370.

unfinished and changing patterns of coherence of the individual life. This should be distinguished from Auden's jealous guarding of personal elements on the one hand, and Spender's increasingly confessional autobiographical openness on the other. MacNeice's idea of the 'honest' voice was one in which any coherence was consciously provisional, whether in terms of the personal or the broadly political life. In *Modern Poetry* he went so far as to reinterpret the old concept of the 'Concrete Universal' of his university years in these terms, announcing that 'The poet is once again to make his response as a whole':

On the one side is concrete living—not just a conglomeration of animals or machines, mere flux, a dissolving hail of data, but a system of individuals determined by their circumstances, a concrete, therefore, of sensuous fact and what we may call 'universals'; on the other side is a concrete poet—not just an eye or a heart or a brain or a solar plexus, but the whole man reacting with both intelligence and emotion (which is how we react to anything in ordinary life) to experiences, and on this basis presenting something which is (*a*) communication, a record, but is also (*b*) a creation—having a new unity of its own, something in its shape which makes it poetry.[12]

This effects a conjunction between 'communication'—of its nature open discourse dependent partly on its audience and the movement of time—and the formal constraint at the heart of poetry. Implicitly, the passage denies distinctions between poetics, politics, and metaphysics, and MacNeice's writing of the late 1930s constitutes an attempt to put such a conjunction into practice, so that finished poems exist in the unsettling context of unfinished histories, both 'private' and 'public'.

The diversity of MacNeice's writing during the period 1936–9 is striking: as well as poetry, he produced drama, literary criticism, and travel writing, along with the unclassifiable 'pot-boiler' *Zoo*. Living in Hampstead rather than Birmingham, he was physically closer to the centre of the 1930s literary milieu than before, at the time when *Poems* was being seen as a significant turn in the poetic tide. 1936 was the year of MacNeice's first trip to Spain, on the edge of civil war, then his journey to Iceland and his travels there with Auden, resulting in *Letters from Iceland* in 1937. 'Our Iceland trip' is the best point at which to begin an analysis of MacNeice's late 1930s work, providing, as it does, a point of departure for the poet's artistic

[12] *Modern Poetry*, pp. 29–30.

engagement with his own particular time and place. Iceland in the summer of 1936 offered at least the possibility of a better perspective on the 'Nations germinating hell' in Europe, and the resultant book allowed Auden and MacNeice to work in an unrelentingly 'public' light whilst employing ostensibly 'private' modes of writing— personal letters. *Letters from Iceland* is designed to embody publicized privacies alongside personal comprehension of, and reaction to, public issues, most specifically the state of contemporary Europe.

One important point of contact between MacNeice and Iceland was in the sagas with which the poet had been familiar since childhood, and in particular the figure of Grettir, 'the doomed tough' who, unable to bear the dark, finds he cannot live in the solitude of outlawry, 'even to save my life'.[13] The Icelandic past, as represented by the sagas, offered a suggestive parallel to contemporary Europe, 'a rotten society' 'with only the gangster values', according to Auden.[14] Grettir makes his appearance in MacNeice's 'Eclogue from Iceland', a poem which is in fact quite different in both form and effect from the eclogues of *Poems*, being much closer now to dramatic dialogue. Here, questions of 'escape', 'home', and solitariness are to the fore, with Grettir presenting a clear analogue with their own times to the travellers Ryan and Craven, projections of aspects of MacNeice and Auden themselves. In the original published version of the eclogue, the travellers begin by congratulating themselves upon their escape from Europe:

> C.   I like this place. My personal choice
>   Is always to avoid the public voice.
> R.   You are quite right, Craven. For people like us
>   This is an enviable terminus.
>
> .   .   .   .   .
>
>   And beside this cold and silicate stream
>   To sleep in sheepskin, never dream,
> C.   Never dream of the empty church,
> R.   Nor of waiting in a familiar porch
>   With the broken bellpull, but the name
>   Above the door is not the same.[15]

In fact, the escape to Iceland, away from the pressures of the 'public voice', is an escape from the dream of home (compare MacNeice's

---

[13] *The Saga of Grettir the Strong*, trans. G. A. Hight (1914), 181.
[14] MacNeice and W. H. Auden, *Letters from Iceland* (1937), 119.
[15] Ibid. 124.

later 'Order to View', with its return to a house where 'The bell-pull would not pull | And the whole place, one might | Have supposed, was deadly ill'). The travellers are interrupted by Grettir's ghost, who shows them that what they have taken for escape is in fact exile. Again, 'home' is a point which, even if access to it is difficult or impossible, acts as a kind of centre of gravity for MacNeice's imagination. Interestingly, Grettir makes much of the possibilities offered by an 'island' home, and brings Ryan to a direct confrontation with his own place of origin:

> Is your land also an island?
> There is only hope for people who live upon islands
> Where the lowest common labels will not stick
> And the unpolluted hills will hold your echo.

The apparent rejection of Ireland which this provokes is an admission of exile rather than a declaration of escape; in effect, Ryan counters Grettir's 'unpolluted hills' with his own description of a 'gangster society' close to that of the sagas, offering another perspective on the same 'history'. Myth is undercut by reality here, but reality is in its turn undercut by the perspectives of myth. Thus Ryan and Craven are schooled by Grettir in the meaning of 'exile', in how to confront with integrity the challenge posed by the 'Voice from Europe'; the advice given is in the imperative:

> Argument will frustrate you till you die
> But go your own way, give the voice the lie,
> Outstare the inhuman eyes. That is the way.
> Go back to where you came from and do not keep
> Crossing the road to escape them, do not avoid the ambush,
> Take sly detours, but ride the pass direct.

As far as MacNeice's contributions to *Letters from Iceland* are concerned, the imperative of 'Go back to where you came from' is important, pushing towards 'home' (however hostile 'home' may be) as opposed to being 'an addict to oblivion | Running away from the gods of my own hearth | With no intention of finding gods elsewhere'.

Although 'home' is a vital pole in MacNeice's work, it does not exist at the expense of 'fact'. In the 'Eclogue from Iceland', oppositions between 'fact' and desire, contemporary reality and myth, are set up by the poet in order to suggest a submerged line of coherence. As in an early draft 'Subjective & objective memory' are 'closer connected

| Than is commonly thought',[16] so there is an implicit concern in the eclogue with the degree to which personal and extra-personal worlds overlap. Whether or not the 'public voice' can be avoided, Europe intrudes as more than 'surface' or 'mere copy'; in some sense, the Voice from Europe speaks for a contemporary manifestation of the flux so pervasive in *Poems*, a glamorous hail of consumer data that 'Will smooth the puckered minutes of your lives'. The glitter of flux alone is not enough now, and its radical undermining of the coherences of history is more clearly realized as a distinct threat:

> The nightmare noise of the scythe upon the hone,
> Time sharpening his blade among high rocks alone.

It is against this background that the eclogue's humanist climax, the 'hatred of hatred, assertion of human values', is set. For MacNeice, Iceland provides a tentative glimpse of some of the implications of 'home' that suggest resistance to the forces of time and flux. In effect, the Northern vantage-point orientates the poet more strongly than before towards the 1930s concern for historical coherence, the construction of form out of chaos. His 'Epilogue' to *Letters*, addressed to Auden, is pitched in an uncertain and threatened present tense, spoken from a domestic interior that is also a 'desert in disguise'[17] and mutates to a sinister scene of isolation and danger. MacNeice effectively destroys a conventionally secure 'home' scene at the end of the 'holiday', putting another crisis in its place:

> For the litany of doubt
> From these walls comes breathing out
> Till the room becomes a pit
> Humming with the fear of it
>
> With the fear of loneliness
> And uncommunicableness;
> All the wires are cut, my friends
> Live beyond the severed ends.

The poem's tense, the present on the very edge of a deferred future ('Still I drink your health before | The gun-butt raps upon the door'), is in miniature that of *Autumn's Journal*'s 1938. The self is completely

---

[16] Quoted in Robyn Marsack, *The Cave of Making: The Poetry of Louis MacNeice* (Oxford, 1982), 32.

[17] Cf. the numerous scenes of desert imagery in MacNeice's poetry of the early 1940s, discussed in Chap. 4 above.

isolated in time, its stability undermined by 'the litany of doubt', the antiphonal voices it pitches against itself. Beneath Auden's cavalier tone when he touches upon a similar subject in parts of 'Letter to Lord Byron' is an awareness of the real deaths of 1936, yet his 'home' is simply where he happens to be, and the poet's individuality is always effectively 'at home' with its own voice. MacNeice's 'All the wires are cut' is closer to nightmare, a scene in which the self shuttles between coherence and chaos, history and mere time. If 'home' is still as impossible in the present as it was in *Poems*, its nature at least has been brought into clearer focus. MacNeice, with the 'luck' of a saga character which affects both the self and those with whom it comes into contact, sets himself in a dilemma designed to be of more than individual significance.

The difficulty posed by Iceland is partly that identified by Tom Paulin: 'Was this coming full circle not the question they asked?'[18] As Paulin has pointed out elsewhere, MacNeice saw aspects of the spiritual desolation in Ireland in the landscape of Iceland, just as Auden was brought back sharply to the problems of totalitarianism, both of them travelling in 'a democratic community which works under the physical shadow of its landscape and the spiritual shadow of its heroic past'.[19] Certainly, MacNeice's work after his trip to Iceland is 'political' in ways that seemed impossible before, reaching a peak in *Modern Poetry* and *Autumn Journal*. The poems that make up *The Earth Compels* (1938) show MacNeice coming to terms with a burden of responsibility which is broadly 'political' in its terms of reference, while sustaining also the concerns already central to his poetry. One preoccupation is of particular importance here, that of time and its relation to history. That the present was in some sense a crucial period was already a truism (too much so, perhaps, in Auden's 'Spain'); one of the most vivid statements of this conviction had been made by Day-Lewis in 1934: 'To-day the foreground is a number of fluid, confused and contradictory patterns. Standing at the end of an epoch, the poet's arms are stretched out to opposite poles, the old life and the new; that is his power and his crucifixion.'[20] In *Poems*, MacNeice made it his business to confuse such patterns even further; after Iceland, the difficulties in the present tense became those of past and future also. Paulin argues convincingly for the

---

[18] Tom Paulin, 'Thinking of Iceland', in *A State of Justice* (1977), 13.
[19] Tom Paulin, 'Going North', *Renaissance and Modern Studies*, 20 (1976), 74.
[20] Cecil Day-Lewis, *A Hope for Poetry* (Oxford, 1934), 48.

burden of the past in *Letters*; but after 1936 there is also the question of the future pressing on MacNeice's present. The predicament of the figure in 'Hidden Ice' 'who sat between the clock and the sun' could perhaps be taken as an analogy for the poet's difficulty in going beyond the strategies of *Poems* in order to write more openly 'responsible' poetry. The 'hidden ice' which intrudes fatally into the world of habit, disrupting 'Our mild bravado in the face of time', anticipates Auden's description of the Icelandic glaciers as 'no glacial flood | But history, hostile, Time the destroyer',[21] or John Cornford's 'The past, a glacier' in 'Full Moon at Tierz'.[22] 'Hidden Ice', written at the beginning of 1936, questions the surface sufficiency while maintaining the value of 'A twitter of inconsequent vitality': the self in the poem is usurped by elements it had ignored. This represents a questioning of the habitual divisions between self and other, and a recognition that the values of surface, of flux, are in this sense incomplete—the self's boundaries are not to be drawn so easily. Coming 'home', for MacNeice, entails discovering the limits of the self as well as affirming patterns of history against the canvas of time.

The first recognition to be made in this process is that flux cannot be entertained by poetry as an end in itself. Like other metaphysical cruces, this has implications on many levels for MacNeice. In 'Sonnet' (a poem printed first in 1937 and later dropped), addressed to a lover who has now gone for good, MacNeice admits that 'The creed I built upon your charm and sex | And *laissez faire* I find no longer tenable'. Here *Laissez-faire* (later to echo through *Autumn Journal*) sums up a past nonchalance and openness that is now abandoned. As in 'Epilogue', the poet ends up sitting alone in his own room:

> Settling now to a grey and reasoned gloom
> Where I shall neither recant the minutes gone
> Nor fumble for the past with backward hands.[23]

The 'reasoned gloom' that settles on MacNeice's post-1936 work (as opposed to the glitter of his earlier writing) is one consequence of his allowing the future as well as the present to become an important

---

[21] Auden, 'Letter to R. H. S. Crossman, Esq.', in *Letters from Iceland*, p. 93.

[22] John Cornford, 'Full Moon at Tierz: Before the Stroming of Huesca', repr. in J. Galassi (ed.), *Understand the Weapon Understand the Wound: Selected writings of John Cornford* (Manchester, 1976), 38.

[23] MacNeice, 'Sonnet', the *Listener*, 30 June 1937, p. 1306 (repr. in *Poems* (New York, 1937), 90).

imaginative co-ordinate. Here it is the very gloominess of MacNeice's vision that contrasts most strongly with what might be considered to be 1930s orthodoxies on the subject. In the minds of a good many poets, 'history' had come to mean the future as much as the past, with the present time being essentially symptomatic of historical change. In Rex Warner's 'Future', for example (published in 1937):

> What is happening will be clear to the men of the future;
> for deceit will not be needed.
> But our here and now to them will look like a dream
> sad, furious, fatal.[24]

MacNeice, for whom patterns of history were compromised by time, also framed the present between past and future, but tended to depict the contemporary crisis as being on the edge of catastrophe rather than historic illumination. This is the setting for 'The Sunlight on the Garden', of course, in which 'the church bells | And every evil iron | Siren' press in upon the individual's occupation of time and space. It is noteworthy that both here and in 'The Brandy Glass', MacNeice freezes the present moment rather than following its movement as 'flux'; just as 'The moment cradled like a brandy glass' is forced away from simile into the near-surreal image of snow falling in a dining-room, so the garden is finally held in one stable focus of 'sunlight'. The intricate construction of the poem is in fact a way of trying to 'cage the minute' by acknowledging the dangers posed by the minutes to come. MacNeice's assonantal development of the final words of lines towards a more threatening form ('garden | Hardens', 'flying, | Defying', 'pardon | Hardened') builds change into the fabric of the poem, while the full rhymes of the first and last lines of each stanza serve to contain each phase of this change, reversing the emphasis in the final stanza (so that it is 'pardon' which now rhymes with 'garden', rather than vice versa). Effectively, MacNeice uses the structure of his poem to supply the closure against which, in fact, the argument runs.[25] 'The Brandy Glass' also has a circular structure,

---

[24] Rex Warner, 'Future', in *Poems* (1937), 62.
[25] Cf. Stephen Spender's poem 'What I Expected', in which structural symmetry, and the final image of 'the dazzling crystal', seem to work against the apparent argument. Extended analyses of 'The Sunlight on the Garden' are to be found in Robin Skelton, 'Celt and Classicist: The Versecraft of Louis MacNeice', in T. Brown and A. Reid (eds.), *Time Was Away: The World of Louis MacNeice* (Dublin, 1974), and Adolphe Haberer, *Louis MacNeice 1907–1963: L'Homme et la poésie* (Bordeaux, 1986), 218–31.

ending at the point at which it began, with everything changed. The snow that falls in the poem carries MacNeice's habitual fear of 'snow's unity':

> From the chandeliers the snow begins to fall
> Piling around carafes and table legs
> And chokes the passage of the revolving door.
> The last diner, like a ventriloquist's doll
> Left by his master, gazes before him, begs:
> 'Only let it form within my hands once more.'

There appears to be a wariness of the caged minute here as leading to repetition and absurd isolation. Perhaps even the very form of 'The Sunlight on the Garden' contains the same wariness, an acknowledgement of the inadequacy of the isolation which the poem's structure, its firm and obvious closure, enacts.

Clearly, difficulties such as these are parts of *Modern Poetry*'s tension between 'communication, a record' and 'creation—having a new unity of its own'. At the same time, they are related to what MacNeice saw as the need for a stable self within poetry to facilitate its function as 'communication', as well as to the idea of 'impure' poetry, 'conditioned by the poet's life and the world around him'.[26] In some ways, all of this is at odds with MacNeice's conception of the 'lyric' voice in poetry, as well as with the strategies of inclusion and self-countering to be found in *Poems*. 'The Sunlight on the Garden' forces a division between the two aspects of form identified in *Modern Poetry*, where 'the form of poetry includes far more than the surface patterns of rhythm or sentence-structure; it is also the juxtaposition of images and the balance of idea against idea':[27] its images go in one direction, and its packed and complete internal design in another. A number of the shorter poems in *The Earth Compels* are written in intricate forms, or forms that suggest music ('The Sunlight on the Garden' was originally simply 'Song'),[28] while their images are premonitions of impending catastrophe, of an ending more final than that of a poem. Often it is the present tense that is the focus of attention, and the world of personal relationships forms its principal value. In 'The Heated Minutes', for example:

> I should not feel the dull
> The taut and ticking fear

[26] *Modern Poetry*, p. v.   [27] Ibid. 63.
[28] MacNeice, 'Song', the *Listener*, 22 Jan. 1937, p. 151.

> That hides in all the clocks
> And creeps inside the skull—
> If you were here, my dear.

It is important that MacNeice tends to switch his focus to the personal at the end of poems, so that the closure which the continuing present tense might otherwise deny seems to be made a little more rooted and secure. The formally intricate sapphics of 'June Thunder', for example, contain the worsening elements beyond individual control that culminate in 'lightning's lavish | Annunciation, the sword of the mad archangel | Flashed from the scabbard'. The poem's final stanza reclaims the present tense for the personal ('If only now you would come I should be happy | Now if now only'), but this, as an ending, sets one present tense against another, the personal against the threateningly impersonal. Another poem in sapphics, 'Christmas Shopping', is more uncompromising; written entirely in the present tense, its form holds it back from being a 'hailstorm of data', but its present is that of 'The eleventh hour', and the future presses dangerously:

> Out there lies the future gathering quickly
> Its blank momentum; through the tubes of London
> The dead winds blow the crowds like beasts in flight from
> Fire in the forest.

Anticipating an image from *Autumn Journal*, the presentation of 'blank momentum' abolishes individual distinctions, and the poem's ending swings towards the completely inhuman, a lighthouse 'like a giant at Swedish drill whose | Mind is a vacuum'. 'Christmas Shopping' itself is an exercise in 'blank momentum' which, unlike 'June Thunder', abandons the personal level of the present tense in favour of the impersonal (and unfinished because continuing) force of the coming future. Like the other poems, though, 'Christmas Shopping' makes a point of 'having a new unity of its own' in terms of form, while in fact abandoning any patterns of coherence or stability in the way in which it treats its subject.

MacNeice's subsequent accounts of his late 1930s writing tend to make it seem almost schizophrenic, part Audenesque journalese and part 'serious' writing. In *The Strings Are False*, for instance, he claims that 'I continued dreaming about bombs and fascists, was worried over women, was mortifying my aesthetic sense by trying to write as Wystan did, without bothering too much with finesse.'[29] Apart from the example cited by MacNeice, *Out of the Picture*, productions like *Zoo*, or *I Crossed the Minch* certainly have all the appearances of rushed composition, yet they are far from beside the point as far as the development of the poet's 'aesthetic sense' is concerned; or, rather, by the time he wrote *Strings*, MacNeice's idea of what constituted an 'aesthetic sense' had changed somewhat. In *Zoo*, a book of 'reportage' steeped in autobiography, MacNeice went so far as to include an argument between the 'Reader' and the 'Writer' on the limits of the imaginative writer's scope, with the political premiss that 'Democracy . . . will rest on the layman's right to criticize':

So the human individual takes in anything you give him and promptly transforms it; he is ready to give you out again his own reactions—first, in thought and emotion, then in voice or action. The human being cannot experience anything—*anything*, mind you—without reacting to it both with his emotions and his intelligence. . . . This being so, it is inevitable that he should go on to let those reactions come out in words or deeds.[30]

The theoretical aesthetic application of this is clearly embodied in *Modern Poetry*, and put into practice, to some extent, in *Autumn Journal*, but it should be noted that MacNeice could never completely follow through the theory in his poetry. The 'aesthetic sense' corresponds with the 'honesty' for which reviewers tended to praise MacNeice, but the reconciliation of 'honesty' with the form of poetry was more problematic for the poet. Certainly, in the themes and persistent concerns of his poetry of the late 1930s, MacNeice made use of areas in which 'honesty' to personal obsessions overlapped with public issues, but the idea of poetic form did tend to work against this. The 'unity' claimed for poems in *Modern Poetry* might be at odds not just with journalistic 'honesty' towards the facts, but with poetry's 'political' side as well. Thinking back to Auden's *The Orators* in 1934, the critic Edgar Foxall wrote of 'the sincere political mindedness which sometimes blinds him to the unity essential in a good art work',[31] and in the late 1930s both Auden and Spender were moving closer towards seeing the unities of poems as

---

[29] MacNeice, *The Strings Are False: An Unfinished Autobiography* (1965), 169.
[30] MacNeice, *Zoo* (1938), 15.
[31] Edgar Foxall, 'The Politics of W. H. Auden', the *Bookman*, 85 (Mar. 1934), p. 474.

the alternatives to those of 'political mindedness'. By the end of the decade, Spender wrote that 'The individual poet has been forced to make a unity in his own soul, where there is chaos all around him',[32] and Auden was firmly embarked upon a more sophisticated analysis of the same position. Where the other poets were, broadly speaking, consolidating their notions of the self in the late 1930s, MacNeice, 'mortifying my aesthetic sense', was attempting both to destabilize the self in his writing and to establish personal 'honesty' more firmly as an imaginative resource. In so far as this meant understanding the isolated self, savouring his existence like the lone diner in 'The Brandy Glass', and opening up the range of the 'ordinary man', MacNeice could use subject as a key resource: poems like 'On These Islands' or 'Rugby Football Excursion' are forms of personalized documentary, and the 1936 essay 'Subject in Modern Poetry' makes the issue sound quite straightforward: 'Every man lives in a contemporary context which is of value and interest. That is the life which, directly or indirectly, he should write about. He must be a craftsman to be able to "put it over", and this he may have to do under various disguises.'[33] Even so, 'contemporary life', which, MacNeice claimed, 'strictly speaking is the only life', entered the 'aesthetic sense' in more complex, and sometimes threatening, ways than summaries like this would suggest.

Measuring MacNeice's 'political' content in the climate of the late 1930s is in some ways liable to be misleading, since it often amounts to accepting various contemporary definitions of political 'commitment' in the light of which the poets tended to be seen. Like Auden, MacNeice is remarkably difficult to pin down in such terms. D. E. S. Maxwell is representative in arguing that MacNeice 'was not just "reporting", and among the attitudes his poems express is a sort of reluctant marxism which accepts the premisses but has no enthusiasm for the conclusion'.[34] Yet this can be seen from another angle as a kind of gruff orthodoxy: certainly, the 'sceptical liberal' tag has been used too easily in MacNeice criticism, as though it did away with the need to consider the pressure of 'political' forces upon the poet's imagination. If the events of the late 1930s, such as the Spanish Civil War and the Munich crisis, affected the poet, they did not do so in

[32] Stephen Spender, 'The Creative Imagination in the World Today', *Folios of New Writing*, Autumn 1940, p. 156.
[33] 'Subject in Modern Poetry', p. 158 (Heuser, p. 74).
[34] D. E. S. Maxwell, *Poets of the Thirties* (1969), 179.

terms of his 'position', Marxist or otherwise, but rather by forcing his imagination outwards, making, as it were, the self encounter the other without pre-conditions. When, in a poem like 'Bagpipe Music', the momentum of horror forces the poetic self into the entrenchment of the satiric voice, the verse is clearly 'political' over and above any specific 'position'. The same is true of another poem, 'Salute',[35] which attacks Fascism in the voice of world-weary cynicism ('The world is going under— | Don't we know it? | . . . Rotten-ripe for plunder | Years fermented'). Like 'Bagpipe Music', the poem can hardly be covered by the 'sceptical liberal' designation:

> Call the carcase
> To its last reveille,
>   *Hail and be damned,*
> Trapped in khaki,
> Drilled to kill and toady,
>   *Hail and be damned,*
> Cheers on the lips
> And ulcers in the belly,
>   *Hail and be damned.*

Again like 'Bagpipe Music', the poem is a phantasmagoria, in the form of a Yeatsian marching-song rather than a reel, with the imagery of Fascism sending the world 'under' ('The Kingdom Comes | With castanets and truncheons'). This recollection of the 'personal' poem 'Intimations of Mortality' is applied to a larger and equally threatening frame of reference; the ironic command to 'Frame the moment, | Kiss the passing harlot' (also recalling aspects of Mac-Neice's earlier writing), suggests the need to renounce the 'private', isolated relation to external reality. In terms of political 'position', the poem is simply 'anti-fascist'; yet it places itself within the context of MacNeice's poetry as well, where its 'political' aspect is more complex, pushing the attitude of cynical resignation, which is sometimes present in *Poems*, to an extreme. At this extreme, there is a recognition that isolation, the self's complete and moment-framing integrity, is perhaps a kind of complicity with the forces of death and decay which it affects to spurn. MacNeice cannot retreat behind the cover of 'sceptical liberalism' and leave 'politics' there; for him, poetry itself is a scene on which 'political' issues are fought out with

---

[35] MacNeice, 'Salute', *In Letters of Red*, ed. E. A. Osborne (1938), 163.

greater seriousness than the language of 'position' or 'commitment' allows.

At the time of composing *Autumn Journal*, MacNeice answered *New Verse*'s request to commit himself 'about' poetry by writing: 'I have committed myself so much already *in* poetry that this seems almost superfluous.'[36] This encapsulates the difference in his work between the politics of 'position' and those of poetry. Although in the late 1930s he tended to avoid the parable art favoured by Auden, MacNeice did write poetry to be regarded as in some sense exemplary, if only in its linguistic wariness and its lack of finality. In 'Homage to Clichés', written late in 1935, cliché and repetition function as signals of an isolation of the self from the other, whether through ignorance or habit; but this isolation is under threat. The poem's wariness of 'the same again' becomes a wariness also of the very habits of mind that make absolutes and finalities out of aspects of experience. The ending, therefore, is a challenge to finality; in terms of the running bar-images, it is something of a startling way of calling time:

> Somewhere behind us stands a man, a counter
> A timekeeper with a watch and pistol
> Ready to shoot and with his shot destroy
> This whole delightful world of cliché and refrain—
> What will you have, my dear? The same again?

The 'counter', semantically transformed in its repetition from the mundane to the ominous, undermines the static nature of 'cliché and refrain'. MacNeice commits himself *in* poetry here in the sense that, as in 'Letter to Graham and Anna', 'we must keep moving to keep pace | Or else drop into Limbo, the dead place', or in the final couplet of 'Chess', one must 'Choose your gambit, vary the tactics of your game | You move in a closed ambit that always ends the same'. The whole poem enacts a wariness of repetition that is intended as exemplary. Similarly, in 'Eclogue between the Motherless', the cycle of maternal–marital affection and disaffection is limiting, with the two voices who shrink the outside world to 'others, isolated by associations', being undermined by the repetitiveness of their personal worlds, 'A gramophone needle stuck on a notched record'. To turn away from the mother to something other than merely her substitute is essentially to forego the easy repetitions of the known for the

---

[36] MacNeice, 'A Statement', *New Verse*, 31–2 (Autumn 1938), 7.

world beyond the self's exclusive control. For MacNeice, this change in personal orientation necessarily implies a different 'aesthetic sense' as well, one in which 'politics' are incorporated as more than modish lip-service to the right causes. Unlike Auden, for whom, as Edward Mendelson has pointed out with regard to 'A Summer Night', repetition 'became the ground of memory, the medium of love',[37] MacNeice's poetry destabilizes firm grounding in the 'personal' or the poetic self. This is a gesture explicitly against repetition, and is even (in a broader sense of the word than that used by the propagandists) a 'political' act, opening up the self to uncertainty and disorientation.

By the second half of the 1930s, MacNeice had considerably complicated the rationale of the optimistic 'school' of *New Country*. Building on the critique of deterministic history implicit in *Poems*, he returned increasingly to the individual, compromised by time and his surroundings, as the centre of attention, but he understood this individual in neither Marxist nor bourgeois individualist terms. In 'Subject in Modern Poetry', MacNeice uses Yeatsian co-ordinates of 'Self' and 'Soul' to place contemporary writers, claiming that 'Auden and Spender follow Yeats rather than Eliot in being more concerned with the Self than the Soul'. He enlarges on this perceptively with regard to Auden:

Auden's admiration for the objective world is founded in that cosmic pride which is distinct from personal pride and which is at the base of Christianity. This explains his belief that 'Pelmanism' is an important factor both in art and in the good life. The Epicurean, like the Artist for Art's sake, will have no use for pelmanism. Why burden his mind with facts *which cannot affect his own life*? The Epicurean does not appreciate Otherness as such.[38]

If MacNeice did not have quite this 'cosmic pride' as an imaginative pole, he certainly did use and need the fascination with 'Otherness as such'. It is interesting that he finds this in accord with the Yeatsian self, which he understands as something entirely distinct from egocentricity. Furthermore, this self is defined dialectically, or by difference, being in itself meaningless without its opposed value of soul. MacNeice's conception of the individual, then, is similarly unstable, part of a whole system of differing values and attitudes. In *I Crossed*

---

[37] Edward Mendelson, *The Early Auden* (1981), 172.
[38] 'Subject in Modern Poetry', pp. 156, 157 (Heuser, p. 73).

the Minch, MacNeice sets down clearly a prescription for this kind of 'individual':

A world society must be a federation of differentiated communities, not a long line of robots doing the goose-step. In the same way the community itself must be a community of individuals. Only they must not be fake individuals—archaizers and dilettantes—any more than the community must be a fake community, a totalitarian state strutting in the museum robes of Caesardom.[39]

MacNeice's Utopias, here as in *Autumn Journal*, can be revealing; the political good resides in individuals rather than in *the* individual. This is a crucial distinction, for it rules out the 'pure' individual, who is defined simply in relation to what the self can control, the archaizer and the dilettante, rather than being defined by the fluctuating world, the other. MacNeice's individual, then, exists by virtue of difference as well as by his own integrity to the self. The self relies upon otherness, and the blueprint for a just society is an enlargement of this openness, a socialized dialogue of self and soul in which one individual is incomplete without others. In his 'Letter to W. H. Auden, of 1937, MacNeice praised Auden's realization that 'one must write about what one knows', adding that: 'One may not hold the bourgeois creed, but if one knows only bourgeois one must write about them.' This apparently liberal programme has a sting in its tail, however: 'They all after all contain the germ of their opposite.'[40] Writing, even writing with the honesty of MacNeice's 'reportage' or 'communication', is conceived of as part of a larger system of differences in which the individual participates by being fully a self rather than merely an observing ego. Instability is therefore built in as part of a larger, ultimately perhaps utopian, strategy far removed from both the determinist history of Marxism or the detachment of the sceptical liberal minding his own business.

For MacNeice, the idea of the 'bourgeois', seen in this light, was of central importance, though its poetic implications were not followed through completely until *Autumn Journal*. Obviously, the term served as a left-wing taunt for most of the 1930s, as did the accusation of 'individualism'. MacNeice's movement towards identi-fication with both the bourgeois and a species of individualism was

[39] MacNeice, *I Crossed the Minch* (1938), 12.
[40] MacNeice, 'Letter to W. H. Auden', *New Verse*, 26–7 (Nov. 1937), 12 (Heuser, p. 85).

in some ways a deliberate affront to leftist pieties, and *Autumn Journal* is itself a refutation of the need to apologize for ideological 'impurity'. If MacNeice's ideas of the self in poetry were becoming more Yeatsian, increasingly parts of an attitude governed by dialectic and difference, the acceptance of the bourgeois as such goes completely against the Yeatsian bias. However, MacNeice's Ireland in the 1930s contained more figures than Yeats; and one important Irishman for him was Stephen MacKenna, whose journal and letters had been edited by Dodds in 1936. In a review of these, MacNeice praised MacKenna (the 'Eclogue from Iceland' 's 'brilliant talker who left | The salon for the solo flight of mind') for having 'the courage of his instincts', being 'a subtle introspecter, a perhaps quixotic adventurer, a master of whimsy, a hundred per cent Irish Republican, an enemy of clap-trap and banality'. MacKenna's two loves, according to MacNeice, 'were Ireland and Greece', the love of Ireland, 'possibly fanatical', being 'tempered by the good sense of his Hellenism' (these were also to be crucial co-ordinates in *Autumn Journal*).[41] One of MacKenna's remarks, quoted with approval by MacNeice, is of particular importance: 'I always saw, however, that bourgeoisism is a hardened mysticism: nearly all the virtues of the bourgeois are the true virtues of the poet too.'[42] This could be seen as confronting Yeats's élitism without conceding imaginative ground to him or giving in to deterministic 'mysticism'; as MacKenna goes on to say: 'The thing is to be bourgeois in act with a free soul.'[43] MacKenna's defence of the bourgeois is very close to MacNeice's use of the idea in his later 1930s work, and offers important hints for *Autumn Journal*: on the one hand it is a democratization of Yeats, but on the other it makes large claims for the capacity of the 'ordinary man' referred to so often in *Modern Poetry* and elsewhere. If the bourgeois can embody 'hardened mysticism', the mystic might also be seen as a bourgeois gone soft.

Of course, there was no shortage of dogma against which to measure these ideas, and it could be argued that the weight of such dogma crushed poets like Spender, and forced Auden further away from the 'commitment' foisted upon his earlier work. Critical analyses of the late 1930s have tended to concentrate on issues such as

[41] MacNeice, rev. of *Journal and Letters of Stephen MacKenna*, ed. E. R. Dodds, in the *Morning Post*, 4 Dec. 1936, p. 19.
[42] MacKenna, *Journal*, p. 99, quoted by MacNeice, ibid.
[43] MacKenna, ibid.

'propaganda' in their treatment of ideological tensions between the poets and the British left. In fact, the question that was usually asked was not whether poets should be writing 'propaganda' (the term was seldom, if ever, defined by those who indignantly refuted it) but how far the 'individualism' inevitable in poetry ought to extend. Alick West, writing in 1937, is representative, claiming that 'The social order which individualism unconsciously asserts, the kind of "we" of which its "I" is the fetish, is the social order of capitalism, with its "freedom" of the individual, capitalist and worker.'[44] The heart of the quarrel was the nature of the 'I' in a poem. Spender defended his practice by pleading the special conditioning of the first person in his poetry, maintaining that 'in every instance the socialist analysis of the problems of the individual in his relation to society gives us a profounder picture of a given situation than any other';[45] yet he also recognized that 'The violence of the times we are living in, the necessity of sweeping and general and immediate action, tend to dwarf the experience of the individual, and to make his immediate environment and occupations perhaps something that he is even ashamed of.'[46] MacNeice's course was strikingly different, meeting more directly the ideological challenge of the 'I''s corollary in the 'we' by extending the scope of the self in poetry: 'Who am I—or I— to demand oblivion?' In the late 1930s MacNeice was willing to grant priority to this question of the self in its context of society, but with certain reservations. In a review of Hopkins in 1937, he acknowledged the return of 'beliefs' in poetry, with their consequences for 'subject':

Perhaps this ruthless puritanism is necessary at the moment. I whole-heartedly admit that the human subject is of supreme importance; if, therefore, the painting of still lives injures the human subject, let still lives go to the scrap-heap. We might remember, however, that man is a ζῷον as well as πολιτικόν and that quite a number of people have an organic sympathy with trees, mountains, flowers, or with a painting by Chardin. Does this sympathy lessen our sympathy with our human fellows? If so, it is a pity.[47]

---

[44] Alick West, *Crisis and Criticism* (1937), 53.
[45] Stephen Spender, 'The Left Wing Orthodoxy', *New Verse*, 31–2 (Autumn 1938), 15.
[46] Spender, Foreword to *The Still Centre*, pp. 10–11.
[47] MacNeice, rev. of *The Note-Books and Papers of Gerard Manley Hopkins*, ed. H. House, in the *Criterion*, 16/65 (July 1937), 699 (Heuser, pp. 81–2).

The mysticism is thoroughly hardened here, but the assertion of a connection between social and individual integrities is emphatic. The 'I', MacNeice implies, is responsible both to itself and its surrounding element in equal measure; private and public are not to be dissociated, and are in fact organically linked.

It is this private–public divide, however, often thought of as centrally important to the work of the 1930s poets, which can be applied misleadingly to *Autumn Journal*. For Hynes, the poem is 'a poignant last example of that insistent thirties theme, the interpenetration of public and private worlds', these two worlds being 'analogies of each other'.[48] Yet the point needs to be pushed further than this: MacNeice makes ideas of 'public' or 'private', considered separately, untenable, since the self in *Autumn Journal* is extended so as essentially to deny any distinction between the two domains. This is an important development of MacNeice's 'honesty': writing in late 1938 that 'It is still . . . possible to write honestly without feeling that the time for honesty is past',[49] the poet touched the mainspring of *Autumn Journal*, an openness which transcends the personal, displacing the usual coherences of the lyric in favour of a form for which any closure must be provisional only. 'Private' and 'public' relate to the self which has settled on its boundaries; in denying the boundaries of lyric closure, of which *The Earth Compels* shows the poet to have been intensely aware, or of the progress towards a conclusion of history, personal or otherwise, *Autumn Journal* denies also the validity of the self's habitual or imposed limits. The individual is fully himself by reason of his openness to 'otherness as such'—Grigson's formula of 'loneliness surrounded by everything' is, as Edna Longley has suggested, at the poem's heart.[50]

At the same time, it is important to recognize that *Autumn Journal* is conceived as inherently unstable—'It is in the nature of this poem to be neither final nor balanced', as MacNeice put it in his introduction. Designedly incomplete in itself, it works according to what might be seen in one light as a strategy of failure; by 1940, MacNeice himself was approaching it in this way:

---

[48] Hynes, *The Auden Generation*, p. 368.

[49] 'A Statement', p. 7.

[50] Geoffrey Grigson, 'Lonely, but not Lonely Enough', *New Verse*, 31–2 (Autumn 1938), p. 17, quoted in Edna Longley, *Poetry in the Wars* (Newcastle upon Tyne, 1986), 80.

'Autumn Journal,' the long topical poem I wrote in the Fall of 1938, is in a sense a failure; it fails in depth. I had foreseen that failure. We shall not be capable of depth—of tragedy or *great* poetry—until we have made sense of our world. 'Autumn Journal' remains a journal—topical, personal, rambling, but, failing other things, honest.[51]

Of course, 'honest' here does not conflict with what MacNeice called elsewhere 'a *dramatic* quality, as different parts of myself (e.g. the anarchist, the defeatist, the sensual man, the philosopher, the would-be good citizen) can be given their say in turn'.[52] Indeed, the design of *Autumn Journal* is in some ways a structural elaboration of the poet's flexible 'lyric' voice into its component parts (compare his 1934 note to Hilton, with its claim that the lyric expresses only 'a particular moment, or else a particular facet in a man's outlook' when 'Different parts of him want or believe different, or even opposite, things'[53]). As a large structural expression of MacNeice's particular kind of 'honesty', *Autumn Journal*'s openness and instability, its form's capacity to expand and contract, loosen and tighten, are all obvious assets; they are also parts of an engagement with time on MacNeice's part that becomes one of the poem's major preoccupations. The 1930s clichés of past and future, the symptomatic present and the design of history, all enter MacNeice's poem to be transformed there, subjected to the test of an open, unfinishable poetic form. The failure 'in depth' is not a consequence but a part of the incoherence of contemporary history for MacNeice, and the instability of the poem is in that sense foreseen. Critics of *Autumn Journal* have generally deplored the more abstract sections, the blueprints for Utopia, or the sections more overtly ethical in tone than the well-known accounts of Spain, Marlborough, Ireland, or Munich, or those concerning a finished love-affair. But this may be to apply the standards of lyric balance and economy to a poem that deliberately moves away from them, and is in a way a principled refutation of the principles themselves. A feeling that *Autumn Journal* does not fully cohere, that the equation does not, in fact, 'come out at last', is also perhaps foreseen in MacNeice's design.

Of course, *Autumn Journal* has its highlights, vividly evocative sections that have never gone short of praise. However, these cannot

---

[51] MacNeice, *Poems 1925–1940* (New York, 1941), p. xiii.
[52] MacNeice to T. S. Eliot, quoted in Marsack, *The Cave of Making*, p. 43.
[53] MacNeice, MS note among John Hilton papers, Bod. Lib.

really be divorced from the larger structure of the poem without losing a certain amount of weight; without the 'hardened mysticism' of MacNeice's more abstract passages, the charges of 'nostalgia' which Hynes makes against the poem have slightly more justification. It should be noticed, however, that for MacNeice abstraction follows experience rather than going in advance of it, so that his philosophizing, if it is that, is drawn from vividly concrete bases. The crucial section, in terms of its 'abstract' content, is XVII, directly after MacNeice's engagement with the Irish version of 'home'; the questions posed here go deeply into the poem itself:

> Why not admit that other people are always
>   Organic to the self, that a monologue
> Is the death of language and that a single lion
>   Is less himself, or alive, than a dog and another dog?
> Virtue going out of us always; the eyes grow weary
>   With vision but it is vision builds the eye;
> And in a sense the children kill their parents
>   But do the parents die?

After section XVI's pouring of scorn on both Irish houses, this has perhaps the force of a qualification, or at least of a change in perspective. If 'other people are always | Organic to the self', the self cannot renounce its past so readily simply by putting that past outside the pale of its approval. While XVI is a kind of killing of the present, XVII recognizes that the murder is finally impossible, since the self is broader than its 'personal' disgust alone, and cannot answer exclusion with exclusion. By analogy, what the self communicates is more than a précis of its rhetorical performance: XVII contrasts with the preceding section in order to prove that 'a monologue | Is the death of language' (XVI could be seen as presenting two mutually uncomprehending 'monologues'). More explicitly:

> . . . if you are going to read the testaments of cynics
>   You must read between the lines.
> A point here and a point there: the current
>   Jumps the gaps, the ego cannot live
> Without becoming other for the Other
>   Has got yourself to give.

This formulation (presumably part of what MacNeice meant by the 'didactic' in his introduction) serves also as a commentary on *Autumn Journal*'s more concretely located episodes, which are all, in some sense, examples of the self being realized in the other, the other in the self.

The major scenes in *Autumn Journal* are symbols shadowed by failure, compromise, and defeat; they are acts of salvage rather than just imaginative retrieval. The poem has three principal imaginative compass points—past, present, and future—which overlap throughout. The symbolic elasticity exploits these temporal directions, past events remembered in the present influencing the future. Time, as it affects the individual, is thus rendered less straightforward, and the disruption of the usual limits of the self seems to go together with this bending of temporal divisions. But time, as the element in which the poem is written and read, is still all too simple, going in one direction—forwards—and resisting the frames offered by historical pattern. In this sense, the individual has to settle for the gesture of action only in order to encounter the future:

> . . . a future of action, the will and fist
> Of those who abjure the luxury of self-pity
>   And prefer to risk a movement without being sure
> If movement would be better or worse in a hundred
>   Years or a thousand when their heart is pure.

Autumn Journal is almost a manifesto for impurity, but it still represents a working-out of the difficulty MacNeice had encountered at least since 1935, of how to reconcile 'communication' and 'honesty' with the 'unity' of form, the complication of temporal sequence that takes place in the mind of the individual with the stubbornly sequential nature of the time that continues around him. If 'history', for example, is always trumped by time, that does not necessarily absolve the poet from the responsibility of giving some kind of coherence to the 'other' as he finds it in his experience. *Autumn Journal*'s symbolic elasticity is a way of negotiating a path between these extremes: London itself, a finished love-affair, the felling of trees on Primrose Hill, the Munich crisis, Spain festering before civil war, and Barcelona on the verge of collapse—all mark points where the 'public' and the 'private', external and internal, begin to overlap and lose any semblance of independence. The antiphonal voice to the desires of the self, always present in MacNeice's work, is expressing itself here on the level of events. Munich, for example, becomes an emblem of the unwillingness to 'essay good through evil' (VII). Isherwood's recollection of his own 'dead-secret, basic reaction' at the time of the crisis is comparable: 'What do I care for the Czechs? What does it matter if we are traitors? A war has been postponed— and a war postponed is a war which may never happen.'[54] MacNeice brings the 'dead-secret' to the surface, by having the voice attempt to plunge it under:

> *We* are safe though others have crashed the railings
> Over the river ravine; their wheel-tracks carve the bank
> But after the event all we can do is argue
> And count the widening ripples where they sank.

Straightforward irony is at one end of the scale, where 'we' is not a development of the poem's 'I', but at the other there is a recognition of helplessness in which 'we' or 'I' tend to be implicated, unable to realize a 'future of action' or to shape what happens in time into the desired endings belonging to history. The problem for this 'I', the self open, expanded, but also frustrated by events, is in fact time as flux, one of MacNeice's oldest and most persistent nightmares. Where the self traces its coherences between past, present, and future, this aspect of time undermines them by denying finalities of any kind.

At this point the question of responsibility becomes pertinent. One aspect of flux for MacNeice had been that of dazzling surface and mesmeric change; another was the inevitability of change leading towards death. 'Flux' for the poet was always an idea of brilliant lights flashed out against a terrifying and disabling darkness. In *Autumn Journal*, the areas of light include memories of Mary, imagined 'Inaccessible in a sleeping wood | But thorns and thorns around her | And the cries of night' (XI); she is joined by Nancy, 'with her moods and moments | More shifting and more transient than I had | Yet thought of as being integral to beauty'. But the recourse to flux as a kind of excuse for failing to open the observing self to the changing other is ruled out in the poem, probably the furthest point reached by MacNeice in his movement away from the aesthetic implicit in much of *Poems*. The tag of Heraclitus which had been a touchstone for MacNeice since his youth is, in the context of *Autumn Journal*, a symptom of culpable self-absorption:

> You can't step into the same river twice so there can't be
> Ghosts; thank God that rivers always flow.
> Sufficient to the moment is the moment;
> Past and future merely don't make sense

[54] Christopher Isherwood, *Christopher and His Kind* (1977), 241.

And yet I thought I had seen them . . .
But *how*, if there is only a present tense?

Even Grettir's advice in 'Eclogue from Iceland', that 'with Here and Now for your anvil | You must strike while the iron is hot', is insufficient in the light of this; whatever the necessity for present action, it has to be considered as part of a larger temporal perspective. The kind of present tense favoured by MacNeice in the late 1920s and early 1930s could be used to undermine deterministic history, but it tended to exist in the vacuum of the self's brilliant perceptions; in *Autumn Journal*, there are responsibilities to both the past and the future that force the self to do more than live for the present moment. Flux in the poem is a condition of enactment rather than a personal tenet; it is embedded in the poem's incompleteness, its 'failure in depth', but it is refuted as a practical matter of belief. This forces MacNeice to face both history and the self directly, with the flexibility offered by *Autumn Journal*'s differing voices and moods. The one constant in the poem is the forward movement of time, but this is never allowed to become an end in itself.

In an obvious sense, *Autumn Journal* is full of 'history', touching on the major events of late 1938 as experienced by one individual; yet, in the 1930s sense of the word, history is almost missing from the poem. The future is far from settled in advance, but is linked instead to the capacity of the self in the present, a matter of vital choice. MacNeice's use of the personal is such as to deny the notion of history as an impersonal force. In fact, late 1930s criticisms from the left miss their target with regard to *Autumn Journal*. Randall Swingler, for example, wrote of poets 'caught in a small circle, which they know to be a refuge against the harder reality of social change', who, although they admit 'that the smaller group depends upon the larger', 'look out through closed windows at history moving inexorably by, and know with a pathetic sadness and resignation that if they are separated it will simply destroy them'.[55] This fear of separation (an acute-enough observation on some of the other poets) is entirely distinct from the loneliness of *Autumn Journal*, where it is not history but time that moves inexorably; the poet's responsibility is to face the future with all the personal resources open to, or opened by, his poetic self:

> I cannot drug my life with the present moment;
> The present moment may rape—but all in vain—

[55] Randall Swingler, 'History and the Poet', *New Writing*, NS 3 (Christmas 1939), 50.

> The future, for the future remains a virgin
>   Who must be tried again.

The image of 'inaccessible' femininity is important in the poem, pursued but never controlled, functioning in a way similar to the Yeatsian paradox of desire and possession. If the women are given all the surface glitter of MacNeice's flux perspectives, they are also lost— the sexual loneliness of *Autumn Journal* parallels the impossibility of reducing time to the impersonal determinism of history. The final resolution of the temporal/sexual imagery in section XXIV into 'The future is the bride of what has been', goes about a provisional settling of the perspectives of flux; it is also in striking contrast to the imagery of 'future' in much 1930s poetry, usually stern and impersonal, like Auden's Icelandic glaciers. 'History' as a marriage of past and future relies on the individual for its success; MacNeice, like Auden, 'believes in a free will, the power of choice; man, so to speak, has to carry history on his shoulders'.[56] But the sexual imagery used for this in *Autumn Journal* adds the implication that a union with history is not to be made by the self in isolation—history cannot be taken, but has to be won. In this sense, MacNeice personalizes a force which 1930s poets were often told was wholly outside their control.

Yet MacNeice's loneliness, whether or not 'surrounded by everything', is important, and the absence of any wedded bliss with the future is one of the problems that *Autumn Journal* has to face. The poet with 'No wife, no ivory tower, no funk-hole', is in fact in a more privileged position as far as the opening-up of the poetic self to be 'no longer squandered | In self-assertion' (XXIV) is concerned. The farewell to the two women in the poem is also a farewell to the values of 'flux':

> And you with whom I shared an idyll
>   Five years long,
> Sleep beyond the Atlantic
>   And wake to a glitter of dew and to bird-song.
> And you whose eyes are blue, whose ways are foam,
>   Sleep quiet and smiling
> And do not hanker
>   For a perfection which can never come.

Though MacNeice himself does not quite load his poem with aspirations to 'a perfection which can never come', he does propose a

---

[56] MacNeice, 'Tendencies in Modern Poetry' (discussion with F. R. Higgins), the *Listener*, 27 July 1939, p. 185.

denoument for the problems of self and other in society which, as Edna Longley points out, 'may seem *impossibly* poetic'.[57] The poem's method forces MacNeice to go further in the way of self-criticism than he had gone before, in poetry at least: the 'archaizer and dilettante', the 'fake individuals' of *I Crossed the Minch*, come through as aspects of the voices of *Autumn Journal*, whether as 'impresario of the ancient Greeks' or the hedonistic connoisseur of 'Shelley and jazz and lieder and love and hymn-tunes'. The analysis of Irish violence and atrophy, too, carries the liabilities of being both part of the problem and disowning it. The prayers that compensate for the poem's negative, or at least self-lacerating, aspects are necessary if only to even the balance. In Barcelona, for instance:

> May God, if there is one, send
> As much courage again and greater vision
> And resolve the antinomies in which we live
> Where man must be either safe because he is negative
> Or free on the edge of a razor.

This is as vital a component of *Autumn Journal*'s matrix of voices as any used in the more widely quoted sections of reminiscence or reportage. What it is not, however, is a précis of the poem's 'meaning' or 'moral', for *Autumn Journal* as a whole embodies 'the antinomies in which we live' as, in their contrast and interaction, the instruments with which the self is to be redefined. The system, if not its emphatically humanist co-ordinates, is one of Yeatsian antinomies. The poem as a whole absorbs MacKenna's formula, 'bourgeois in act with a free soul', in combining an acceptance of particular social conditioning and habit with the instinct for non-exclusive imaginative scope. This is, inevitably, to be 'free on the edge of a razor', to build a castle that is also 'falling', or to try to keep a lover who cannot finally be possessed. The 'meaning' of all this is not in conclusion but in process, and *Autumn Journal*'s ending is thus pitched into the future, a wish rather than a statement, and is itself part of the drama of conflicting impulse that the poem embodies. As MacNeice recognized in 1940, any absolute coherence or direction in the poem is linked to the events in the midst of which it exists, and any finalities are therefore provisional.

The achievement of *Autumn Journal* was essentially to bring to maturity an 'aesthetic sense' implicit in a good deal of 1930s poetry, rather than to inscribe the headstone over its grave. The tensions

[57] Longley, *Poetry in the Wars*, p. 88.

between completion and inconclusion, history and time, were all too often found by poets to be disabling. Spender's solution, which bears comparison with Auden's development after 1939, was to pin his faith on the idea that 'As long as somewhere in society, in individuals, there are centres of isolation, there is also a possibility of development and change';[58] Auden's 'September 1, 1939' includes similar 'centres of isolation', where 'the Just | Exchange their messages'.[59] The stakes for MacNeice were higher than this, and entailed a denial of isolation along with an admission of its seductive power. Yet *Autumn Journal*, written at a time when endings were in the air, resists the unity of the closed poem or completely defined self; it accepts time rather than a pattern of history, albeit along with the imperative of responsible individual action and choice. MacNeice provided a triumphant example of the rationale of homelessness without allowing the idea of 'home' to lose any of its strength.

As the decade drew to a close, the tension between 'communication' and 'unity' was undiminished for MacNeice, and in this he is true to the most basic of difficulties haunting 1930s poets, that of responsibility towards society and responsibility towards form. Whatever its prescription for the individual, *Autumn Journal* creates a poetic self wide enough to hold these responsibilities in equilibrium, even though the condition of such a balance is that it shall be provisional, subject to time. MacNeice's late 1930s work has as one of its poles the Yeatsian need 'to hold in a single thought reality and justice',[60] but at the other pole is time's subtle undercutting of poetry itself. MacNeice as well as his audience had to move on from the long poem's exemplary 'failure': as Margot Heinemann remembered, 'the moment of unity passed with 1939'.[61] Yet 1939 was also the year in which the time *for* unity arrived, officially at least, presenting MacNeice with new difficulties and different equations to be solved.

[58] Stephen Spender, 'September Journal', *Horizon*, 1/2 (Feb. 1940), repr. in *The Thirties and After* (1978), 102. Cf. Spender's account of this prose journal, not dissimilar in intention to MacNeice's poem: 'what I was trying to do in "September Journal," was not to state considered opinions to which I was prepared to commit my whole future, but to set down my immediate reactions to events from day to day. The responsibility I undertook in writing this document was not to discover a consistent attitude, but to make a truthful record of my immediate reactions to a violent and rapidly altering situation. . . . It is a difference in the kind of responsibility one is undertaking.' (Letter in the *Partisan Review*, 7/5 (Sept.–Oct. 1940), 405.)

[59] W. H. Auden, 'September 1, 1939', *The English Auden*, p. 247.

[60] W. B. Yeats, *A Vision* (1937, repr. 1962), 25.

[61] Margot Heinemann, 'Louis MacNeice, John Cornford and Clive Branson: Three Left-Wing Poets', in J. Clark *et al.* (eds.), *Culture and Crisis in Britain in the Thirties* (1979), 115.

4

The Desert's Purge: 1939–1944

MacNeice's trip to Ireland with Ernst Stahl in the late summer of 1939, a stay protracted until the end of the year, and his departure for America at the beginning of 1940 marked the start of the most turbulent period in the poet's career, by the end of which his work was to be decisively reorientated. That world events were equally turbulent at the time is a truism, but the question of how far external circumstances might impinge upon the nature and direction of artistic activity was by no means a dead issue for MacNeice then, and may be seen as a pressure which often bore significantly upon the work itself. If the outbreak of the Second World War marks a suspiciously neat point for the literary history of the 1930s to end, that neatness is missing in MacNeice's development, even though the period 1939–41 is, properly speaking, still a turning-point in his work. This is not to say that the poet had no part in the general rush to tidy up the 1930s, for praise or blame, which was already evident before the departure of Auden and Isherwood for America in January 1939; MacNeice's own *Autumn Journal*, appearing in May of that year, contributed to the sense of ending and account-balancing already prevalent in England. The 'immediate nostalgia for America' that MacNeice felt on his return from a lecture tour that Easter was in part prompted by the feeling of 'imminent disaster', 'the caterpillar wheels of enormous tractors rearing on every horizon' in London;[1] his decision to leave Bedford College and return to America, already made in June,[2] was an obvious break with a world that seemed, in any case, as good as finished. However, MacNeice's attempt at a new start, in both personal and artistic terms, was compromised by events in the next two years in such a way that it resulted in

---

[1] MacNeice, *The Strings Are False: An Unfinished Autobiography* (1965), 207, 208.

[2] See letter to E. R. Dodds, 1 Jun. 1949 (Bod. Lib., Dodds fo. 44): 'Actually I am not too displeased at it turning out this way as London is very difficult these days & I shouldn't be surprised if during the next year I could do more work over there' [i.e. the USA].

something very different from that envisaged by the poet in the summer of 1939.

Writing on the affinities between Yeats and Rilke, MacNeice observed that 'both are primarily interested in their own relationships to a world which seems extraordinarily *other* to them'.[3] The problem of the self in writing and in its contact with the other, the world of events breaking in on the integrity of the individual imagination, preoccupied MacNeice in the war years, despite his occasional attempts to dismiss it or even to ignore it altogether. In the crudest version of this difficulty, he found himself accused of escapism, 'Running away from the War', in the words of one of his own poems;[4] his attempts to refute this kind of charge, both on his own account and to some extent on that of Auden, influenced the direction of his poetry before and even after his return to London at the end of 1940. The artistic difficulty raised by this 'escapist' label was not a simple one, however; for MacNeice, it involved the persistently troublesome crux of the status of the self within and outside poems, which he had earlier met in terms of 'voice', making special claims for that of the 'lyric' as a means of reconciling self and other. In *Autumn Journal*, the instability of the self, and the uncertainty as to its boundaries, had been central to the poem's design; with the events of 1939, such strategies began to seem inadequate as a way of containing the tensions building up in MacNeice's work between external disruption and internal coherence. In both the poetry and the prose of these years (crucially *The Poetry of W. B. Yeats*), MacNeice effected a significant readjustment of the balance between such elements, which was in turn to alter the whole course of his career. The present chapter will examine this writing in an attempt to clarify the nature and causes of the readjustment.

The poems composed during MacNeice's Irish trip with Stahl, published in the short Cuala Press volume of 1940, *The Last Ditch*, as 'The Coming of War', mark the poet's transition away from his 1930s writing: they exhibit a certain self-consciousness with regard to their own transitional nature. In its original form, the sequence (which MacNeice reduced from ten poems to seven, and then eventually to five[5]) made Ireland the middle ground between dream

---

[3] MacNeice, *The Poetry of W. B. Yeats* (1941, repr. 1967), 159.

[4] Poem v of 'The Coming of War', *The Last Ditch* (Dublin, 1940), 7.

[5] Poems II, IV, and V of 'The Coming of War' were omitted from MacNeice's *Poems 1925–1940* (New York, 1941), and poems VIII and IX from *Plant and Phantom* (1941).

and nightmare—his relationship in America with Eleanor Clark being the dream, the situation in Europe the nightmare. If Ireland at this time presented MacNeice with 'tangents away from reality',[6] it was not a sufficiently unreal scene to allow him to escape the pressure of contemporary events: on the other hand, by playing off its love-poems against more public poems of foreboding, 'The Coming of War' attempts to salvage a place for the personal which cannot be considered mere escapism. This can lead the poet into an uncharacter-istic clumsiness ('God damn Hitler | That she is not here', for example), but the fundamental difficulty for MacNeice, that of understanding the nature of his own position between war 'Casting a blight on the Irish day' and peace 'beyond the clamour of Manhattan', can be expressed here only in negative terms—America, for instance, is:

> . . . a land which is a legend for me already
>   A dream that has come untrue,
> For now, my love, there is more than the Atlantic
>   Dividing me from you.[7]

'The Coming of War' exploits the ambiguity of the poet's 'position' in both geographical and ethical senses—and neither can be defined satisfactorily. MacNeice's later reduction of the sequence, removing the love-poems, may well give 'the final poem greater poignancy', as Robyn Marsack claims,[8] but it also shifts the emphasis away from the original ambiguity. The later title, 'The Closing Album', is a piece of hindsight—at the time of composition, the poet was far from certain as to the nature of the change which the war might represent. The difficulty involved in MacNeice's understanding of Ireland here is paralleled by that of knowing the 'position' of the self, or the extent of its significance at a time of crisis.

MacNeice's apparent intention to apply for the Chair of English at Trinity College, Dublin prolonged his stay in Ireland into the autumn of 1939. In September he wrote to E. R. Dodds with some uncertainty: 'I dare say this will scandalise you as being a kind of escapism but I can't really see that I should be doing any more for civilisation by what they say the intellectuals must do—propaganda work.'[9] Raising

---

[6] *The Strings Are False*, p. 213.
[7] Poem IV, *The Last Ditch*, p. 7.
[8] Robyn Marsack, *The Cave of Making: The Poetry of Louis MacNeice* (Oxford, 1982), 59.
[9] MacNeice to Dodds, 24 Sept. 1939, Dodds fo. 47ʳ.

the spectre of 'propaganda' here is in line with the attitudes of Auden or Spender in the late 1930s, and opposing this to 'escapism' is perhaps something of a melodramatic heightening of the issues (albeit one which did not originate with MacNeice himself). Even so, a concern with the integrity of the self is unmistakable in MacNeice's writings at this time, and is felt heavily throughout *The Last Ditch* as a burden that cannot be shrugged off by external or personal commitment alone. Writing to Dodds from Dublin in October, MacNeice could not let drop this question of the self's confusion, caught between external events and personal values as though between rival unrealities:

Down here one gets quite de- (or dis)orientated. It all sounds like a nightmare algebra which you have to change back into people being killed. It is all very well for everyone to go on saying 'Destroy Hitlerism' but what the hell are they going to construct? I am now falling into a sort of paradox which is:—if the war were a rational war leading somewhere, I should want to stay out of it in order to see where it led to: but if it is a hopeless war leading nowhere, I feel half inclined to take the King's shilling & escape— more likely than not—the frustration to come. The motives in each case of course being selfish.[10]

The disillusion here is not simply a consequence of isolation, but also to some extent a cause; what MacNeice calls 'selfish' motives go back to a self that is unable to decide upon the external context within which it has to exist. It is this which makes 'The Coming of War' a sequence in which personal and public pressures result in a virtual paralysis of the self as an agent, a profound passivity. Similarly, in the letter to Dodds, MacNeice wrote: 'It is difficult not to be egotistical over here. Yet I got the impression that in England it must be difficult to avoid wishful thinking. I would rather be quit of thinking altogether & just let people order me about. All this boosting up democracy—it seems to me just throwing the sand against the wind.'[11] Both egotism and 'wishful thinking' elevate the importance of self over other: in so far as MacNeice concentrated on the problem, he tried to preserve a balance between the extremes, but the feeling of passivity, both in his letters of the time and *The Last Ditch*, comes close to artistic inertia. This dilemma is behind poem VIII of 'The Coming of War', 'Clonmacnois':

[10] MacNeice to Dodds, 13 Oct. 1939, Dodds fos. 48^{r-v}.
[11] Ibid., fo. 48^v.

> You millenarian dead, why should I arraign,
> Being a part of it, the stupidity of men
> Who cancel the voices of the heart with barbarous noise
> And hide the barren facts of death in censored posts?[12]

The poet's voice is powerless here because it is a part of the conspiracy of noise which may falsify reality; even if it is inadequate to convey these 'barren facts', MacNeice's voice is also, at this stage, unwilling to do so. The impulse to sink the poetic voice altogether follows from this:

The tiresome corollary of this from my point of view is that, *if* it is my war, I feel I ought to get involved in it in one of the more unpleasant ways. Ignoring the argument that writers are more use writing. No doubt they are. But writers also unfortunately seem to be expected to express opinions on these subjects, & if, *qua* writer, one were to say that one was pro-War, then one ought to be prepared to accept the nastier parts of the war just as much as anyone else.[13]

Yet, early in the new year, MacNeice left for Cornell and the spring semester. To all appearances, he had joined Auden, Isherwood, and the rest in 'escapism'.

The best way of accounting for MacNeice's departure is perhaps provided by his work on Yeats, which he had begun in the summer of 1939. Although *The Poetry of W. B. Yeats* was, in part at least, a way of distancing himself from the public image of the 'Auden generation' ('whom', according to Samuel Hynes, 'he writes of . . . as though it were the School of Ben'[14]), MacNeice allowed the process of writing the book to include, and further, his own change of attitude with regard to the question of 'escapism'. It was of course this aspect of Yeats's significance which Auden seized upon in 'The Public vs. the Late William Butler Yeats', which appeared in the *Partisan Review* in spring 1939, and in the poem 'In Memory of W. B. Yeats', the first version of which was published in the *New Republic* that March. MacNeice's active engagement with Yeats cannot be so easily isolated, but an intense and important phase of this difficult relationship began in the months following the older poet's death. With his

---

[12] *The Last Ditch*, p. 10.

[13] MacNeice to Dodds from Belfast, 10 Nov. 1939, Dodds fo. 53ᵛ.

[14] Samuel Hynes, 'Yeats and the Poets of the Thirties', R. J. Porter and J. D. Brophy (eds.), *Modern Irish Literature: Essays in Honor of William York Tindall* (New York, 1971), 9.

critical work on Yeats already under way, MacNeice wrote 'Dublin', the first poem of 'The Coming of War'. This piece is cast in one of the characteristically Yeatsian metres, identified by MacNeice as 'the short-line poem with three or four stresses to a line', in which the technical difficulty is 'so to control the rhythms that the poem does not get into a skid'.[15] 'Dublin' recalls Yeats's 'Easter 1916' with its imagery of stone and water, and its equivocal attitude with regard to the historical characters who harden into figures of national myth ('O'Connell, Grattan, Moore'). The poet might at first appear to provide an alternative, and a warmer, perspective on Ireland than that of 'The Black | North, the winch and the windlass, | The drum and the Union Jack' elsewhere in the sequence[16]—as 'Train to Dublin' complemented 'Valediction' in *Poems*—but any softening of focus is deceptive. Dublin, for all her 'seedy elegance' and 'gentle veils of rain', is less susceptible to the poet's understanding than the North, and presents him with a concrete example of otherness that remains unapproachable. Apparent closeness and real separation are at the heart of the poem—the easy and attractive images (such as the sun 'Like barley-sugar on the water') are the falsifications of illusive objectivity:

> And the mist on the Wicklow hills
> Is close, as close
> As the peasantry were to the landlord
> As the Irish to the Anglo-Irish,
> As the killer is close one moment
> To the man he kills,
> Or as the moment itself
> Is close to the next moment.

There is more than just national or political alienation involved here: like the progression of time from moment to moment, the relationship between separate individuals, the self and the other, shows continuity and discontinuity at once. Whereas Yeats attempted to make 'Easter 1916' a means of overcoming, or transcending, the problems raised when 'He had built an Ireland out of words and now he saw them translated into action',[17] MacNeice moves from the apparent security of tourist description to a realization of dangerous otherness, of action undercutting words. 'Dublin' has no room for

[15] *The Poetry of W. B. Yeats*, p. 105.
[16] Poem v, *The Last Ditch*, p. 7.
[17] *The Poetry of W. B. Yeats*, p. 108.

any 'terrible beauty'; it leaves the poetic voice separated from its subject, the self touching the other only briefly and with suspicion.

'The Coming of War' is as resigned to the impossibility of escape as it is to the impulse towards escapism; like *The Last Ditch* as a whole, it embodies an impasse between art and events, a realization that MacNeice's 1930s perspectives were no longer useful. David Daiches saw MacNeice as 'marking time' in this short volume, still in the process of 're-adjusting himself to the foreseen yet shattering present'.[18] That the present upheaval had been foreseen—and even experienced by some writers in advance in Spain or China—was certainly a difficulty hampering artists, and it helps to explain the eagerness of a number of literati to tidy away the 1930s into poetic mythology. MacNeice's poetry in the autumn of 1939 did not dry up altogether, but it did dwindle to eight-line 'kind of epigrams'[19] (their number was drastically reduced in subsequent collections); an attempt to write a poem on Barcelona, whose fall had provided another formal ending to 1930s concerns, had to be abandoned, the original idea of a work in *terza rima* ending up as yet more impressionistic eight-liners.[20] MacNeice preserved the best of these short poems,[21] but all of them originally shared a small number of images relating to the themes of ending and powerlessness. The image of 'the reflected, the wrong, sky' in 'Didymus', for example, combines water and mirror images that run through the poems, both carrying associations with death. In 'Radio', voices are 'bubbles'—'I count them and remember | Men can drown'—while in 'The Lecher', memories are 'The same coral sea | That often drowned him', and in 'November Afternoon':

> I look into the dim
> Mirror in the hall and see
> A faded portrait, a drowned
> Face looking back at me.[22]

---

[18] David Daiches, 'The Honest Man Alone', rev. of *The Last Ditch*, in *Poetry* (Chicago), 57/2 (Nov. 1940), 157.

[19] See MacNeice to Dodds from Belfast, 22 Nov. 1939, Dodds fo. 56ʳ.

[20] See MacNeice to Dodds, 28 Nov. and 8 Dec. 1939, Dodds fos. 57ᵛ, 58ᵛ.

[21] Four of the poems survive in *Collected Poems* (1966) as 'Entered in the Minutes': *Poems 1926–1940* had included a further 5. The poem entitled 'Barcelona in Wartime' was in fact excluded from *Plant and Phantom* in 1941, and reinstated in *Collected Poems 1925–1948* (1949).

[22] *Poems 1925–1940*, 'Octets': 'Radio' (IV), p. 312; 'The Lecher' (VIII), p. 314; 'November Afternoon' (III, p. 312).

Images of the self, like those of the past, are deceptive for MacNeice in these poems: even the image of the swallow's wings in 'Didymus', recalling 'An Eclogue for Christmas' where 'the swallow's tangent wings' represent one point at which perception can hold and draw value from flux, are their own 'shadows' here, part of the feeling of being removed from reality which is pervasive in these short pieces. The self is almost incapable of registering anything other than its own obsolescence: the 'Idealist' who 'lived among blue prints | For a castle in the air' finds that he 'has not even the air | To build his castle on'.[23] The intrusion of events upon the imagination seemed to have brought MacNeice's writing to something of a dead end.

The Poetry of W. B. Yeats was one way in which MacNeice chose to approach such difficulties. Begun in July of 1939 in the British Museum, where readers were 'searched for I.R.A. bombs when we entered the gate',[24] and completed in America with Europe at war, the book was written in the shadow of conflict, and of conflicting claims on its author's allegiance. Just as in 'Dublin' Yeats featured as a powerful presence against which MacNeice measured his own inability fully to transcend the pressure of events, the elder poet's ability to absorb external conflict and transform it into poetic strength prompted MacNeice to question the possibility, and propriety, of following Yeats in his apparent elevation of self over other. Such questioning, however, is not the same thing as outright rejection, and much of the book's preliminary skirmishing with the idea of the poem as either contextually conditioned and accountable or else a self-contained and self-justifying aesthetic whole may be seen as an attempt to contain Yeats's influence whilst also laying claim to him as a precedent. MacNeice asserts, for instance, that 'a poem does not exist in a vacuum, but a poem at the same time *is* a unity, a creation', and while maintaining that 'I am not one of those who hold that each one poem in the world must be isolated and appreciated in a vacuum', he also speaks of poetic form as 'a spiritual principle which calls for expression in matter'. MacNeice's definition of the instinctive 'mystical' urge as a stage where 'the individual does not distinguish the forces within him from the forces outside him' is perhaps significant in this respect.[25] As a poet, Yeats had been able to harness this urge, but with the coming of war MacNeice found the impulse a

---

[23] MacNeice, 'Idealist', *New Statesman and Nation*, 9 Dec. 1939, p. 820.
[24] *The Strings Are False*, p. 208.
[25] *The Poetry of W. B. Yeats*, pp. 18, 147, 24.

debilitating confusion rather than an increase in strength, blurring the self's boundaries so as to threaten extinction instead of promising expansion.

In some respects, this could be seen as a continuation of the 1930s quarrel between history and imaginative autonomy, but MacNeice was no longer certain of the direction in which history was moving; his attacks on the intellectual left of the 1930s have their place in the general movement away from that decade by those who were among the leading protagonists of its literary history, but, despite these, the idea of history as in some sense the artist's domain still exerted an attraction for the poet:

The critic's view of art is essentially static; the artistic process is essentially dynamic. The critic tries to fit a particular artist into a niche in history as if history were a long corridor with all its niches there already. The artist on the other hand would never have become an artist if all he had to do were to walk down a ready-made corridor. History for the artist is something which is evolving and he himself is aiding and abetting it.[26]

This, like the qualification of Auden's 'poetry makes nothing happen' at the end of the book,[27] brings MacNeice closer to accepting that the pressure of events implies a change within the artist, that self and other may be actively related rather than mutually alienated. In 'The Gates of Horn', a poem written in October 1939, this possibility of relation is raised in connection also with temporal perspectives of past and future. The past here is aligned with falsity, and the future with truth, even though the figure who comes through the gates of horn, of true dreams, holding 'the future in his hand' is ominously silent, and strikes the poet dumb. The past, however, is associated with romance, a woman 'gone | As she had come— | Passing through the ivory gate':

> The night she came
> The clock had stopped

[26] Ibid. 26. The first sentence here echoes Rupert Doone's comment on his production of Aeschylus' *Agamemnon*: 'Aeschylus is static, I am dynamic, so fuck all'; MacNeice adapted this in a letter to Dodds of 13 Oct. 1939: 'Aeschylus is static, Hitler is dynamic, so f--- all' (Dodds fo. 49ᵛ).

[27] *The Poetry of W. B. Yeats*, p. 192: 'The fallacy lies in thinking that it is the *function* of art to make things happen and that the effect of art upon actions is something either direct or calculable. It is an historical fact that art *can* make things happen and Auden in his reaction from a rigid Marxism seems in this article to have been straying towards the Ivory Tower.'

> And the room no longer
> Was the same,
> I felt the cornice
> Closing in
> Like the petals of
> A closing flower[28]

The echoes of 'Meeting Point', in which 'the clock | Forgot them'
with 'all the room a glow'[29] and silence 'a flower', are clear, but the
scene is being rewritten as a falsehood: the clock has started again,
though the future is both unknowable and inarticulate.

MacNeice's critical work on Yeats has to be read in terms of the
charges that he found being levelled against him during his absence
from England. Writing in November 1940, Stephen Spender was to
ask him and the other literary exiles 'whether they think that there is
a chance of escaping from history altogether', repudiating such
attempts as 'simply putting the clock back for yourself, using your
freedom of movement to enable yourself to live still in pre-Munich
England'.[30] MacNeice's awareness that, far from putting back or
stopping the clock, time had in some ways caught up with his
generation, helped him to project Yeats's career as 'a miracle of
artistic integrity', open to the currents of history without being
completely at their mercy—'it is a lucky thing for the artist that his
work usually outruns his ideology'.[31] At the root of this was the idea
that, as one reviewer of *The Poetry of W. B. Yeats* noticed, 'A man
can no more be static than his poetry can be', and since 'Both
represent a process of becoming', the reader 'will not ask for finality'.[32]
MacNeice's own poetry of this period offers no finalities other than
those of past history, and searches for new patterns of beginning, but
it was not until the move to Cornell at the beginning of 1940 that
such patterns began to appear to be poetically feasible. In an exuberant
letter to Dodds, the reunion with Eleanor Clark prompted the
reflection that 'I must have been merely aberrent the last six months
or so', and a determination to change direction:

[28] *Poems 1925–1940*, pp. 283–4.
[29] MacNeice altered this phrase to 'one glow' in *Eighty-Five Poems* (1959).
[30] Stephen Spender, 'Letter to a Colleague in America', *New Statesman and
Nation*, 16 Nov. 1940, p. 490.
[31] MacNeice, 'Yeats's Epitaph', *New Republic*, 24 June 1940, repr. Heuser,
p. 117.
[32] Rev. of *The Poetry of W. B. Yeats*, in *TLS*, 29 Mar. 1941, p. 150.

Don't ask me what's going to happen next because I don't know. I think maybe it's about time I had a bout of irrationality. I feel I've been fitting myself into patterns for so long & (though you may be sceptical about 'romance'?) it is so exciting to find oneself timelessly happy; also I am going to write (at least I hope so) quite new kinds of poems. After which, no doubt, the deluge but I can't think about that now.[33]

Of course, it was MacNeice too who had been sceptical about 'romance' and the side-stepping of time through happiness. It is important to bear in mind the extent to which a statement of personal intent such as this is conditioned by the external pressures against which it reacts, in particular the questions of 'escapism' and putting the clock back, which MacNeice could not leave behind. The poems that he wrote during his stay in America also reveal how much the external was in fact internalized for him at the time, and how the theme of *'Poète, prends ton luth'* figured increasingly in his work.[34] Even Yeats's 'remedy', as MacNeice saw it, 'was to put his clock back, not forward';[35] MacNeice's attempt to disown both courses (he still associated the latter with the Utopianism of the 1930s intellectual left) led him back to the stopped clock with its attendant connotations of inertia and irresponsibility.

One of MacNeice's eight-line poems of the autumn provided a concentrated image for the forebodings about to find their historical fulfilment, centred upon the dangerous element of time. The poem itself was entitled simply 'The Clock':

> In the Nineteen-Twenties
>   Life was gay,
> They made the clock run
>   Until it ran away.
>
> Ten years later
>   In a desert place
> They met the clock again
>   With murder in his face.[36]

Again, there is a reference back to 'Meeting Point' in this sinister little poem, in its return to the desert where 'The camels crossed the miles

---

[33] MacNeice to Dodds from Cornell, 5 Feb. 1940, Dodds fos. 65ʳ–66ᵛ.

[34] See *The Strings Are False*, p. 27: André could 'look at one piercingly and say in a manner less than half whimsical, more than half pathetic: "*Poète*, why are you doing nothing? You must show us a course, it is your business. *Poète, prends ton luth . . .*".'

[35] *The Poetry of W. B. Yeats*, p. 97.

[36] MacNeice, 'The Clock', *New Statesman and Nation*, 6 Jan. 1940, p. 11.

of sand'. The desert was to figure as one of MacNeice's central images for the experience of the individual in wartime, culminating in the landscape at the end of *The Dark Tower*, where 'The desert is the only clock';[37] its associations with solitary trial are balanced by a sense of that trial's communal significance. In 'Stylite', written in America in March 1940, the saint looking over 'the sand | Where no one ever comes | And the world is banned', sees the Greek god who represents the antithesis of his ascetic denial of external reality only once he is able to feel 'The conscience of a rope, | And the hangman counting'. That MacNeice should use 'conscience' here suggests also an awakening of ethical responsibility, so that what Marsack calls the saint's 'instinctive reaction in the face of death'[38] is in the face of others' deaths as well as his own. The poles represented are those of denial and acceptance of the world of external events, and it is the desert stretching between these poles which is the poem's true focus, as well as the area of experience towards which MacNeice was increasingly drawn. The desert's possible apocalyptic significance was of course one aspect of Yeats's poetic legacy, and 'The Second Coming' is felt behind a number of MacNeice's poems of the time. 'Jehu', written in August 1940, begins with the 'Peace in New England', depicted in terms of abundant fertility, but moves to a parable set again in the desert, a 'deceiving | Mirage of what were once ideals or even motives'. The killing of the woman whose face was 'a Muse's possibly once but now a harlot's', suggests the painful and necessary break with the rotten side of Western culture which MacNeice saw as one possible consequence of the war, and the final stanza of the poem does in fact bring the trial of the desert right into wartime Britain:

> And now the sand blows over Kent and Wales where we may shortly
> Learn the secret of the desert's purge, of the mad driving,
> The cautery of the gangrened soul,

Although the neatness of 'Jehu''s final presentation of the choice between 'The charioteer, the surgeon' and 'the pampered | Queen', along with the careful symmetry of the whole poem's design, may seem a little overworked, it does suggest another aspect of the connection between the desert symbol and the trial of the war over which the poet brooded. 'Perhaps', MacNeice wrote in July 1940,

---

[37] MacNeice, *The Dark Tower* (1947, repr. 1964), 57.
[38] Marsack, *The Cave of Making*, p. 66.

'we all need a dose of the desert, and perhaps that is just what we shall get, whether we want it or not.'[39] Writing from the fertile landscapes of New England in Connecticut, MacNeice depicted even that abundance in such a way as to imply its potential connection with 'the desert's purge': in 'Order to View', written in March, a shrubbery is a 'crypt | Of leafmould dreams', and 'the whole place, one might | Have supposed, was deadly ill'; while 'Evening in Connecticut' allows signs of Fall to pun on 'The fall of dynasties'. Writing to Henry Church from Hertford, Connecticut that August, Wallace Stevens observed that 'We live quietly and *doucement*, but, for all that, the climate is changing, and it seems pretty clearly to be becoming less and less a climate of literature.'[40] MacNeice, too, had one eye on the New England landscape, while with the other he was 'scanning | Miles of desert and sky'.

The relation between the isolation of the solitary ordeal in the desert and its implications for the larger, un-solitary community outside was more difficult for MacNeice to imagine, especially while situated on the far side of the Atlantic. Isolation was precisely what a *Times Literary Supplement* editorial criticized in MacNeice and the other literary exiles in April 1940:

There is the fatal self-consciousness of the intellectual the world over, his frequently complacent sense of isolation from the general run of society . . . The middle-class thunderers and the lyricists of the left were often enough driven by sincere ideals; but what in the first place drew their feet irresistibly to follow the Communist gleam was . . . the impulse to emphasize their distinction from the common herd, or else the longing to escape from their own annihilating isolation and merge themselves in the herd.[41]

Those who had been identified with the literary left in the 1930s were now, with the coming of the war and in the wake of the Russo-German pact, unlikely enough to receive a fair hearing. Those, like Spender, who stayed in Britain, could hardly afford to voice much support for the exiles' positions, and were in fact prone to join in the charges of escapism and self-isolation. In the light of this, the tone of MacNeice's first 'American Letter' in *Horizon* was perhaps less than well-chosen:

[39] MacNeice, 'American Letter', *Horizon*, 1/7 (July 1940), 464.
[40] Wallace Stevens to Henry Church, 23 Aug. 1940, in *Letters of Wallace Stevens*, ed. Holly Stevens (1967), 365.
[41] 'The Communist Cult', *TLS*, 20 Apr. 1940, p. 195.

I hear people are still fussing in England about the ethics of his [Auden's] migration to America; why bother? The explanation he gave me seems reasonable enough—that an artist ought either to live where he has live roots or where he has no roots at all; that in England to-day the artist feels essentially lonely, twisted in dying roots, always in opposition to a group; that in America he is just as lonely, but so, says Auden, is everybody else; with 140 million lonelies milling around him he feels he need not waste his time either in conforming or rebelling. . . . It is no question of *il gran refiuto*; he feels he can work better here than in Europe, and that is all there is to it.[42]

'Speaking for myself', MacNeice continued, 'I must say that at the moment I prefer being in America to being in England.' The grounds, as well as the jaunty tone of the defence of Auden indicated just that isolation which the *Times Literary Supplement* had deplored in a whole generation. However, MacNeice's poems of the time, as well as the elaborate defensive strategies employed in *The Poetry of W. B. Yeats*, do indicate a dissatisfaction with this self-centred (or at least self-protective) conception of art. Privately, MacNeice was already convinced that 'Freedom means Getting into things & not getting Out of them',[43] but this in itself, or even the mere intention to return to wartime London (which the poet had decided upon by the summer), did not quite answer the charge of an 'escapism' that expressed a profound and debilitating isolation on his part. In America, Archibald MacLeish made a shrill attack on the contemporary writer as one who 'thinks without responsibility to anything but truth of feeling', and 'observes with honesty and truthfulness and without comment'.[44] The attack had more bluster than substance, but MacNeice's sensitivity to it is not surprising. His 'Ballade for Mr. MacLeish' is an attempt to defend that 'honesty'; it does not deny the charges, but asserts instead the integrity of a position not solely his:

> We have not set the epoch right,
> We would not if we had to lie;
> Writers by trade we have tried to write
> By evidence of mind and eye;

---

[42] 'American Letter', p. 464.
[43] MacNeice to Mrs Dodds, 22 Mar. 1940, Dodds fo. 67[v].
[44] Archibald MacLeish, *The Irresponsibles: A Declaration* (New York, 1940), 30–1. The polemic was first published in the *Nation*, 13 May 1940.

> The day for that is perhaps gone by,
> Truth is unfashionably slow
> And shuns the opportune reply:
> You need not tell us what we know.[45]

The echo of 'Under Ben Bulben' here, along with the general reminis-
cence of 'The Grey Rock', are probably no more accidental than the
Yeatsian cast of MacNeice's identification of poetry in October of
1940 as 'my road to freedom and knowledge'.[46] All of the five
ballades written in August affect a plain-spoken defiance, managing
to be at once admissions of defeat and assertions of integrity—for
this kind of stance, Yeats is an exemplary figure. What lies behind
this is the knowledge that honesty alone is not enough to guarantee
artistic autonomy or independence from what appear to be the
demands of the external world, in the same way that a suspicion of
poetry's unreality in the practical world provides *The Poetry of
W. B. Yeats* with a dark side of doubt and distrust of the older poet's
'constitutional inhumanity'.[47] MacNeice was sure, at any rate, that
the poetic self's relation to the other had to be more than simply a
representational fidelity: other fidelities—to society, if not to 'history'
—were involved, and the war was bringing these more forcibly to the
poet's attention.

Contemplating his eventual return to England, MacNeice wrote in
August that 'Half of me is pleased to be coming back';[48] but the
return itself was still regarded by the poet as a transfer from one
unreality to another. His admission, even in the July 'American
Letter', that although 'There is a theory that when one gets over here
one can see things in perspective', 'I don't find that myself, am still
desperately out of focus',[49] revealed that the real artistic result of the
American stay was to bring the self rather than things into focus. And
yet, when MacNeice tried to do this in verse, it was 'things' that
constantly intruded. The conclusion of 'Plain Speaking', that 'I am I
although the dead are dead', rings slightly hollow in comparison
with 'Bar-Room Matins' or 'Cradle Song for Eleanor', with their
suggestions of the futility of the horizons of self-concern. Yet Mac-

---

[45] MacNeice, 'Ballade for Mr. MacLeish', *Poems 1925–1940*, p. 296. Cf. Mac-
Neice's later reference to MacLeish's book as 'This piece of artistic treason (and
nonsense)', in 'Touching America', *Horizon*, 3/15 (Mar. 1941), 211.

[46] Foreword to *Poems 1925–1940*, p. xiv.

[47] 'Yeats's Epitaph', p. 169 (Heuser, p. 116).

[48] MacNeice to Dodds, 18 Aug. 1940, Dodds fo. 70ʳ.

[49] 'American Letter', 464.

Neice had always, and especially since the 1930s, been aware of the poetic possibilities of *things*, the elements of a heterogeneous world of flux; the tension between the perceiving self and these elements was hardly new to him, but his particular ways of coping with it were beginning to seem obsolete. Far from a studied melancholy at the passing of time, or a descriptive accuracy in registering the flux of experience, the war had begun to impose new ideas and feelings for 'time' which MacNeice's American poems started to sense, but it also demanded a frame of reference wider than that of the consciously isolated self. 'Coming from Nowhere', a poem written shortly after MacNeice's arrival in America, already implies the necessity of losing a concept of the self which, however serviceable it might have been for an artist in the 1930s, was now resembling that of 'A pillared saint | With knees drawn up | And vacant eyes': the saint 'waits | Till time erodes | The walls of thought, | The thoughts of self', and finally, in an apparently miraculous change of climate and surroundings (like that at the end of 'Order to View'), 'the sun | Unrolls a carpet':

> Then he leaves
> His rock and with
> Deliberate feet
> On golden water
> Walks the world.[50]

Like the other poems of 1940, this is oblique in its relation to MacNeice himself, in so far as its symbols remain, to a great extent, abstract. 'Jehu' is the only (and not entirely successful) attempt to relate symbols to events, and MacNeice's efforts to open himself further to events and sensory phenomena reached their peak with 'The Sense of Smell', a long and almost pointless enumerative exercise. The gap between 'reportage' (from which the poet was distancing himself in the introduction to *The Poetry of W. B. Yeats*) and more personal writing, with its symbols for the necessity of some kind of commitment, was largely one between other and self, compounded by an awareness of time that no amount of stylistic elegance was sufficient to contain.

In September 1940, when the London Blitz had begun in earnest, MacNeice was convalescing after peritonitis, and preparing to return to Britain, while also finishing the book on Yeats and turning again explicitly to the subject of time:

[50] MacNeice, 'Coming from Nowhere', *Poems 1925–1940*, pp. 269–71.

We still tend to think that, because a thing is in time, its value can only be explained by an abstraction from the thing of some supposedly timeless qualities; this is to explain the thing away. That a rose withers is no disproof of the rose, which remains an absolute, its value inseparable from its existence (for existence is still existence, whether the tense is past or future).[51]

This question of time and specific value (characteristic of MacNeice in fact since his schooldays) had been at the centre of his remarkable poem 'Plurality' of the previous month. There, a jingling verse form was employed to accommodate abstruse metaphysics (or rather repudiations of metaphysics). The poem, one of MacNeice's most elaborate attempts to come to terms with the idea 'That only change prevails', tries to salvage value in a philosophical system where flux is paramount and a static universal impossible. The definition of each thing as 'a denial of all that is not it', leads MacNeice to a view of each entity as

> An absolute and so defiant of the One
> Absolute, the row of noughts where time is done,
> Where nothing goes or comes and Is is one with Ought
> And all the possible sums alike resolve to nought.

Aligning the Yeatsian state of 'Soul' with a sterile universal,[52] MacNeice tries to lay claim to a more modest absolute that need neither transcend nor fear time. Yet it is questionable whether the poet changes this 'Absolute' by anything more than stripping it of its capital letter: the poem's energies are concentrated upon the fragility of the self which perceives and reasons, 'Conscious of guilt and vast inadequacy and the sick | Ego and the broken past and the clock that goes too quick'. The extreme artificiality of the verse, and the rather showy verbal cleverness that it demands, are in some ways self-defeating: they reflect, perhaps, the poet's need to formalize excessively his response to the demands being made upon him by the seemingly destructive force of time. The belief that 'existence is still existence whether the tense is past or future', is part of an uncertainty as to which tense the poet must live in. 'Exile', a poem written in March, showed a figure 'Tired of what he wants | And sick of what he ought', who watches 'The window fill with snow | Making even the Future |

---

[51] *The Poetry of W. B. Yeats*, p. 15.
[52] Cf. the Soul in Yeats's 'A Dialogue of Self and Soul': 'For intellect no longer knows | *Is* from the *Ought*, or *Knower* from the Known.'

Seem long ago'. The allusion back to the scene of 'Snow', with its endorsement of plurality, the separateness of specific existence, is ironic here, and without the assurance of self-sufficiency; the uncertainty of the tense of existence is rooted in pressures of the present:

> Knowing that in Europe
> All the streets are black
> And that stars of blood
> Star the almanac,
> One half-hour's reprieve
> Drowns him in the white
> Physical or spiritual
> Inhuman night.[53]

This suggests that 'Plurality''s 'dead ideal of white | All-white Universal' is allied with the limbo between escapism and commitment which is represented as an escape from, or evasion of, time—which America was coming to represent for MacNeice. Departure for Britain meant also accepting the possibility of a new relation to an idea of time as a force more complex than either the 1930s perspective of history stretching from the past into the future, or the philosophical recourse to the instability of flux and constant change.

In his account of the so-called 'Atlantic tunnel' which begins *The Strings Are False*, MacNeice conveys a temporal disorientation in 'going back to a past which is not there': from America, 'which for me is mythical future, I am going over to somewhere without tenses'.[54] If America was indeed a 'future' for MacNeice, it was proved 'mythical' by developments in the European present: a 'future' centred on the integrity of the self came to seem untenable. The letter written in March 1940 to Mrs Dodds, claiming that 'one must keep making things which are *not oneself*', on the grounds that 'it seems high time neither to be passive to flux nor to substitute for it, Marxist-like, a mere algebra of captions', was in fact not such a final and decisive manifesto as critics have made it: the actual artistic consequences of these instinctive feelings remained unclear to MacNeice in anything other than abstract terms, but they already depended upon their personal corollary, that 'freedom means Getting Into

---

[53] MacNeice, 'Exile', *Poems 1925–1940*, p. 58. The poem's original title, 'Three Thousand Miles', makes the exile in question more explicit (printed in *Poetry* (Chicago), 66/11 (May 1940), 66).

[54] *The Strings Are False*, p. 17.

things & not getting Out of them'.[55] As a poet, making things 'which are *not oneself*', MacNeice was in a position of responsibility which could not be occupied satisfactorily by writing with reference primarily to the self. As the American poems of 1940 show, the nature of the relation between self and other was difficult, if not impossible, for the poet to establish. Coming, then, from a 'mythical' future to one which, existing independently of the self's instincts, was unknowable, MacNeice took stock:

I am 33 years old and what can I have been doing that I am still in a muddle? But everyone else is too, maybe our muddles are concurrent. Maybe, if I look back, I shall find that my life is not just mine, that it mirrors the lives of the others—or shall I say the Life of the Other? Anyway I will look back. And return later to pick up the present, or rather to pick up the future.[56]

This was MacNeice's second new start within a year, but it entailed a change in artistic direction that was to influence the rest of his work; the polarities of self and other had been identified by now as more than abstract problems, and it could be argued that almost everything that MacNeice wrote afterwards was an attempt to bridge the gap between them, that the process of composition itself came to be regarded as a kind of battleground for these antinomies. London in 1941 was a real enough scene of conflict, but it seemed to MacNeice also a crucial testing-ground for personal and artistic integrity, and the poems which this produced were closer to the prescription for 'things which are *not oneself*' than those written in America. However, verisimilitude, whether to the feelings of the self or in terms of external 'reportage', was a means rather than an end for much of MacNeice's writing from 1941 onwards.

While MacNeice's return at the beginning of 1941 was certainly to a new and different London, under attack and constant threat of attack from the *Luftwaffe*, the literary world, if rather more tightly grouped than before, had survived more or less intact. The 1930s arguments over the writer's responsibility were still being conducted, though with Auden now amongst the easy targets; MacNeice himself, while in America, had been referred to by John Lehmann as a writer who 'will, one feels, always be able to produce lyrics of the same liveliness and easy grace, whatever happens in the world'.[57] The

---

[55] MacNeice to Mrs Dodds from Cornell, 22 Mar. 1940, Dodds fo. 67[v].
[56] *The Strings Are False*, p. 35.
[57] John Lehmann, *New Writing in Europe* (Harmondsworth, 1940), 116.

1930s myth, established for good by Orwell's *Inside the Whale* and
Virginia Woolf's *The Leaning Tower*, was only strengthened by the
ways in which the literary bickering contrived to continue. In
February 1941, for example, Arthur Calder-Marshall wrote how the
1930s writers 'are like me in looking back on that decade with a
sense not of triumph, but of shame and failure', and went on:

Those who held back, 'for their art's sake,' will find their sterility exposed
the more familiar their technical virtuosity becomes. Their contribution, as
Mrs. Woolf has pointed out, lies chiefly on their autobiographical work; the
sensitive revelation of their experience. Their 'political' writing is bad, not
because it is political, but because it was never lived.[58]

Spender's rather odd reply to this, that 'If a future generation
condemns us, it will be because we lacked sufficient faith in ourselves
to take our own work seriously',[59] was in effect another instance of
'so much flagellation, so many *Peccavis*, going on in the literary Left',
repudiated by MacNeice on the grounds that 'We may not have done
all we could in the Thirties, but we did do something.'[60] MacNeice's
criticism of arguments such as Woolf's or Calder-Marshall's hinged
on the fact that, as Calder-Marshall himself admitted, they were not
written to recapture 'the puzzled conflicting moods with which in
1935 we approached the future, but as one, like posterity, wise after
the event'.[61] In place of hindsight, MacNeice offered a reassessment
of the nature and aims of poetry, using Christopher Caudwell (who
was often cited by mythologizers such as Spender as a kind of
cautionary example of the dangers of mixing art and ideology) for
his point of departure:

Even an orthodox Communist Party critic, Christopher Caudwell, in his
book *Illusion and Reality*, insisted (rightly) that poetry can never be reduced
to political advertising, that its method is myth and that it must represent not
any set of ideas which can be formulated by politicians or scientists or by
mere Reason and/or mere Will—it must represent something much deeper
and wider which he calls the 'Communal Ego'. It is this Communal Ego with
which Auden and Spender concerned themselves.[62]

---

[58] Arthur Calder-Marshall, 'The Pink Decade', *New Statesman and Nation*, 15
Feb. 1941, pp. 157–8.
[59] Stephen Spender, 'Letter to Arthur Calder-Marshall', ibid. 22 Feb. 1941, p. 183.
[60] MacNeice, 'The Tower that Once', *Folios of New Writing*, 3 (Spring 1941), 41
(repr. Heuser 124).
[61] Calder-Marshall, letter in *New Statesman and Nation*, 1 Mar. 1941, p. 214.
[62] 'The Tower that Once', p. 40 (Heuser, p. 122).

MacNeice always saw Caudwell's stress on how 'men are affected by each other's emotional experiences and experiences of reality' so that they 'make each other what they are', as much more important than his specifically political views;[63] MacNeice's attempts to understand and employ this 'Communal Ego' began with his return to Britain, and lay behind the poems which were eventually to comprise the 1944 collection *Springboard*: picking up the future was to entail, in theory at least, some serviceable compromise between the individual and the community. As often in the poet's work, the self and the other refused to be reconciled quite so easily as this kind of reasoning tended to suggest.

The signs of MacNeice's determination to open his work to a sense of community (rather than simply a resigned abandonment of the self to oblivion, as suggested by some of the letters to the Doddses[64]) are present in the prose pieces written on his return to London. In 'Traveller's Return', published in *Horizon* in February, MacNeice was still defending Auden, reporting that he 'had repudiated propaganda', and attacking Spender's notion that the expatriates were 'trying to put the clock back' ('we might remember that there are people over here . . . whose clocks, it seems, have stopped'); at the same time, he distinguished his own case from that of Auden's, who in *Another Time* and *The Double Man* 'is now attempting a new synthesis of his material', and claimed that 'not being on the track of a synthesis and being more attached to things than to ideas I might have felt I was only marking time in America'.[65] MacNeice expanded upon this in 'The Way We Live Now', published in Lehmann's *Penguin New Writing* in April, remembering that 'By autumn I had reached a point where, though England had not regained its reality, my Americans had begun to lose theirs.'[66] England, though, had gained a certain reality for the poet, as he made clear in answer to his own question 'So what?' (which also begins *The Strings Are False* as 'This modern equivalent of Pilate's "What is truth?"'):

So this: I have never really thought of myself as British; if there is one country I feel at home in, it is Eire. As a place to live in or write in I prefer the U.S.A. to

[63] Christopher Caudwell, *Illusion and Reality: A Study of the Sources of Poetry* (1937), 213.

[64] C.f. MacNeice to Dodds, 18 Aug. 1940, Dodds fo. 70ᵛ: 'What do you think they'll make me do? By this stage I am on for doing anything—cleaning sewers or feeding machine guns, but preferably nothing too intelligent.'

[65] MacNeice, 'Traveller's Return', *Horizon*, 3/14 (Feb. 1941), 114, 112–14, 116.

[66] MacNeice, 'The Way We Live Now', *Penguin New Writing*, 5 (Apr. 1941), 11.

England and New York to London. But I am glad to be back in England and, in particular, in London. Because London since the Blitz has become more comprehensible. Because this great dirty, slovenly, sprawling city is a visible and tangible symbol of freedom.[67]

This declaration of allegiance turns away from the stress on 'myself as an example of uprootability',[68] to embrace the shared existence of war in a city under bombardment. 'We play Rummy here every night', MacNeice wrote from London, adding that 'It occurs to me that even playing Rummy in London now is a kind of assertion of the Rights of Man, whereas in America it would be nothing but playing Rummy.'[69] In his *New Writing* article, the poet extended the political implications of this mere daily existence in London during the Blitz, asserting that 'there is just a chance that the other tunnel we are in at the moment may lead us up into a more concrete kind of socialism', and going on to defend the values of 'the typical Englishman': 'The notorious defects of the English are at least the defects of a people who respect the individual being. A world view? All right, we need a world view (we can't be mere empiricists for ever) but the world is made of human beings. Any ideology which ignores the individual human being is ripe for the scrap-heap.'[70] Politically, MacNeice's reconciliation of the experience of war with the idea of communal advance towards socialism was hardly unique;[71] the stress on 'the individual human being', however, had definite artistic implications for the poet, which may be seen as culminating in his lengthy piece, 'The Kingdom'. The weakness of that poem's celebration of 'the Kingdom of individuals', its excessive deliberateness, should be traced back to the tensions beneath MacNeice's artistic commitment to ideas of both community and individuality during the war years.

[67] MacNeice, 'The Way We Live Now', *Penguin New Writing*, 5 (Apr. 1941), 13.
[68] 'Traveller's Return', p. 114.
[69] MacNeice to Mrs Dodds, 10 Feb. 1941, Dodds fo. 74ᵛ.
[70] 'The Way We Live Now', p. 14.
[71] Cf. *Guilty Men* by Michael Foot, Frank Owen, and Peter Howard, published by Victor Gollancz in July 1940 (just after Dunkirk), a highly critical assessment of the Chamberlain government, drawing conclusions for the socialist future; or George Orwell's 'My Country Right or Left' (*Folios of New Writing*, Autumn 1940): 'There is no real alternative between resisting Hitler and surrendering to him . . . Within two years, maybe a year, if only we can hang on, we shall see changes that will surprise the idiots who have no foresight.' (Repr. in *The Collected Essays, Journalism and Letters of George Orwell*, ed. S. Orwell and I. Angus, i (1968), 591.)

Experiencing the Blitz in the first half of 1941, MacNeice found that his reactions were divided between 'mere chaos'[72] and the desire for coherence. In March he wrote to Dodds about his autobiographical book (later to be published as *The Strings Are False*), announcing that 'as the result of living in London in war-time, I want to re-do the whole thing'.[73] It is perhaps fortunate that he did not in fact take up the project again at that time. The new direction MacNeice had in mind for his autobiography was probably towards the 'unconscious over-ruling of heterogeneous realism for the sake of that coherence which we never achieve in our lives but which, as an implicit ideal, acts in our lives as a mainspring',[74] another gesture in the direction taken by Yeats, on a path which MacNeice himself was still beginning, sometimes rather clumsily, to follow. Between pattern and 'chaos', disordered experience and individual coherence, MacNeice tried to keep to the track of an 'empiricist'—'someone who follows an ideal that is always developing, implicit rather than explicit'.[75] The intention was tested severely by events.

In April and May of 1941 London suffered heavy bombing: MacNeice, working by then for the BBC (though not, until May, on a permanent basis), was in some ways journalistic in his artistic response to events. Besides his 'London Letter' to the American journal *Common Sense* from April to July, the poet gave a detailed account, for home consumption, of the aftermath of one of the heaviest raids, that of 16th April (known afterwards as 'the Wednesday') in *Picture Post*.[76] The article, 'The Morning After the Blitz', begins with a description of the sounds of the raid itself—'Just one long drawn-out lunatic symphony'—which is immediately reminiscent of the poem 'The Trolls': 'the banging of all the tea-trays and the loosing of all the fireworks and the rumbling of all the tumbrils and the breaking of all the oceans in the world'. The account of a walk through the devastated areas of London after the attack reveals something of the nature of MacNeice's attempts at coherence in the face of apparently overwhelming destruction; in

---

[72] See MacNeice, 'London Letter', *Common Sense*, July 1941: 'sometimes I say to myself "This is mere chaos, it makes no sense," and at other times I think "Before I saw war-time London I must have been spiritually colour-blind"'.

[73] MacNeice to Dodds, 21 Mar. 1941, Dodds fo. 85ᵛ.

[74] MacNeice, 'Autobiographies', *New Statesman and Nation*, 17 May 1941, p. 512.

[75] MacNeice, 'Broken Windows or Thinking Aloud', in MS.

[76] MacNeice, 'The Morning After the Blitz', *Picture Post*, 3 May 1941, pp. 9–14.

fact, the whole article makes much of the efforts of Londoners to re-establish a kind of order out of chaos. MacNeice's artistic order, however, is sometimes almost obtrusively apparent. The concern for precise literary representation of visual phenomena is in excess even of that which might be expected of a photographically illustrated article. While allowing one or two figures apart from himself to make their way through the rubble, MacNeice describes London in such a way as to dehumanize the scenes, making it seem as if they were only material for literary working-up. There is no callousness behind this—'People's deaths were another matter'—but MacNeice's deepest reaction is to find 'this fantasy of destruction' 'enlivening'. Looking at a ruined bookshop, the poet converts 'the paradox of *distance*' involved in his reactions into something more positive:

All those shattered shops and blazing stores, this cataract of broken glass, this holocaust of dog's-eared property—there was a voice inside me which kept saying, as I watched a building burning or demolished: 'Let her go up!' or 'Let her come down. Let them all go. Write them all off. Stone walls do not a city make. Tear all the blotted old pages out of the book; there are more books in the mind than ever have got upon paper.'

Even allowing for the article's propagandist function of delivering illustrations of the 'London can take it' slogan (which was also the purpose of MacNeice's radio scripts in the series *The Stones Cry Out* at this time), the authorial transition from 'distance' to affirmation here is more than a little forced. The order which MacNeice elicits from the surrounding chaos is precisely that which cannot be described in anything other than near-clichés—'That London can take it may no longer be news, but it remains—and will remain—a national asset'—and cannot compete in poetic attractiveness with the livid forms of chaos themselves. The self-consciously artistic cast of MacNeice's account of the Blitz damage perhaps serves to draw attention to the problematic nature of 'the paradox of *distance*' in which the poet found that he had been caught.

Something of this problem may be seen also in 'The Trolls', written after the same air raid. Against the powerfully farcical description of the attackers 'Barging and lunging out of the clouds, a daft | Descent of no-good gods', 'our answer' is simply denial—'they happen | To be—for all their kudos— | Wrong, wrong in the end'. Death enters rather more prominently than in the Blitz report, in order to clarify the reasons for destruction's ultimate futility. In the fourth section, for instance, there is a personification of time which

Swings on the poles of death
And the latitude and the longitude of life
Are fixed by death, and the value
Of every organism, act and moment
Is, thanks to death, unique.

This transformation of an image of time first employed by the poet in the 1930s is echoed by the prose piece 'Broken Windows or Thinking Aloud' (also probably from 1941), in which war is 'applied science' that, 'by shattering a town overnight, by superimposing upon ordered decay a fantastic but palpable madness, has shown us the integral function of death'. The definition of death as 'the opposite of decay; a stimulus, a necessary horizon', works in 'The Trolls' as a way of assigning value to moments of time as well as to individual actions. A clear corollary of this is the celebration of the individual himself; uniqueness is finally the only answer to the trolls' negation. The actual results of this in poetry, however, did not always strike a balance between the uniqueness of individuality and the reality of the external, destructive pressure of war.

The weaker aspect of MacNeice's poetic interpretation of the individual's dilemma may be seen in 'Convoy', written at the end of 1942. The description of the ships 'keeping in line' and the 'little whippet warships' scurrying around them leads to a final stanza that makes explicit the comparison hitherto suppressed:

This is a bit like us: the individual sets
A course for all his soul's more basic needs
Of love and pride-of-life, but sometimes he forgets
How much their voyage home depends upon pragmatic
And ruthless attitudes—destroyers and corvettes.

The honest integrity of this is not sufficient to enable the lines to recover from the bathos of 'This is a bit like us', yet the poem's lack of success in this respect is arguably no more than a concrete example of how little MacNeice felt individual integrity and its strategies for survival could in fact be reconciled without forcing—the forcing is, in real terms, the strain imposed upon the artist by the war itself. To some extent, *The Poetry of W. B. Yeats* had prepared the ground for the kind of problems MacNeice encountered in wartime London, with its reasoned equivocation on the relation between the poetic self and external reality, but its qualified rejection of Yeats as a poetic model for the times ('If the war made nonsense of Yeats's poetry and all works that are called "escapist", it also made nonsense of poetry that professes to be "realist" '[77]) was not enough for some readers when the book was published in February of 1941. Almost immediately, Stephen Spender offered a more scathing view of Yeats (close, in fact, to that of Auden's 'Public Prosecutor') that went well beyond MacNeice's double-edged reservations: 'Yeats wrote by saving himself from the mud of Flanders and the mud of the common mind of his time. He is an isolated figure who achieved greatness. Other poets may admire him, but they cannot follow him, because he does not wrestle with the problem of interpreting the surrounding life of his time into poetry. He is only himself.'[78] Of course, 'the war' as understood by MacNeice while writing on Yeats in 1939–40 was quite different from the war as he experienced it in London in 1941, and the pressures exerted by 'pragmatic | And ruthless attitudes' had not perhaps been fully understood then by the poet: yet Spender's condemnation of Yeats for being 'only himself' serves well to illustrate the very quality which MacNeice was coming to value, that of individuality against the odds. Developing his definition of an 'empiricist' in 'Broken Windows', he wrote:

To live either happily or usefully, as to make works of art, requires a method which is in this sense empirical—that each case is unique. The number 2 may always be the number 2 but no two men or no two pictures are identical. This does not preclude recognition of men as men or pictures as art but it means that, to judge them, you need an open mind.

This turns out to be not quite so simple (even simplistic) as it appears: MacNeice adds that 'The Open Mind is good but it encourages Laissez-Faire. & Laissez-Faire is bad.' This awareness of both the necessity and the danger of extending the limits of self-interest while at the same time celebrating individuality is widespread in MacNeice's poetry from 1941 to 1944, resulting in a number of failures as well as undoubted successes.

The emphasis on destruction as 'enlivening' in MacNeice's Blitz accounts and poems is seen by him as a wiping-clean, an opportunity to begin afresh. In 'Broken Windows' this is made explicit: 'Let them all go if they must. Take out your razor & shave away the houses;

---

[77]   *The Poetry of W. B. Yeats*, pp. 17–18.
[78]   Stephen Spender, 'Tragedy and Some Modern Poetry', *Penguin New Writing*, 4 (Mar. 1941), 147.

shave away the soil & the subsoil. If the human animal remains, it remains—an animal & human; instincts, ideals remain.' It is noteworthy that MacNeice yokes together instincts and ideals at the same level, with the individual 'an animal & human'. This implies an ethical element in mere existence. Criticizing Auden's dictum that 'Others must be regarded aesthetically and only oneself ethically', MacNeice wrote that he had 'sold out', adding that 'Ethics presupposes not only judgement upon others but calculated interference with them.'[79] In 'Troll's Courtship' (May 1941), MacNeice alludes to Auden's 'Now the leaves are falling fast', where 'Starving through the leafless wood | Trolls run scolding for their food':[80]

> Nostalgia for the breast that never gave nor could
> Give milk or even warmth has desolated me,
> Clutching at shadows of my nullity
> That slink and mutter through the leafless wood
> Which thanks to me is dead, is dead for good.

Whereas in 1936 Auden used 'the leafless wood' as an image of desolation and finality, in 1941 MacNeice transforms the image into an illustration of mere desolation's futility in the face of values it cannot comprehend (the troll 'cannot accurately conceive | Any ideal, even ideal Death', and so must remain frustrated). What in the 1930s was an end can appear in 1941 as a beginning, positive values having been brought into focus by their widespread negation. In 'Brother Fire', the finest of MacNeice's Blitz poems, the destructive fire is no longer a fanatical imposition but now a necessary element, both 'enemy and image of ourselves'; what the fire and its survivors have in common is expressed as 'Destroy! Destroy!', but the resultant knowledge is more subtle: 'Thus were we weaned to knowledge of the Will | That wills the natural world but wills us dead'. This Hardyesque 'Will' is being classicized by MacNeice, for here the ability to define satisfactorily 'the human animal' comes only as a consequence of understanding the difference between its 'human' and 'animal' aspects: 'ideal Death' as 'a stimulus, a necessary horizon', is thus a distinctively human inheritance. Where, in 'Troll's Courtship', the troll starved, the inhabitants of London now are 'suckled

---

[79] This quotation occurs in the 'Notes to Letter' section of *New Year Letter*, p. 133.
[80] *The English Auden*, ed. Edward Mendelson (1977), 159. The poem was included in *Look, Stranger!* (1936).

with sparks': again, MacNeice implies that direct experience of the war has acted as a kind of vital nourishment for the 'human' element within that irretrievably clichéd unit, the individual.

Claiming that a new start has been made is not, of course, the same thing as making a new start. Spender's somewhat glib assertion that 'The faith that enables a true poet to write poetry is the faith that the universal conditions of life prevail behind all existing appearances', is a watered-down version of MacNeice's 'shave away the houses', and leads on to another commonplace which is nevertheless important for understanding a good deal of the poetry of the period, that 'the crisis of modern poetry turns on the challenge of modern organization when it seems to over-ride all the feelings of individuals'.[81] On the BBC Overseas Service in June 1941, George Orwell observed that 'We live in an age in which the autonomous individual is ceasing to exist—or perhaps one ought to say, in which the individual is ceasing to have the illusion of being autonomous.'[82] For both Spender and Orwell, the pressures upon the idea of the individual were those which were seen to begin in the 1930s, and which the war was serving only to intensify; it was as though the intellectual in the 1940s found himself resisting those forces that existed for him as ideas in the previous decade, but which were not translated into real terms—the fact that in some cases he himself might have embraced these ideas, complicated issues further. Poets like Spender, and to some extent also MacNeice, had to confront in wartime London the humbling of that individualism whose downfall they had both prophesied and, sometimes, advocated in the 1930s. MacNeice's poetry of these years tries to accommodate that measure of humbling alongside a surviving integrity of the self. Adapting Yeats's apparently eccentric estimation of Keats in 1941, MacNeice agreed that 'Keats in life could not have the world he wanted; he tried to build up a world in poetry', but added that 'The value of such a world depends upon how egocentric its author is or rather, perhaps, upon how far he is a man like other men.'[83] However earnestly democratic its principles, MacNeice's poetry did not quite work according to this formula, nor entirely along the lines proposed in his introductory note to *Springboard*, with its 'imagined individual' who 'seems to me

[81] Stephen Spender, 'The Poets in Revolt', *Penguin New Writing*, 11 (Nov. 1941), 125–6.

[82] George Orwell, the *Listener*, 19 June 1941, repr. in *Collected Essays*, ii. 134.

[83] MacNeice, 'John Keats', in *Fifteen Poets* (Oxford, 1941), 352.

to have an absolute quality which the definite article recognizes'.[84] Instead, the poems tend, at their best, to feel acutely the lack of complete contact between individuals along with a self-consciously futile regret for their obsolescence—where affirmation is to be made, the poet experiences more difficulty in translating private values into public celebration. In this respect, the epigraph to *Springboard*'s first section, George Herbert's 'Even poisons praise thee', is appropriate to the shorter poems' dominant tone of loss and absence, a sometimes sinister *via negativa* to the positive values.

The problem of the self's relation to the other, with which the 1930s had ended for MacNeice, is solved only in *Springboard*'s weaker poems. In the first section of 'The Kingdom' (1943), this solution is expressed most explicitly, but even here MacNeice finds it necessary to use negative terms to define his ideal individuals, 'Not merged nor yet excluded' from the external world. The self, it seems, accommodates the other only according to its own valuation (it is apart 'from such as being false are merely other'), but this has to relegate a great deal to the barbarous reality of 'merely other', outside 'The Kingdom', with which in fact a great many of the poems in *Springboard* are preoccupied. Amongst the criteria for member-ship of 'the Kingdom of individuals' is the capacity of the voice 'To break the inhuman into humanity' with words which, 'Whether in code or in clear, | Are to the point and can be received apart from | The buzz of jargon' (section VIII); and it is this quality for which the poems in *Springboard*'s first part search. The repeated line in 'Babel', 'Can't we ever, my love, speak in the same language?', is complemented by 'The Mixer': 'like a Latin word | That many languages have made their own', 'often spoken but no longer heard'. Language is seen here as one of the barriers between the self and the other, transcended only in the gesture of articulation and commun-ication which is the poem itself. Yet the barriers return throughout the book's first part, most insistently in 'Schizophrene', where the self is rendered impotent through division; the inability to 'speak up', and the consequent need to 'deny, deny, deny', stem from the impossibility of containing the other as it is manifested in the intimation of formlessness ('The Dark, the Flood, the Malice', or bells ringing—a very deeply rooted nightmare image for MacNeice —till 'Chaos be itself and nothing felt'). All of this is akin to

---

[84] MacNeice, *Springboard* (1944), 7.

MacNeice's abiding fear of the destructive powers of flux and time, though the poem, like others in the volume, distances such concerns somewhat by replacing the poet's characteristic 'lyric' first-person voice with the apparent detachment of the third-person depiction. When the barriers come down in 'Schizophrene', all that is left is denial, the assertion of final chaos; similarly, in 'The Casualty' in the book's second part, the possibility of Graham Shepard's finding 'a Form | Grow out of formlessness' is obscured by death's impenetrable silence. The barriers between self and other, form and chaos, provide the poetry with its necessary condition; their removal remains either a nightmare or an impossible speculation. The poems, in *Springboard*'s first part especially, attempt to approach these barriers with a degree of objectivity, implying that the method of approach, as much as the poems' 'content', is in some sense exemplary.

In poems preoccupied—albeit often negatively—with value, MacNeice had to distinguish between individual integrity and the culpably isolated self. Just as 'Broken Windows' complained that 'we've shrunk back into individualists with an airy fairy conception of freedom', so *Springboard* resists ideas of individualism that entail the contracting of personal horizons—'isn't it a pity if you have to choose between the Astral Plane & High-Mindedness? Aren't there other choices?' ('Broken Windows'). The individual of 'Bottleneck', who once 'dreamt of barricades' at his 'progressive school' (the first of a number of Everyman-figures from the 1930s generation to be used by MacNeice), finds that 'The permanent bottleneck of his highmindedness' will not permit any 'compromise with fact'. This kind of 'compromise' is denied in much the same way by what MacNeice calls 'the Astral Plane' in the 1940s; certainly, the poetry of 'Apocalypse' was to the fore in England during the war. Though its subsequent decline in reputation was as sudden, for the most part, as its rise, the astral plane does not end there. Once again, Spender provides a useful point of reference, contemplating enthusiastically the possibility of transcending 'the world of action' through the knowledge that 'humanity is greater than individuals, and the eternal continuity of what exists greater than humanity'.[85] As early as his return from America, MacNeice had warned that although 'Mr. Yeats did return to the Upanishads and he got away with it', 'we

---

[85] Spender, rev. of *The Geeta*, trans. Swami, in *Poetry* (London), 2/9 [n.d.], 52.

don't all have to go to Birmingham by way of *Shangri-La*'.[86] Given this, it is not surprising that parts of *Springboard* identify the dangerous isolation of the self with spiritual yearning, the times, as in 'Nostalgia', at which 'Aloneness is too ripe | When homesick for the hollow | Heart of the Milky Way'. Yet MacNeice also included poems with a clearer direction which, while not 'bound for the Holy Mountain' ('Broken Windows'), still attempt a kind of spiritual affirmation. Both 'Prayer in Mid-Passage' and 'Prospect' come directly to the theme of time—'Though the evil Past is ever present | And the happy Present is past indeed'—recalling the poet's preoccupation with the change in personal life and its corollary in the shifting tenses of 1939/40:

> We were the past—and doomed because
> We were a past that never was;
> Yet grant to men that they may climb
> This time-bound ladder out of time
> And by our human organs we
> Shall thus transcend humanity.

The hymn-like metre here imposes another barrier between the poetry and its object, the transcendence in question remaining clearly an act of faith, or will, not to be realized within the writing self, who prays to something that depends upon his own finality: 'Thou my meaning, Thou my death'. There is a neat conjunction here of the 'necessary horizon' with the literal reality of the self's mode of existence as writing. MacNeice's claim that 'we need all the senses we were born with; and one of those is the religious' ('Broken Windows'), while it did not set a course for the holy mountain, entailed a growing awareness of the importance of wartime experience as a trial with more than just individual significance. In 'Thyestes', a dark poem of 1943, the idea of complicity is central, and the borders between the self and the other are blurred accordingly: 'Thus Here and We, neither of which is what | The mind and map admit, in perfidy are linked'. The poem's suggestion of complicity between spectator and murderer, especially bitter in wartime, is expressed in terms of the classical myth until the last two lines, where Christian imagery breaks in dramatically—'we' are 'messmates in the eucharist

---

[86] MacNeice, rev. of *A Golden Treasury of Scottish Poetry*, ed. Hugh MacDiarmid, *New Statesman and Nation*, 18 Jan. 1941, p. 66.

of crime | And heirs of two of those three black crosses on the hill'. It is characteristic of *Springboard* that religious elements should make themselves felt more strongly in the context of doubt and self-accusation than that of transcendence and affirmation.

The burden of spiritual affirmation weighs heavily upon the second part of *Springboard*, with its optimistic epigraph from Dante promising 'sweet fruits' in place of Herbert's 'poisons' which prefix the first part. Two deaths in 1942, of his father and of Graham Shepard, elicited MacNeice's literary response: where 'The Casualty' is an elegy for one friend in particular, 'The Kingdom' absorbs Bishop MacNeice in a series of fulsome celebratory epitaphs aspiring to a representative status for the poet's conceptions of individuality and value. Between these two lengthy poems is placed 'The Newsreel', a short piece in which MacNeice attempts to see through the historical debris of wartime experience with intimations of 'the intrusions | Of value upon fact' (compare the 'compromise with fact' of 'Bottleneck'). As in all his wartime writing, the poet has to feel for the value through fact, and not by leaving fact behind. In 'The Casualty', the effort to resist the easy transcendence belonging to the standard elegiac tropes is strongly felt. Among this poem's many evasions is the avoidance of Yeats's unrestrained celebration in 'In Memory of Major Robert Gregory'; this is made all the more difficult for MacNeice by the fact that Shepard does, in many ways, measure up to the Gregory blueprint as given by Yeats. Following the method of Yeats's poem, in which MacNeice understood that 'the hero is conceded full individuality, his Marxist conditioning is ignored', 'The Casualty' takes Yeats's 'explanation of a man not by his daily life but by one or two great moments',[87] and uses it as a pattern for content which is, in the older poet's terms, determinedly unheroic:

> Here you are gabbling Baudelaire or Donne
> Here you are mimicking that cuckoo clock,
> Here you are serving a double fault for set,
> Here you are diving naked from a Dalmatian rock,
> Here you are barracking the sinking sun,
> Here you are taking Proust aboard your doomed corvette.

MacNeice democratizes Yeats at his most aristocratic, without losing the essential continuity between the two elegies; 'The Casualty' is

---

[87] *The Poetry of W. B. Yeats*, p. 110.

the best example in *Springboard* of the Hopkinsian 'Go thou and do otherwise' at the end of *The Poetry of W. B. Yeats*.[88] The poem holds back from making explicit 'some momentous truth' aside from 'inklings', 'a footprint here and there | In falling snow', and both this and the major image of the sea that drowns Shepard recall MacNeice's talismanic points of poetic contact with the pervasiveness of flux. It is noteworthy that 'The Casualty' is the only poem in the volume to rely heavily on flux and 'the integrity of differences', perhaps because Shepard is being played off against the fixed and rather monumental virtues assigned to Robert Gregory by Yeats. What marks the poem so characteristic of its period in MacNeice's work, however, is the leaving-open of the possibility of a form growing out of formlessness, though there is no offer of an answer: the 'great moments', and their value, are all that are left. In this respect, it is the ghostly presence of Yeats's elegy which enforces upon 'The Casualty' a reticence with regard to generalization and transcendence, 'talking big', that 'The Kingdom' unfortunately lacks.

In contrast to the confident portraits of 'The Kingdom', none of which matches the depth and intensity of the seventh (that of the poet's father), two of *Springboard*'s strongest poems, 'Epitaph for Liberal Poets' and 'The Springboard' itself, confine their affirmations of value to those inherent in, and not coaxed out of, the reality of individual defeat. The poems come from an acknowledgement that the war represents defeat for many of the values of the 1930s generation. Discussing these writers in 1943, Henry Reed wrote: 'Perhaps their world seems doubly solid as compared with the world which has succeeded it, for its more sensitive members were drawn together by a knowledge of its impending collapse', and added that: 'It is less easy to-day to reach out across the rubble and the fallen masonry; and perhaps it does not greatly matter.'[89] 'The Springboard' transposes this difficulty of a generation into a surrealistic Blitz nightmare, its atmosphere anticipating strikingly that of *The Burning Perch*, in which the individual, faced with the collapse of his supporting environment, has to set a price on his own head. The poem postulates the sacrifice of the individual in the context of 'unbelief'; he goes down in the knowledge that his destruction can have no practical consequences, that 'His friends would find in his

---

[88] Ibid. 197.
[89] Henry Reed, 'The End of an Impulse', *New Writing and Daylight*, Summer 1943, p. 117.

death neither ransom nor reprieve | But only a grain of faith—for what it was worth'. The nature of such a 'grain of faith' is left obscure in favour of the dramatic dive itself which is the poem's conclusion. Here MacNeice balances impressively the completion of the surrealistic image with its moral and religious overtones:

> And yet we know he knows what he must do.
> There above London where the gargoyles grin
> He will dive like a bomber past the broken steeple,
> One man wiping out his own original sin
> And, like ten million others, dying for the people.

As in 'The Casualty', death functions as a 'necessary horizon' rather than as an excuse for a sermon; here, too, affirmation is the more effective for being a matter of 'inklings'. The individual's separateness is the essence of his integrity, but it is not the same thing as isolation; the third-person mode characteristic of *Springboard* includes finally the writer and audience—'we know he knows what he must do'. As a provisional reconciliation of self and other, 'The Springboard' does begin to 'reach out across the rubble'—which means getting beyond the rubble as well—by means of directly presented and unelaborated symbolism, in its surface simplicity the germ of what MacNeice was later to call 'parable'. 'Epitaph for Liberal Poets', which enacts a similar reconciliation, does so without the symbolism: the death here is unambiguously that of the self and, perhaps, of a whole culture centred upon the self. Even so, MacNeice still uses the epitaph as a means of affirmation as well as an admission of defeat, suggesting a continuity of artistic endeavour that is greater than the individual, while still requiring full individuality as a prerequisite.

With *Springboard*, MacNeice's transition from the 1930s to the 1940s was completely achieved. The volume elicited little enthusiasm from critics, especially since it seemed to be bad war poetry (as, in the propagandist sense, it is): one American writer complained that 'These are not poems to rally resistance but are poems of shared guilt', adding that 'MacNeice cannot see the beam in his enemy's eye for the mote in his own.'[90] The *Times Literary Supplement* remarked, more perceptively, on 'the depths of mystery with which he has yet to integrate his impulsive interest in the social surface'.[91] MacNeice's

---

[90] Coleman Rosenberger, rev. of *Springboard*, in *Poetry* (Chicago), 68/1 (Apr. 1946), 48.   [91] Rev. of *Springboard*, in *TLS*, 3 Feb. 1945, p. 57.

propaganda work was in another medium in the war years, but the 'depths of mystery' impinged more closely on the 'social surface' of his poetry than ever before. Yet the real change in direction went unremarked: the war forced MacNeice to confront the metaphysical problem of the self and the other, hardly new to him or his work as an idea, in far from metaphysical contexts; the result of this was poetry that understood and used more fully than before the 'individual' as its central figure. 'Poems of shared guilt' were the result of the poet's determination to reassess the nature and the limitations of the self. In a sense, the circumstances of everyday existence led back persistently to the metaphysical crux of self and other—both the concept of 'the self' and MacNeice's own self, tangled in personal and public pressures. The inextricability of these selves can be felt in 'Prayer before Birth':

> I am not yet born; forgive me
> For the sins that in me the world shall commit, my words
>   when they speak me, my thoughts when they think me,
>   my treason engendered by traitors beyond me
>   my life when they murder by means of my
>   hands, my death when they live me.

This represents a vital deepening of MacNeice's instinct, already in evidence at the time of *Poems*, that 'I not only have many different selves but I am often, as they say, not myself at all. Maybe it is just when I am not myself . . . that I feel like writing poetry.'[92] In 1939 the poet had envisaged the experience of war as a trial, a desert purgation, almost the nemesis of the self. With the publication of *Springboard* at the end of 1944, it was clear that 'the desert's purge' meant neither the abandonment of the self nor the unqualified adoption of social criteria for the value of poetry: rather, the poetic self was to be both more open and more fully individual. One result of this was plain speaking that could verge on the obvious or the trite; 'The Kingdom' was not to be without its successors in the next decade. Another result, however, was the mode of writing which MacNeice was eventually to identify as 'parable'.

[92] *The Poetry of W. B. Yeats*, p. 146.

5

Experiment: 1945–1953

ONE of the few points on which there is a significant degree of consensus between MacNeice's favourable and unfavourable critics concerns his poetry of the immediately post-war years, from parts of *Holes in the Sky* (1948) to *Autumn Sequel* (1954). This period tends to be referred to as 'the middle stretch', a term supplied, conveniently enough, by MacNeice himself.[1] To claim that the poetry of these years is consistently at the level of his best would be perverse, but although some poems may be, as W. H. Auden suggested, 'a bit dull',[2] much of what MacNeice achieved in this period was to prove of great importance to the lyric poetry of his last three volumes, and has seldom received serious attention. In particular, *Autumn Sequel*, which MacNeice himself always defended, has been done a critical disservice which obscures the importance of myth and parable in the poet's work as a whole. It is important not to judge the productions of this period by primarily lyric criteria; the discipline of writing for radio offers an alternative frame of reference which critics seldom put to use. Without the painstakingly unlyrical poems of MacNeice's 'middle stretch', the modified lyricism of the late poems would have been impossible.

By the time of *Springboard* (1944), MacNeice's writing had begun to lead in two directions: towards expository and ethically orientated verse; and towards more compressed, symbolic, double-level poetry. Both impulses may be seen clearly in an article of late 1945 for *La France libre*, 'L'Écrivain brittanique et la guerre',[3] where the end of the war is regarded as an important starting-point for new developments, a necessary humbling of the 1930s generation, whose form of pride has been changed by events. The responsibilities here go beyond surface verisimilitude to observation, just as they go beyond

---

[1] In the poem 'Day of Renewal' (*Ten Burnt Offerings*), *Collected Poems of Louis MacNeice*, ed. E. R. Dodds (1966), 309.

[2] W. H. Auden, Introduction to MacNeice, *Selected Poems* (1964), 9–10.

[3] MacNeice, 'L'Écrivain brittanique et la guerre', *La France libre* 11/62 (15 Dec. 1945), 109.

the commitment to 1930s theory: they are, in fact, far more complicated than either of these, involving the artist and the external world in a difficult interaction. 'Notre tâche', MacNeice writes, 'est de trouver un rapport entre l' « objectif » et le « subjectif ».' He encounters the objections to this overtly metaphysical approach directly: 'Certains critiques obtus ont deploré que ces poèmes se soient éloignés du monde lequel nous vivons—parce qu'ils sont presque essentiellement métaphysiques, évoulant autour de l'idée de temps. Mais le monde dans lequel nous vivons *est* métaphysique, et les paradoxes du temps *nous* concernent.' To illustrate this, Mac-Neice goes on to quote from Eliot's 'The Dry Salvages'. The 'metaphysical' concerns of *Four Quartets* are close to the heart of Mac-Neice's argument in this article, and Eliot's poems leave their mark on a good deal of his post-war poetry. As they become more openly metaphysical in their concerns, so MacNeice's poems rely more upon form to achieve their effects. MacNeice's treatment of the idea of time and the paradoxes of objectivity and subjectivity, self and other, depend in these years on the poetic medium's capacity for balance and opposition. Eliot's *Four Quartets* offered MacNeice examples of the successful combination of metaphysics with discursive form which, along with Rilke's *Duino Elegies*, lie behind poems like 'The Stygian Banks' or those of *Ten Burnt Offerings*. The *France libre* article of 1945 mapped out MacNeice's concerns for the next eight years in ambitious and uncompromising terms—as early as the spring of 1944 he had been projecting ideas for *Autumn Sequel*[4]—and the ways in which this writing of the middle stretch handles the topics raised there are similarly controlled and organized.

However, MacNeice's control and organization have often been seen as cold and premeditated in these post-war poems. The *France libre* article gives some indication of the degree of determination which was certainly involved for the poet—the need, as he saw it, for a reassertion of poetic 'pride' over and above the virtues of journalistic fidelity—but this has to be understood in the context of the immediately post-war period. Already in *Springboard* MacNeice has been concerned with the liabilities of war for the individual, with poems like 'Thyestes' articulating profoundly uneasy speculations on the degree of complicity between self and other. With 1945, the war could be seen as having forced a confrontation with some difficult

[4] See MacNeice to T. S. Eliot, 7 Apr. 1944, quoted in Robyn Marsack, *The Cave of Making: The Poetry of Louis MacNeice* (Oxford, 1982), 101.

issues, as well as an evasion of others. 'Hiatus' marks out this quarrel:

> Yes, we wake stiff and older; especially when
> The schoolboys of the Thirties reappear,
> Fledged in the void, indubitably men,
> Having kept vigil on the Unholy Mount
> And found some dark and tentative things made clear,
> Some clear made dark, in the years that did not count.

Wartime had muddled the clarities of peace, and the years after 1945 brought to the surface many of the contradictions and difficulties of Britain's role in world affairs. MacNeice's BBC work, especially in India, meant that he was often a professional commentator on the changing patterns of power and the dismantling of Empire; his poetry of these years, too, is preoccupied with a reassessment of the influences of world and self upon one another. The metaphysical character of much of this is a response to the foreseen anticlimaxes of post-war history, sometimes even a wilfully abstract gaze turned on immediately pressing real situations. In the same way as Britain, slowly at first, turned from victory in 1945 to an uncomfortable realization of the limits of her own influence (the climax of this coming with Suez in 1956), MacNeice's post-war poetry turned determinedly inwards, stripping itself of illusions in order to understand better the assumptions upon which it depended. For MacNeice the enterprise was less than comfortable, and, despite his 1945 protestations of 'pride', it was in some ways humbling—indeed, *Autumn Sequel* compounds its Yeatsian celebrations of friendship with a distinctly un-Yeatsian humility.

Two principal difficulties faced MacNeice at the end of the war: on the one hand, peace was proving an anticlimax; on the other, those lessons that could be drawn from the war were close to truism and seemed to lead in no direction. The first of these problems figures in 'Aftermath' (1946), where, in a Blitz-less London, 'The joker that could have been any moment death | Has been withdrawn':

> the bandaging dark which bound
> This town together is loosed and in the array
> Of bourgeois lights man's love can save its breath:

Where MacNeice's Blitz poems had gestured towards a removal of the barriers between the self and others in a community in time of crisis, 'Aftermath' recognizes that those barriers have been erected again, and unity replaced by separation—'What was so large and one | Is now a pack of dog's-eared chances'. The 'future' which has been 'ransomed' is far removed from that of the 1930s left, dividing 'luck' and 'lack' as before. The efforts to redeem this anticlimax and change it into a positive moment tend to fail through forcing: 'The National Gallery' and 'Street Scene' both employ modes of Mac-Neice's own 1930s poetry—the catalogue and the precise, glittering detail—as attempts at celebration, but neither is successful. However, the final stanza of 'The National Gallery' does point forwards to the concerns which MacNeice was to make central in the coming years:

So fling wide the windows, this window and that, let the air
Blowing from times unconfined to Then, from places further and fuller than
    There,
Purge our particular time-bound unliving lives, rekindle a
    Pentecost in Trafalgar Square.

The window image (later, of course, to prove important to MacNeice, from 'The Window' of 1948 onwards) signals new beginning and the opening-up of a restrictive environment—it first appears in this way in 'Order to View' (1940) in relation to a parable 'house' rather than a public gallery—but in 'The National Gallery' it fails to carry conviction. MacNeice's attempt to effect a transcendence of time and place through shorthand abstraction ('Then', 'There') is forced, pointing forwards to poems like 'The Stygian Banks'. A need for decisiveness and clarity overrides the poetic instinct for caution. The effort to deny anticlimax is sometimes damaging, and can lead instead to the over-obvious or trite, in the same way as the heartfelt assertion of individual integrity had been too much for a poem like 'The Kingdom' to contain.

MacNeice is more successful when his poems acknowledge the disjunctions imposed by war along with the disappointments of peace. 'Tam Cari Capitis' (1946) admits a basic truism in the first line ('That the world will never be quite—what a cliché—the same again'), but fixes attention on personal loss instead of broader social upheaval.[5] Rather than in moments of epiphany which, the poem implies, can be left to look after themselves, a friend's absence is felt

---

[5] The poem's reviewer in the *TLS* noticed that 'what a cliché' does not save the phrase from remaining one.

most strongly in the habitual strategies for 'Killing | Time where he could have livened it'. Another poem of 1946, 'Bluebells', also concentrates on anticlimax without attempting to force through any abstract transcendence; here, neither woman nor man is able to break free of the imposed solitudes of wartime separation, and, with 'no peace to be waiting for', they are reunited without the expected 'enrichment of surprise'. The only tentative reconciliation is suggested by the image of the bluebells, 'a merger of blue snow' mixing the elements of sky and cold, man and woman, in the 'dark beneathness' of a wood. MacNeice's concerns are more effective beneath poems than on their surfaces at this time; the basic problems of anticlimax and truism, though acknowledged ('O bathos that the years must fill— | Here is dull earth to build upon | Undecorated' ('Twelfth Night')), are never quite left behind. Beneath these, too, are the perennial difficulties of MacNeice's poetry, those of time and identity. In 'The Drunkard' (1946), the anticlimax following 'That hour-gone sacrament of drunkenness', becomes the hangover left by God's disappearance. Reeling away on a train from this intoxication, the drunkard recedes from God to godlessness, from 'the absolute moment' to the time of the clock, and from the community of 'we' to the isolated self:

Such was the absolute moment, to be displaced
By moments; the clock takes over—time to descend
Where Time will brief us, briefed himself to oppress
The man who looks and finds Man human and not his friend.

The poem concentrates the disillusion of the end of the war impressively, though it packs a great many of MacNeice's preoccupations into a small space. In much of his work from *Holes in the Sky* to *Autumn Sequel*, MacNeice puts himself in the position of the drunkard here (the train journey was to remain a common motif in his poetry), oppressed by time and isolation while haunted by the lost possibilities of a 'sacrament' glimpsed in wartime London. The longer poems of this period, however, tend to work back towards 'the absolute moment' rather than tracing a course away from it, but to do so they employ more than purely lyric resources.

As always, MacNeice's attempts at coherence are tinged with a feeling for chaos. In an article of 1946 the poet wrote of how 'the new thought of to-day, especially when correlated with world events, appears to have a trend that moves more and more towards chaos', and questioned the surrender to the unconscious in art, whether romantic, Freudian, or surrealist. Against this, the role of the poet is to assert the values of reason and construction: 'the word "poet" means *maker* and in Europe they have usually known what they were making'.[6] In the late 1940s, such an assertion was not entirely without point, given the productions of the 'New Apocalypse' school, which represented a romanticized Surrealism then much in fashion. In 'An Alphabet of Literary Prejudices' of 1948, MacNeice took issue with G. S. Fraser's contention that the war had taught poets 'to depend on ourselves and the universe, the intermediate social worlds having been largely destroyed',[7] by insisting that 'language cannot be divorced from some sort of social world'. The responsibility imposed by this involvement is that of the 'maker' rather than the 'modest registering machine' of either unconscious-dominated Surrealism or surface reportage. The idea of form has an intermediary function to fulfil here: 'All pattern is artificial and most patterns need smashing up on occasions; we cannot, for all that, get away from artificiality. The writer who despises form must still formalize even in selecting his material. To despise "form" will not bring him any nearer reality but may very easily take him further from it.'[8] Increasingly in these years MacNeice puts such ideas into practice, placing more emphasis on the careful architecture of his longer poems as a means of disciplining both the irrational and the journalistic elements within his own poetry. Reflecting on the root meaning of 'poet' in 1949, MacNeice insisted that 'he is something more than an impressionist', and went on to consider the relation between poetic form and the formlessness of its contexts:

Does he live in a world of chaos? All right: perhaps he can do nothing about it as a man; he *can* do something about it as a poet. A poem must have some relation to life—and perhaps that life is messy—but it must also emerge as a thing in itself, an organism. And therefore it must be shaped, it must have an internal structure. And by that I do not mean merely a formal pattern; I mean also the sort of structure which will creep in, willy-nilly, if a poet has some positive values or beliefs.[9]

    [6] MacNeice, 'The Traditional Aspect of Modern English Poetry', *La cultura nel mondo*, Dec. 1946 (repr. Heuser, p. 138).
    [7] MacNeice, 'An Alphabet of Literary Prejudices', *Windmill*, 3/9 (Mar. 1948), 38 (repr. Heuser, p. 142).
    [8] Ibid.
    [9] MacNeice, 'Poets conditioned by Their Times', *London Calling*, 10 Feb. 1949, pp. 12, 19.

'Structure', then, presupposes for MacNeice 'positive values or beliefs', and is in fact itself an aspect of such values. His apparent acceptance of the division between poet and man of action might, therefore, carry with it at least a trace of Yeats's 'envy', since poetry's assertion of the right 'form' is seen as being closely aligned with the right forms of action, and is almost paradigmatic in relation to them. Above all, the objectives which MacNeice sets himself in these years· take for granted an active engagement of text with context, in terms of structure and form as well as—or even, perhaps, more than— specific subject. Terms from the 1930s return in this new context, as parts of a programme of action very different from that given in *Modern Poetry*:

We are all conditioned by our times, and the times, it is quite likely, are against major poetry proper. But we can always have honest poetry, and I would even hope that soon we may once more be able to achieve two things at once, two things which are found apart in the pure and impure poets of our day, but which Shakespeare shows you blended: I mean common sense and imagination.[10]

It is important to remember that metaphysical abstraction falls into the domain of 'common sense' for MacNeice, and is a pre-condition of full 'honesty'; 'common sense and imagination', to go together, demand the careful balances provided by the poet's experiments in structure at this time, though the difficulty of their combination does remain a 'fertilizing paradox'.

If abstraction in MacNeice's ideas comes to compromise the banalities of surface observation, that surface itself can also compromise the abstractions. Travel, and in particular the working trip to India in 1947, was for MacNeice an exercise in imaginative expansion and compromise, a reordering of abstract assumptions in the light of actual observation. In 'Mahabalipuram', the experience of India unsettles, changes, and consolidates MacNeice's poetics; the poem's form, with stanzas made up of long, loosely classical lines and two short rhyming lines, is unstable, sprawling, and concise at once. After work like 'The Stygian Banks', 'Mahabalipuram' registers an alternative ordering (or disordering) of the familiar patterns of the one and the many, yet the poem seems to disallow any abstraction of the ideas it contains. The poem is set not so much in India as between India and the sea; the temple facing the ocean is immediately

<hr>

[10] MacNeice, 'Poets conditioned by Their Times', *London Calling*, 10 Feb. 1949, p. 19.

reminiscent of MacNeice's old clash of images, rock and water (as
for example in 'Ode'), which is always charged with some measure of
'metaphysical' significance for the poet. For MacNeice, the rock-
carvings of Mahabalipuram are intermediaries between the rival
immensities of the sea and India, but their message for him is far from
clear: these images 'live to excite | And at once annul the lust and
envy of tourists', but a lot depends on how far the tourist perspective
is the one accepted. Although the reliefs can be interpreted as 'the
earnest of what we aspire to | Apart from science and chance', this
frame of interpretation is not enough. Another reaction is 'an awe
and a horror', the tourists taken 'out of themselves to find themselves
in a world | That has neither rift nor rim'. Here the lingam of the
poem's opening is seen again:

Created things for once and for all featured in full while for once and never
The creator who is destroyer stands at the last point of land
Featureless; in a dark cell, a phallus of granite, as abstract
    As the North Pole; as alone.

This is a long way from the reassurances offered by the tourist
perspective; 'at the last point of land', the meeting-point of stone and
water, land and ocean, the symbol is cold, rigid, and 'featureless'.
After this, the last stanza draws back—'But the visitor must move on
and the waves assault the temple'—returning to the more comfortable,
because familiar, features of MacNeice's symbolism: 'Living granite
against dead water, and time with its weathering action | Make
phrase and feature blurred'. Yet the poem's ending, with its play on
'relief', is not a resolution but a stepping-back, a tentative, relieved
resumption of particular interpretations of the carvings. The ex-
perience, finally, is recast in intellectual and poetic form, the long
lines clinched with rhymes; none the less, the 'featureless' lingam has
effectively undermined the poem's resolution.

This may be compared with MacNeice's reactions to India as
represented in 'The Crash Landing', a radio feature of 1949, where
'the Visitor' attempts to 'forget all my own preoccupations—every-
thing I've heard and read', 'to start from scratch, get my own
impressions', only to find that 'No one can start from scratch'. The
Visitor is told by 'the Still Voice' of 'a whole sub-continent crowding
upon you and here stand you, enmeshed in your background'.[11] The
'background' to 'Mahabalipuram' is in part that of MacNeice's own

[11] MacNeice, 'The Crash Landing', *Botteghe Oscure*, 4 (1949), 380.

characteristic ideas, his approach to symbols and to 'form' itself. If that background is not abandoned, it is at least seen for what it is. India's 'efflorescence of grace-notes, her topless towers of wreathing and writhing sculpture, her intervolutions of high metaphysics',[12] strike a chord in MacNeice's imagination, their multiplying variety leading back to something resembling the kaleidoscopic world of *Blind Fireworks* (a volume MacNeice was to reconsider in some detail in 'Experiences with Images' in 1949). Yet the resemblance is an unsettling one: where MacNeice looks back on his early writing to reflect that 'technique begins in the junkshop, in a process— conscious or unconscious—of sorting out',[13] he sees India as offering her own 'junkshop' from which the visitor can only select. Between the Western observer and India, 'With my gods that dance in the rock, with my living dancers timeless as they keep time',[14] this selection and interpretation is interposed (even the dancer image here seems to have come to MacNeice from Yeats by way of Eliot). Writing in 1953, MacNeice saw India as somewhere that 'being too large and too complex to be "comprehended," invites us to select from her vastness only our own pet properties, rediscovering in fancy dress things which we have always fancied'.[15] This admission, already implicit in 'Mahabalipuram', is complemented by the aware- ness of India as something alien, beyond the reach of individual 'sorting-out'—the lingam 'at the last point of land | Featureless', or the menacing expanse of 'The Crash Landing': 'Here in the middle of my great plain, my aggressively featureless plain, my immutable imponderable interminable plain—here there's no rise in the ground to be seen—no shadows even for the sun is straight above you—here in this desert that buzzes with people, here where the eye has nowhere to rest and the restless hawk circles for ever.'[16] The scene recalls strikingly the desert of *The Dark Tower*, and before that the desert landscapes of MacNeice's poetry from early in the war, both the settings for decisive trials of strength between self and other, the individual and time.

[12] MacNeice, 'The Crash Landing', *Botteghe Oscure*, 4 (1949), 385.
[13] MacNeice, 'Experiences with Images', *Orpheus*, 2 (1949), 130 (repr. Heuser, p. 161).
[14] 'The Crash Landing', p. 385.
[15] MacNeice, rev. of Edward Lear, *Indian Journal*, in *New Statesman and Nation*, 4 Apr. 1953, 402.
[16] 'The Crash Landing', p. 381.

Of course, the trial in India was not so decisive as MacNeice might have wished; some of the things encountered there were all too familiar, notably the violence of the Punjab massacres. The events at Sheikhupura set MacNeice thinking of religion and 'the root of evil', the realities of the West and of Ireland; if India was a case of 'Everything at ground level or over your head', the 'ground level' experience was as unsettling for MacNeice as the implications of the 'high metaphysics' at another level.[17] The poem 'Letter from India' charts this disquieting area, without the excited observations of 'Mahabalipuram' and with a much flatter deliberateness on the edge of horror. Part of this horror lies in recognition: 'The lid is off, the things that creep | Down there are we, we were there always'. This feeling is still clearer in 'India at First Sight', where the Punjab comes very close to home: 'And who were we to feel superior? Did we not come from twentieth-century Europe? And were we quite sure that the British themselves were not responsible for some of this?'[18] Travel, even with the reporter's brief ('we looked and reported what we had to and cast no stones'), brings into focus familiar troubles rather than alien ones; in this sense, the Indian trip resembles the Iceland journey of 1936. India seems to have compromised Mac-Neice's responses at every turn, whether by means of difference or similarity, and the degree of compromise in the poetry is perhaps limiting. In 'Letter from India', physical and metaphysical clash without resolution:

> And always also, doubtless, ruthless
> Doubt made us grope for the same clue,
> We too sat cross-legged, eyes on navel,
> Deaf to the senses and we too
> Saw the Beyond—but now the view
> Is of the near, the too near only.

'The Beyond', unlike that glimpsed rather unconvincingly by Brandan in 'Western Landscape', is brought into the frame of reference of MacNeice's Indian poems without being approached. The intrusion of the near, whether as the familiar response or as the unavoidable, sometimes brutal, reality, means that the poetry remains compromised by the breadth of its context. Behind all the 'features', the 'feature-less' is present but unapproachable.

[17] Ibid. 370.
[18] MacNeice, 'India at First Sight', in *BBC Features*, ed. L. Gilliam (1950), 62.

After India and *Holes in the Sky*, MacNeice's poetry might be seen as having written itself into a corner. 'The Window' of 1948 is an attempt to reopen horizons—a rewriting of 'The Stygian Banks' in the light of India—but succeeds rather in promise than in achievement. MacNeice is able to chart, in terms of imagery, where he wants to go, but the middle section's abstract analysis of the 'tentative | Counter attack on the void' seems if anything to impede his progress. It is as if images alone are not felt by the poet to be enough, and need to be buttressed intellectually to make sure of their function as symbols. For all his emphasis on form and structure, by the late 1940s MacNeice's poetry seems to have stalled, at least as far as its more ambitious aspects are concerned. However, by 1949 regrouping was under way, and MacNeice was both consolidating his writing and reassessing the pattern of his career with *Collected Poems 1925– 1948* and the article 'Experiences with Images'. In both, the poet brings his own work into focus and clarifies the basis for continuity and development.

'Experiences with Images', the most valuable of all MacNeice's assessments of his own writing, is in some ways a defensive text; at the same time, it is also a determined statement of intent, more explicit, in its way, than even *Modern Poetry*. The discussion of imagery goes deeper than the images themselves; the admission that 'I have tended to swing to and fro between descriptive or physical images (which are "correct" so far as they go) and *faute de mieux* metaphysical, mythical or mystical images (which can never go far enough)',[19] delineates well the kind of conflict which had been going on in MacNeice's poetry at deeper levels than simply that of imagery. Yet this admission is qualified by what appears to be a theoretical solution to the problem in terms of both 'form' and a clearer definition of the impersonal, 'dramatic' element of poetry. Although there is nothing new for MacNeice in stressing the link between 'lyric' and 'dramatic' voices, his emphasis on the 'Opposition', 'on their toes in the wings—and crowding the auditorium', and his appeal to 'the *rest* of the truth which lurks between the lines',[20] serve to open ground in which the longer poem, as well as the lyric, can be free of some impediments. The principal fault with poems like 'The Stygian Banks' or section II of 'The Window' is that they set down exhaustively 'the *rest* of the truth' around their arguments; however

---

[19] 'Experiences with Images', 126 (Heuser, p. 156).
[20] Ibid. 125 (Heuser, p. 155).

carefully structured this may be, in the context of poetry's special properties it may in the end be unnecessary. MacNeice writes of a 'structural tightening-up' in his work, involving 'a single theme which itself is a strong symbol', 'a rhythmical pattern which holds that theme together', 'syntax (a more careful ordering of sentences, especially in relation to the verse pattern)', and 'a more structural use of imagery'.[21]

This amounts to a strategy for the longer poem as much as for the lyric, and although MacNeice gives 'The Stygian Banks' as an example (in line with Rilke), the ideas were not to be put into practice successfully until the poems of *Ten Burnt Offerings*. The essay's other direction, towards 'dream logic', 'a blend of rational allegory and dream suggestiveness',[22] was eventually to be subjected to similar 'structural tightening-up'; it is worth noting, though, that the foundations for the structural techniques of *The Burning Perch* were laid when MacNeice was grappling with the idea of structure involved in the poetry of his 'middle stretch'.

A division between discursive, expository writing and more obliquely ordered and presented material, between 'plain speaking' and 'dark saying', is evident in *Holes in the Sky*. This second category includes a poem like 'Godfather', carefully structured according to syntactic, rhythmic, and imagistic criteria to offer sidelights on a figure who may be God the Father, death, or both. Similarly, 'Hands and Eyes' (quoted as an example of tight structure in 'Experiences with Images') times its mixing of images in order to build up to a culmination in which they merge into a general sense of waiting, provoking the final open question, 'Oh would He, were there a God, have mercy on us all?' The logic of verse structure achieves something which would leave discursive logic severely strained, bringing disparate images into a common relation: it also achieves, in a more modest way perhaps, what 'The Stygian Banks' sets out to do, stripping disparate images of their otherness, and breaking down the apparent barriers between them. In 'Corner Seat', the essential issues in much of MacNeice's discursive writing are compressed powerfully:

> Suspended in a moving night
> The face in the reflected train
> Looks at first sight as self-assured
> As your own face—But look again:

[21] Ibid. 130 (Heuser, p. 162).
[22] Ibid. 131 (Heuser, p. 163).

> Windows between you and the world
> Keep out the cold, keep out the fright;
> Then why does your reflection seem
> So lonely in the moving night?

The basic image here, one of the most common in MacNeice's work, of confronting one's reflection in a railway carriage at night, brings together two central concerns: the disorientations of travel, and the problematic stability of the self. 'Corner Seat' is a poem sharply aware of the self-regarding imagination's essential marginality; the 'Windows between you and the world' both make possible an image of the self, and deny contact—other than that of the observer—between that self and the 'cold' and 'fright' of the world outside. Thinking of the self *as the self* is a means of isolation, blocking access to the other; this is the burden of much of 'The Stygian Banks', but 'Corner Seat' is a much more successful poem, and points forward to the tensions of MacNeice's later writing just as clearly as any of the more abstract pieces.

MacNeice's attention over the next four years, however, was given to the longer poem, in *Ten Burnt Offerings* and *Autumn Sequel*. The conventional assumption that this was something of a disaster is hardly tenable: nothing in these volumes is as weak as 'The Stygian Banks', and their function within MacNeice's work as a whole is such that they make his later kind of poetry possible. The progression from 'Corner Seat' to the poems of *Solstices* (1961) could not have been made without the poetry of the early 1950s. It is in these volumes that the poet comes to terms most fully with the metaphysical issue of the self and the other in its less metaphysical guise of individual and society, text and context. Certainly this coming to terms is done with a great deal of effort: the poetry does not come as naturally as leaves to a tree, but it is hard to imagine MacNeice himself having much sympathy with that criterion.

Ten Burnt Offerings, written mostly in Athens in 1950–1, follows the strategy for the longer poem outlined in 'Experiences with Images', and most of its poems are more successful than MacNeice's previous attempts in controlling their symbolic range. If one theme dominates the volume, it is that of myth—whether seen as religious, classical, literary, historical, or even personal. The volume's ten poems juggle various aspects of myth within which dominant themes do emerge, notably that of sacrifice, the 'burnt offerings' offered to 'a god who needs no name'. The ways in which myths are manipulated by the poet owe something to his own reassessment of the mythic 'junkshop' of *Blind Fireworks* in 'Experiences with Images': in fact, the whole volume reads like a much more disciplined and mature attempt to blend myths in the manner of some of MacNeice's ambitious juvenilia. Where that juvenilia found itself sometimes pointlessly lost, with myths running out of control to no apparent purpose, *Ten Burnt Offerings*, stiffened by its overall structure, is buoyed up by the metaphysical problems behind its dialectic; its 'direction' is never in doubt. From the 'holocausts' of blossom' of 'Suite for Recorders', through the imagery of Easter and blood-sacrifice in subsequent poems, the theme of the actual cost of foregoing the interests of the self emerges, a recognition of the sombreness of the context in which the text finds itself. 'The rest of the truth that lurks between the lines' is insistent, though seldom forced, the background against which the more vivid celebratory sections are set. In 'Areopagus' IV, 'The blood of all the world lies doubtless at our door | But at whose not?'; in the light of this, sacrifice is a way of attaching significance to the real cost of understanding what is meant by 'self'. The principal myths employed by MacNeice lead back to this kind of understanding, and the effect of the whole is to emphasize elements of religion to such an extent that *Ten Burnt Offerings* is MacNeice's most obviously 'religious' book.

The religious content is perhaps not entirely surprising: MacNeice's shorter, more oblique poetry of the 1940s had often returned to religion, and in particular Christianity, as an enigmatic centre— 'Place of a Skull', for example, makes the fraying of Christ's garments after the Crucifixion a metaphor for the decay of 'the seamless coat | Which is the world'. In the context of *Ten Burnt Offerings*, Christianity with its Easter sacrifice is one form of the faith that is juxtaposed with doubt and frustration throughout the book. Two of the most successful pieces, 'Areopagus' and 'Didymus', bring these elements together with reference to classical, Christian, and Indian cultures. 'Areopagus' refers back to Paul in Athens, and further to the Eumenides, the Furies made into the 'kind ones' in the service of the same city. Hebrew and Greek, 'Iron faith in the city of irony', juxtaposed in Paul's visit and his words on the subject of the Athenians' altar to the 'Unknown God', are presented sharply by MacNeice:

> he whetted the blade
> Of the wit of his faith to slice their pagan
> Prides to the quick; they nudged and doubted.
> Diamond cut diamond. Something new.

The confrontation between faith and doubt is seen as vital rather than destructive, and the unknown god at the crux of their argument is approached by MacNeice in terms of both systems, of Christ and of the Eumenides, both 'Cursing or kind'. In section III the application of this clash of cultures and myths is made clearer:

> Christ, if we could, having Christian fathers;
> But Furies, if we must. For no
> Life is for nothing, all must pay,
> Yet what unknown is dread, we know
> Can yet prove kind; our selves can pay
> Our sons atonement for their fathers.

A conflict between known and unknown comes to the surface here, and the myths in question are seen as different ways of appeasing this 'unknown' outside the self. In both Christian and Greek systems, such appeasement or trust is a sacrifice of sorts, but in the terms used by MacNeice, 'our selves can pay | Our sons atonement'. The sacrifice here is that of the isolated self. The poem's four-part structure functions by accelerating the mythic dialectic of this theme, the clear presentation of the first section being complicated, enlarged upon, and finally celebrated by the subsequent sections. In 'Didymus', the dialectic is even more marked, with Indian art and mythology being set against the simple figure of St Thomas; as 'Doubting Thomas', he represents a special aspect of faith, not merely as one 'Who has come here armed with two plain crossed sticks | To flout your banyan riot of dialectic', but as a figure whose inclinations are not primarily mystical or religious. Against this, in the midst of the mythic and artistic flux of India, MacNeice posits a mystic 'still centre', whether the 'purposeful indifferent phallus' of 'Mahabalipuram', or the 'fir-cone' held in Shiva's hand:

> the dainty embryo
> Of all that is and the end of all, the core
> That never moves nor melts yet holds the dance,
> Innumerable limbs reduced to one
> Black pencil of pure fire.

Doubting Thomas serves as a foil to the transcendent claims of mysticism, yet his religious mission contradicts also the flux-like variety of Hinduism, asserting the claims of the one against the many. Just as the impulse to sacrifice of the self's limitations is transformed in 'Areopagus' into appeasement of the unknown, doubt in 'Didymus' is made into an empiricism that manages to transcend, because it can accept, the immediacy of flux. Together, the two poems hint at a development of MacNeice's characteristic scepticism towards a more religiously defined goal.

The dialectic of *Ten Burnt Offerings*, however, is such as to ensure that religious goals are glimpsed rather than achieved. Other aspects of myth, the historical and the personal, compromise the movement of the religious motifs by making clearer the implications of sacrifice and appeasement in secular contexts. Byron's activities in Greece, in 'Cock o' the North', are presented as literary and historical myth-making, and are brought together with the Greek Orthodox Easter and the ancient myths of Meleager and the resurrection of Adonis. Byron's self-conscious part in the process is made into a kind of glamorous melodrama by MacNeice. Similarly, in 'The Island', the theme of isolation is given immediate rather than religious implications; myths of Calypso and Hermes are used to emphasize the limitations of insular worlds, with specific political overtones. Most important, however, is the use of personal elements as ingredients in the pattern of interacting myth. 'Day of Renewal', a meditation on the poet's forty-third birthday (hardly the doldrums of middle age that most critics suggest), sets the patterns of autobiography firmly in their elements of fictional shaping and of other lives—'One's birthday is a day that people die on' (III). The poem's fourth section re-approaches the unknown god ('Thrusting burnt offerings on a god | Who cannot answer to his name') with another transformation in mind:

> And purged of flowers that shone before me
> I find in roots beyond me, past
> Or future, something that outlasts me
> Through which a different I shall last.

The self of the first section of 'Day of Renewal', charged with the potent images drawn from MacNeice's own life, is what enters and is transformed by the dialectic of the poem. The different 'I' that is hoped for is one with its sights fixed outside the self, and with one eye on the unknown, 'a god who needs no name'. Religion as such is not accepted exclusively, even though the openness envisaged by Mac-

Neice includes the openness to religious faith. It is in 'Day of Returning', however (the third section of which opens with a translation of the Homeric verses on a homeland which Auden remembered MacNeice 'muttering into his beard' in Iceland[23]), that the religious implications of 'home' are qualified by other important images:

> A stiff climb—and at the top? Will Wesley hand us a gold
> Chalice of nectar—immortal and islanded life,
> A home from home? But is it a window or mirror
> We see that happiness in or through? Or is it
> Merely escape from the clock?

'Islanded life', window, mirror, and clock are all characteristic MacNeicean images of limitation, with only the window holding the possibility of escape. A Protestant Grail filled with the food of the Greek gods makes a fittingly ambiguous goal for the religious aspect of 'home' in the poem: MacNeice cannot allow this to transcend the threats and possibilities inherent in the rest of the imagery. Like Odysseus on Calypso's island, the self with its sights fixed on purely religious goals is liable to have 'found that bliss a prison', and 'escape' may have been only from one island to another. Just as in 'Ode', the sea in 'Day of Returning' is the element of dialectic and difference, 'changing unchanging'. Once Odysseus is cut off from actual contact with this element, he becomes truly 'No Man'; Jacob, by contrast, having 'wrestled all night with God Eternal', comes back to a home whose status for him has been undermined—though 'holding my own', he must admit that 'My own is nowhere':

> And I wake in a sweat, still in the darkness
> Which might be nowhere—but I am most practical,
> I put out my hand to finger the darkness
> And feel the map of it, it is my own,
> Enclosed by myself with walls and enclosing
> My family;

If the idea of 'home' is complicated by religious uncertainty now, it is no more settled than before in MacNeice's work, even though it still functions as a crucial imaginative pole. The myths of Odysseus and Jacob are inflated so as to deepen the 'changing unchanging', 'somewhere', or 'nowhere' ambiguity in the idea of 'home'.

---

[23] MacNeice and W. H. Auden, *Letters from Iceland* (1937), 238.

By comparison with some of MacNeice's more ambitious longer poems of the late 1940s, *Ten Burnt Offerings* is clearly a success, going further towards making good the poet's claims for the possibilities of form and structure. The discipline which the formal organization of the poems enforced on MacNeice's mythic material serves to hold in check what had been a sometimes disabling eclecticism, while it also reduces the amount of purely abstract material, so that the poems are both varied and mutually coherent in terms of their contents and concerns. In all these respects, the volume marked a significant progression for MacNeice, an experiment amply justified by results. The fact that he did not repeat this experiment, that his later poetry seems to have abandoned the longer, 'dialectical' form, has misled critics into seeing *Ten Burnt Offerings* as something of a dead end, when in fact the achievements of the volume, structurally and otherwise, offered the poet important ways forward to the techniques of his shorter poems of the late 1950s and early 1960s.

The volume's cool reception when it was published was in line with the widespread critical reassessments of MacNeice at the time of *Collected Poems 1925–1948*. The complaint of *Poetry Review*, that 'he has yet to prove himself a true poet by going beneath the surface . . . he has spent all his talents on the flesh without attempting to touch the bone',[24] was matched by the *Times Literary Supplement* in 1949, which mentioned 'the type of personal meditation or marginal comment usually associated with maps or diaries or letters', and 'the ease with which it lapses into a kind of journalism in verse'.[25] Topicality seemed to haunt MacNeice's reputation; as a *Times Literary Supplement* reviewer put it: 'The different successes of the thirties are still against him, as they are against Mr. Auden, in achieving this new quality, an intensity and outlook which are alien to their early work.'[26] Like Auden, MacNeice found his reputation languishing under the weight of a misconceived stereotype, itself, ironically enough, largely a journalistic one. It was as though the poet was to be pigeon-holed forever as the author of (a misread) *Autumn Journal*, and therefore deemed to be either limited or out of his depth in subsequent books.

In this sense, *Autumn Sequel*, written in 1953, may be seen as in part a reaction to a critical myopia that misjudged a whole career

---

[24] R. L. Cooke, 'Louis MacNeice: An Appreciation', *Poetry Review*, 38/3 (May–June 1947), 169.

[25] 'A Poet of our Time', *TLS*, 28 Oct. 1949, p. 696.   [26] Ibid.

rather than just its latest phase. A long poem written explicitly for radio, retracing the ground covered in *Autumn Journal*, *Autumn Sequel* meets the critical objections head-on, redefining the terms on which the poet operates, and setting them clearly outside the realm of journalistic values. Here, certainly, the 'external' context of Mac-Neice's career suggests in part the direction of the 'internal' logic of his work. The poem is, then, necessarily something of a revisionist exercise, but it is an attempt at progression also, principally in the areas of the 'rhetorical' aspects of form and the more personal implications of an understanding of the patterns of myth. Instead of the form and subject juxtapositions and balances of *Ten Burnt Offerings*, the poem sustains one voice throughout its twenty-six cantos, centred on the poet himself. At the same time, *Autumn Sequel* is not a poem 'about' Louis MacNeice: rather, it is a poem in which the self is approached mythopoeically in the context of its surroundings, both those of environment and, more importantly, of the 'characters drawn from my personal friends' who, 'for mythopoeic and other reasons, are represented under pseudonyms' (introductory note). In the opening canto, the poem confronts the arguments of the critics by refuting *Autumn Journal*'s 'hand of unformed smoke', and confronting critical objections to 'rhetoric' directly:

> Rhetoric? Why, no doubt. To contrive the truth
> Or the dawn is the bloom and brief of days ahead,
>
> In the teeth of ponce and newshawk, nark and sleuth,
> Who deal in false documentaries.[27]

'Rhetoric', then, is the weapon with which the demands of journalistic truth are to be defeated; in this case, rhetoric is indeed that of radio, the speaking voice contriving a coherent and natural development of ideas. MacNeice intends the effect of his *terza rima* to be one of seamlessness, a developing rhyme-scheme which does not necessarily dictate the length or particular structure of the argument it carries. *Autumn Sequel* uses this essentially open-ended form, together with an aural principle of 'rhetoric', in order to examine the conflict between the self and its context, and the need for others felt by that self. All of this is done, or at least intended, in mythopoeic terms. On all these counts, the poem seems almost calculated to offend the critical orthodoxies of the mid-1950s.

---

[27] *Autumn Sequel*'s subtitle, 'A Rhetorical Poem' (omitted by Dodds in the 1966 *Collected Poems*), is of course relevant here.

Two important modes within the scheme of *Autumn Sequel* are celebration and elegy. Celebration ranges from straightforward roll-call (as in canto VI), to ebullient portraits (Evans and Maguire in canto X), to set pieces such as canto VII's 'Fanfare for the Makers'; the most outstanding elegy is that for Gwilym (cantos XVII and XX), but the elegiac mode is also used for Gavin (canto II) and the Oxford of the 1920s (canto XII). The modes themselves are those of which Yeats took possession in his poetry, and MacNeice's incorporation of his friends into the context of his writing is necessarily in Yeats's shadow in this respect. Obviously, one danger—to which critics have seen MacNeice succumbing—is to allow fulsome encomiums to write the self out of the poem altogether. However, part of the point of *Autumn Sequel* is that the self must to some degree actually include the friends, or what is found essential in them. 'Wimbush', for example, for whom the model was the sculptor Gordon Herrickx, 'Chiselled his vision in a midland shed | Chip upon chip, undaunted and unknown' (I): his determination, celebrated so early in the poem, becomes an essential part of its whole strategy. The terms in which MacNeice praised Herrickx himself (as opposed to 'Wimbush') are suggestive: 'Unlike many modernists, he loved to "finish" his work, and when this finish meant polish . . . it sometimes seems a liability.' Even so, MacNeice went on, this 'polish' was 'a good fault—or at any rate a healthy reaction against much modern idleness'.[28] This is representative of MacNeice's reasons for cele-bration: pitched against the critical or fashionable odds, and often also against the fact of death, achievement in life and art is a matter of determination and 'finish' as much as instinct and inspiration. Again, the ideas recall Yeats, although MacNeice holds them with-out quite the theatricality of the older poet; if they are the mainspring of *Autumn Sequel*, they also pose a problem which, with its particular 'rhetorical' resources, the poem can only solve in part, namely that of how far the personal sphere can accommodate the public, along with which, and against which, it must exist. MacNeice's mythopoeia sometimes comes close to sealing one sphere off from the other, using the tension between the two, particularly as manifested in death, to provide rhetorical momentum. Thus, celebration and elegy depend upon each other, but this can lead to a simplified scheme: 'Boyce', for example, who 'Alike in shelves and plots can plant a Yea | Against

---

[28] MacNeice, letter in *New Statesman and Nation*, 25 July 1953, p. 104.

that obstinate No', occasions such a schematization from MacNeice, making his positive gestures

> While the great No-God winces. This is the age
> He has made his own by making nothing in it
> Appear worth while; we can throw down our gage
> Regardless, this very minute, and every minute,
> And fight him to the death, without expecting
> That he will lose that fight. And yet He need not win it

The danger here is that the difficult and shifting tension between self and other is being simplified into one between us and them, a black and white presentation for the sake of, or even generated by, rhetorical effectiveness.

However, MacNeice does resist the danger in a number of ways. Firstly, the world beyond the circle of friends is not written off for long as simply the alien province of the 'No-God', and part of the kind of heroism proposed by the poet consists in active engagement both in the workings of that world and in the principles of its design. Secondly, the poem's rhetoric is often employed self-consciously: 'to contrive the truth' is recognized throughout as something of a paradoxical undertaking, yet the centre of all the contrivance, the self, is also seen as a maker, in an active rather than a passive relation to the circumstances that are its context. One of *Autumn Sequel*'s principal images is that of the parrot, 'symbol of a mechanical civilization',[29] and it is refuted in both these ways. An important part of the symbol's power for MacNeice is its aspect of mocking repetition (compare its use in *The Dark Tower*): to 'throw the Parrot's lie | Back in its beak' entails an assertion of individual uniqueness, but also an acceptance of change rather than futile stasis. Clearly, it is such an acceptance which gives impetus to the best of MacNeice's elegiac passages, celebrating various makers, but the poet also allows a more problematic area to enter the poem, that of the course between change and repetition plotted by history. 'The Master', Thucydides, seen in canto 1 behind a door 'marked In Exile', 'a cool head but no cynic', balances the pros and cons of history, and knows

> How little, a precious little, in life is fixed:
> On the one hand this but on the other that;
> Justice must lie between and truth betwixt.

---

[29] MacNeice, note on canto 1, in *London Magazine*, 1/1 (Feb. 1954), 104.

This even-handedness and objectivity is portrayed in the light of the historical crux at which *Autumn Journal* was written, and of the inadequacy of that time's prophecies to the later truths: 'Did we know | That when that came which we had said would come, | We still should be proved wrong?' In fact, *Autumn Sequel* is itself an attempt to represent such truths that go beyond the facts of historical interest; Thucydides, then, is a different species of maker from that celebrated by MacNeice in other sections, an intermediary figure between public and private knowledge. This tension comes to the surface in canto XIX, where the ancient historian gives a balanced assessment of Gwilym, tempering his praise (which is similar to that just delivered in the 'Lament for the Makers' of the previous canto) with the fact that 'He played his part regardless of the whole, | By which I mean society, and spurned | The civic virtues'. This personally rooted division provokes a confrontation between poet and historian, between the celebratory voice of affirmation and that conditioned by 'a just analysis' of 'On the one hand this | But on the other that'. The argument prompts a reassessment of Greece, and in particular of Athenian history, retracing the course of *Autumn Journal* IX, though now the earlier rhetoric of condemnation has been exchanged for that of weariness. Far from being of little relevance to the present, the dealings of the Athenian Demos with subject states like Melos, to which Thucydides gave his attention, have a sombre message for the present: 'The war which broke us? Which war? Or which peace?' With 'The Master' back on his shelf, there is news that 'experimental bombing should proceed | Quite equably in Kenya', and a gruff conclusion of the argument: 'Yes, history makes bleak reading after all | And exile is the place for it'. A last glimpse of Thucydides, on the train journey of canto XXVI, suggests the particular kind of maker that his historical openness forces him to be, simply 'another Greek who makes | A virtue of necessity'. History itself need not owe its allegiance to 'the Parrot' for MacNeice, but it is also far from consoling for the celebrant or elegist, the maker proper. Taken to an objective extreme, history undermines patterns, although it bears witness to the capacity of humanity to repeat its own mistakes. All of this is unsettling for the makers of patterns in life and art whom MacNeice celebrates, but *Autumn Sequel* allows it an important place, analogous to (though perhaps finally more threatening than) the antiphonal voice that sounds in parts of *Autumn Journal*.

The weaknesses of *Autumn Sequel* have received more than their share of critical attention: certainly, the poem has certain formal problems; most notable is that of MacNeice's handling of *terza rima*, which does not quite disprove T. S. Eliot's warning of 1950, that 'to the modern ear . . . a modern long poem in a set rhymed form is more likely to sound monotonous as well as artificial, than it did to the ear of a hundred years ago'.[30] Yet recourse to an 'aural' technique is not entirely spurious as an excuse; economy as such is not one of *Autumn Sequel*'s needs, and rhyme functions aurally to bind together the ideas and images in a continuous form. MacNeice took comfort from greater examples in this respect: reviewing E. M. W. Tillyard's book on the epic in 1954, the poet noticed that 'when he begins by lamenting that "the long poem itself is out of favour" he seems not to have noticed the renewed interest in long poems indicated by the successful recent broadcasts of such works as *Paradise Lost*, the *Aeneid*, *The Canterbury Tales*, and *The Faerie Queene*'.[31] Any optimism that MacNeice might have entertained was misplaced: the poem which he intended to refute the 'journalist' tag for good, earned criticism largely for its deficiencies in journalistic content. The most damaging criticism of all came from A. Alvarez, who took *Autumn Sequel* as an opportunity to put an end to 'The reign of the Auden group' as a whole, complaining that 'Being so exclusively of their particular moment, these poets of the Thirties are on their way to becoming as unreadable as the political ballad-writers in, say, *The Rump*.'[32] His condemnation of MacNeice may perhaps be seen as setting the terms of the poet's work in the coming years, making exceptionally clear the need for reassessment and reassertion of the issues faced in the 1930s by a determined misreading of a generation:

perhaps it is that that vast popularising medium is the logical end to what Auden started, and that the Oxford poets of the Thirties have nearly always demanded just such a banality of response. . . . The Thirties entertained. It was not, finally, enough. *Autumn Sequel*, like *The Age of Anxiety*, shows that they have become weary and knowing and bored with it all. All we can do is, with them, lament the makers they might have been.[33]

---

[30] T. S. Eliot, 'What Dante Means to Me' (1950), in *To Criticize the Critic* (1965), 129–30.

[31] MacNeice, rev. of E. M. W. Tillyard, *The English Epic and its Background*, in *New Statesman and Nation*, 19 June 1954, p. 804.

[32] A. Alvarez, rev. of *Autumn Sequel*, in *New Statesman and Nation*, 11 Dec. 1954, p. 794.

[33] Ibid.

Criticism this damning can be answered only through more poetry, and MacNeice's work after *Autumn Sequel* might be seen as in some ways a reply to this radical kind of attack from a new and hostile generation, armed with answers of their own.

The success of MacNeice's reply in his last volumes should refocus critical attention on the work of his 'middle stretch' in something other than the terms used by Alvarez (which even the poet's admirers seem to have inherited). Whatever its weaknesses, the experimental poetry of 1945—53 is nothing less than crucial for MacNeice's poetic development. The grappling with tensions between self and other, unity and diversity, or stability and change is matched by a testing of the limits and the possibilities of form as an integral part of meaning —the 'dialectic' of *Ten Burnt Offerings*, or the sustained, open voice of *Autumn Sequel*—which later, when applied to the 'lyric', enabled MacNeice to give structural expression to the 'dream logic' that had always been present in his imagination. Myth, too, became an indispensable part of MacNeice's poetry during these years: again, this is a matter of possibilities and limits, explored further by the poet as 'parable', a concept no less vital to his later poetry than 'dream logic'. Without a proper understanding of MacNeice's 'middle stretch', 'Where neither works nor days look innocent', important aspects of the achievements of his later years will remain obscure.

6

Parable

THE centrality of the idea of parable to MacNeice's writing is clear, and was often insisted upon by the poet himself, especially in his later years. The nature of this idea, however, is more difficult to clarify, and even MacNeice found 'parable' an awkwardly wide term for critical analysis; yet 'a kind of double-level writing, or, if you prefer it, sleight-of-hand' is at the heart of much of his post-war work.[1] This 'parable', for MacNeice, concentrates elements that had always been of crucial importance—identity, the limits of self, the experience of time—but does so by existing in a context that compounds the contemporary with longer mythic and literary perspectives, and ultimately with those of deep personal memory. The notion of parable and its implications change for MacNeice in the course of his career: the present chapter examines certain points in this development, and attempts to make clearer the contexts against which MacNeice's parable is defined as well as those upon which it tends to draw. In making sense of MacNeice's career as a whole, the late intensification of parable elements is suggestive, seeming to mark the poet as a thoroughgoing member of the 1930s generation for whom, as Samuel Hynes has proposed, parable was never far beneath the surface. Here, too, a degree of context complicates the picture; one of the important backgrounds against which MacNeice's parables are played is the 1930s and its arguments, but the comparative scarcity of parable in his own work of that period is also relevant. It will be argued here that MacNeice's later work represents an exploration of the limits of parable as much as its possibilities, and that it is just such an exploration, often conducted in dramatic form, which made possible the poetry of his last two volumes.

In one sense, MacNeice's parable writing began with his juvenilia, just as his reading of parable literature is rooted in *The Fairie Queene* and Hans Anderson. The writing of parable as part of a considered literary strategy, however, seems to have begun during the war, and

[1] MacNeice, *Varieties of Parable* (Cambridge, 1965), 3.

in particular after *Springboard* (1944). Parable poems such as 'Order to View' (1940), 'The Dowser' (1940), or 'The Springboard' (1942) continued through the 1940s to be juxtaposed with poetry of a more didactic or conversational character—the 'dark saying' contrasted with 'plain speaking' in MacNeice's style. One strain of MacNeice's parable writing seems to reach a climax with cantos XIV–XVI of *Autumn Sequel*; but the main developments in parable which were to prove valuable beyond this point were those reached through dramatic experiment in the post-war years. Most obviously, *The Dark Tower* (1946) represents a major success in parable; yet subsequent dramatic work may be seen as searching out the weaknesses in that parable, and it is here that MacNeice's poetry darkens further the dreams and quests of his plays. Edna Longley's view that 'The plays were a workshop for parable and for redirected legend long before MacNeice's full poetic capitalisation on these assets',[2] may be something of an over-simplification, but it is certainly true that the parable poetry cannot be understood fully without some recourse to the drama which it implicitly revises.

Much of MacNeice's post-war writing is in any case effectively revisionary in character: it often relies upon the past, and especially the experiences of members of the 1930s generation, to supply the co-ordinates for its 'special world'.[3] The 1930s are felt strongly in MacNeice's late *Varieties of Parable*, though half-deplored as over-journalistic. Remembering that 'we used to say that the poet should contain the journalist', MacNeice warns that 'now I would tend more often to use "contain" in the sense of control or limit'.[4] For MacNeice to dismiss the 1930s as a decade of pure reportage would be for him to join in the chorus of his own least friendly critics; the 1930s are remembered differently when he meets the problem of how far the 'special world' of parable 'must be also a private world':

Given the same geographical and historical background, many people's privacies tend to overlap. This has not only been proved by the psychologists, whether Freudian or Jungian, but was maintained even by a Marxist critic, Christopher Caudwell, in the objectivist, over-topical 1930's. Caudwell, who quite rightly insisted that poetry was by its nature subjective, went on to describe it as the medium through which man retires into his inner self, *thereby to regain communion with his fellows.*[5]

[2] Edna Longley, *Poetry in the Wars* (Newcastle upon Tyne, 1986), 231.
[3] MacNeice's term in *Varieties of Parable, passim.*
[4] Ibid. 8.   [5] Ibid. 27–8.

MacNeice had used Caudwell to make the same point as far back as 1941, in reply to Virginia Woolf's accusations of over-topicality in the 1930s writers, when he refuted her argument by claiming that poetry's 'method is myth'.[6] Developing away from the decade, some of the 1930s generation tended not just to read the books of that time as parables rather than directed reportage, but to transform the decade as a whole into a parable of the difficulties of artistic integrity in the face of political pressure. In its turn, this 'myth' has influenced Hynes's reading of the 'Auden generation', for whom parable is 'functional' rather than 'didactic'—'Rather it is an *escape* from didacticism; like a myth, it renders the feeling of human issues.' Furthermore, Hynes has seen 1930s parable as 'non-realistic' and 'moral, not aesthetic, in its primary intention; it offers models of the problem of action'.[7] All of this comes very close to MacNeice's post-war parable; it suggests, in fact, that the later MacNeice was engaged upon a revival of a distinctively 1930s mode of writing. However, MacNeice's subsequent use of parable has also to be seen in the context of his own writing during the 1930s, which was remarkably thin in parable content in Hynes's terms. What brought MacNeice back to the ideas of Caudwell in 1963 was perhaps a fascination not with the parable that 'offers models of the problem of action', but with that having as its crux the relation between 'inner self' and the outer world. The overlapping privacies presupposed in *Varieties of Parable* represent a development from the problem posed by identity in the poet's 1930s work which reached a culmination in the question put in *Autumn Journal*, 'Who am I—or I—to demand oblivion?' The problem remained unsolved, but the development of parable as a mode of thought and expression enabled MacNeice to set it out more clearly. As he wrote in *Varieties of Parable*: 'The questions put by poets like Rilke admit of no answer: the nearest one gets to an answer is in the sheer phrasing of the question.'[8] Between the 1930s and the 1960s, parable became one of MacNeice's most successful changes in phrasing.

Hynes's insistence on parable as a central and even defining 1930s mode means that the question of MacNeice's originality in these

    [6] MacNeice, 'The Tower that Once', *Folios of New Writing*, 3 (Spring 1941), 37–41 (repr. Heuser, p. 122).
    [7] Samuel Hynes, *The Auden Generation: Literature and Politics in England in the 1930s* (1976), 15.
    [8] *Varieties of Parable*, 124.

respects must be answered. Certainly, one of the most important
vehicles for parable writing during the 1930s was drama, and in
particular the dramatic work produced for Rupert Doone's Group
Theatre by Auden and Isherwood, Spender, and MacNeice himself.
It is in this area that one might expect MacNeice's indebtedness to
1930s parable aesthetics to be most in evidence. However, the
principal debts are limited to the stylistic, even in the close relation
between *Out of the Picture* (performed 1937) and *The Dog Beneath
the Skin* (performed 1936). MacNeice's other plays of the decade,
apart from his translation of *The Agamemnon of Aeschylus* (per-
formed by the Group in 1936), *Station Bell* (1934) and *Blacklegs*
(1939), are further removed stylistically from the Auden and
Isherwood idiom.

In Auden and Isherwood's *The Dog Beneath the Skin*, dramatic
parable entails a mixture of cabaret-style stage business with a plot
close to the traditional quest pattern. In MacNeice's *Out of the
Picture*, on the other hand, there is no basic quest or Everyman
pattern to be discerned; instead, the play adopts the revue-style of the
Group productions, taking as its central figure an artist, Portwright,
of high ideals. In the course of the play, Portwright's painting *The
Rising Venus* (MacNeice's original title for the whole piece) is at the
centre of a mainly farcical plot involving a film star, a psychoanalyst
and a Minister for Peace, among others. The war, of which a radio
warns throughout, finally intrudes (more spectacularly in the pro-
duction than in the published text),[9] and Portwright, having unlearned
his idealism, dies amid mere farce. The parable content is one of the
play's least interesting aspects: Portwright's education is one of
MacNeice's standard sermons against Plato ('I am an artist who has
no need of models', he declares at the beginning; 'The true artist has
his eye not on a particular person but on a transcendent model which
exists in the world not of Becoming but of Being.'[10]). The play's
world of becoming undoes the complacency of art, violently in the
end, to prove that, as Portwright's lover Moll puts it: 'All this
concentration on self | Means in the end a mutilation of self.'[11] The
play is a parable of compromise, but its other, less obvious or
accessible levels are not so easy to fit into a 1930s context, being
closer to MacNeice's more personal obsessions. In one choric passage,

[9] See Michael Sidnell, *Dances of Death: The Group Theatre of London in the
Thirties* (1984), 223.
[10] MacNeice, *Out of the Picture* (1937), 16.   [11] Ibid. 51.

the 'Radio Announcer' and the 'Listener-In' tell the audience a 'little
fable' in which an eighteenth-century picnic party, 'with their lutes
and beakers', call to 'the lady Echo' (the whole scenario is reminiscent
of those in *Blind Fireworks*), but their 'Phrases of music and gallant
phrases' meet with a rude reply:

> Echo like a gorgon glared from the sudden rocks
> And cried in a stony voice the one word 'Death'.
> These possibilities should always be remembered
> But for the moment let us go back to our farce.[12]

This particular 'little fable' concentrates the motif of sudden disaster
which looms over the play's plot, but it also functions on its own
account as an exemplary reversal of exploitations, juxtaposing
mannered formality with the 'sudden rocks' of a nightmare landscape.
Another such passage, later excerpted by MacNeice as 'War Heroes',
presents in miniature a frustrated, or unexpectedly horrifying, quest.
The war heroes come to a port 'they seemed to have seen before':

> There were dead men hanging in the gantries,
> There was a lame bird limping on the quay.
> When were we here before? one of them said.
> The captain answered: This is where we were born
> And where we have now returned. Dead to the dead.[13]

Again, the nightmare element of the parable overrides the political or
satirical interpretations to which it may be subject. Where Auden
and Isherwood organized the quest motif in *The Dog Beneath the
Skin* in accordance with broadly satirical effects, MacNeice in his
play contrasts dream or nightmare logic with the intrusion of
disorder into the various kinds of order of his characters' lives. What
the dream logic represents, however, is impossible to say; it has no
messages to deliver, and leaves few conclusions to be drawn.

Although it adopts a good many stylistic devices that mark it
clearly as part of the Auden school (as MacNeice himself knew), *Out
of the Picture* rejects the kind of parable which *The Dog Beneath the
Skin* and, later, *The Ascent of F6* or Spender's *Trial of a Judge* were
to embody. It has its focus less on contemporary society (for all the
intrusions of the impending war on the plot) than on the forces that
work upon the individual imagination: the figure of Venus herself,

---

[12] MacNeice, *Out of the Picture* (1937), 47.
[13] The Listener-In, *Out of the Picture*, p. 78 (repr. *Collected Poems* (1966), 79).

only imperfectly integrated into the play, carries most weight in her parable aspect, and represents for MacNeice a principle of affirmation that can reject stasis. In a speech delivered when she steps out of Portwright's painting (later reprinted separately by MacNeice),[14] Venus talks of a place resembling Yeats's Byzantium ('There is a city beyond this life, no flesh or blood there'), where humanity is reduced to a static image of itself: renouncing their living and loving, 'they do not even think this renunciation | For their brains are solid, of stone, | Their heads and their eyes are of stone'. Venus expands upon this familiar nightmare image for stasis ('Let not man be contriving a frozen beauty; | While he is here and now let him deal in here and now'), calling herself 'the principle of Unity and Division', 'Spawning of worlds from a discord | Always recurring'.[15] Clearly, Venus represents the element which, in MacNeice's poetry of the 1930s, celebrates flux and change, setting this against static, petrified images of stability. *Out of the Picture* as a whole brings this celebration of 'becoming' into the context of the later 1930s, with insistent signs of both international collapse and individual neuroses; its parable content may well be summarized as one with reference mainly to MacNeice's own art, a representation of the author of *Poems* confronting that of *The Earth Compels* or *Autumn Journal*. This self-involvement on the level of parable, in comparison with Auden and Isherwood's work, is a weakness.

It is significant that MacNeice's parable poetry only began properly once the 1930s, and the literary climate associated with that decade, had ended. In America in 1940, the poet was able to return to the dream logic which he had mentioned in a 1936 essay on Malory: 'Sometimes in dreams the dream becomes palpably more substantial. The process is like scrambling eggs. From an indefinite froth comes, seemingly instantaneously, something with a recognizable texture, something one can put in one's mouth. When a dream behaves in this way, it is becoming a work of art.'[16] In 1936, at the height of the English fashion for Surrealism, dream material, treated often in psychological terms, was much discussed. Auden had seen the

---

[14] MacNeice, *Poems 1925–1940* (New York, 1941).

[15] *Out of the Picture*, pp. 116–17. Sidnell quotes from the differing text of the performance copy in the Berg collection, New York (Sidnell, *Dances of Death*, pp. 222–3).

[16] MacNeice, 'Sir Thomas Malory', in D. Verschoyle (ed.), *The English Novelists: A Survey of the Novel by Twenty Contemporary Novelists* (1936), repr. Heuser, p. 46.

Freudian idea of the artist's elaboration of day-dreams and the ability 'to modify them sufficiently so that their origin in prohibited sources is not easily detected', as evidence that 'no artist, however "pure", is disinterested', and that 'he starts from the same point as the neurotic and the day-dreamer, from emotional frustration in early childhood'.[17] MacNeice's interest in what 'makes the dialectic of the dream concrete' was distinct from surrealist or Freudian interests, but in the 1930s it was almost impossible to raise the topic at all without involving these to some extent. Contemporary English Surrealism tended to qualify Breton's definition of 'Pure psychic automatism by which it is intended to express . . . the real process of thought, without any control exercised by reason, outside of all aesthetic or moral preoccupations', by reference to the systems of Marx and Freud.[18] For Hugh Sykes Davies in 1936, Surrealism was 'faced by a violent divorce between the worlds of action and dream',[19] while for David Gascoyne in 1935, the purpose of Surrealism was 'to reduce and finally to dispose altogether of the flagrant contradictions that exist between dream and waking life'.[20] Beneath all this, as Herbert Read saw, was the idea that 'This "self" is not the personal possession we imagine it to be; it is largely made up of elements from the unconscious.'[21] MacNeice seems to have regarded these ideas, in some ways close to his own, as serving up the eggs raw rather than scrambled: 'The Unconscious undoubtedly has a great say in poetry, as most good critics have always recognized, but, whether you call it the Unconscious or Inspiration, it is a mistake for the poet to sit back in cold blood and ask it to do all the work.'[22] To employ dream material in writing in the mid-1930s was inevitably to court identification with the Surrealism which Spender saw, with some justification, as 'the real well of loneliness and subjective romanticism',[23] a

[17] W. H. Auden, 'Psychology and Art To-Day' (1935), repr. *The English Auden* ed. Edward Mendelson (1977), 333, quoting S. Freud, *Introductory Lectures on Psycho-Analysis* (1929), 314–15.

[18] André Breton, quoted in Paul C. Ray, *The Surrealist Movement in England* (Ithaca, 1971), 3.

[19] Hugh Sykes Davies, 'Surrealism at this Time and Place', in Herbert Read (ed.), *Surrealism* (1936), 147.

[20] David Gascoyne, *A Short History of Surrealism* (1935), p. x.

[21] Herbert Read, Introduction to *Surrealism*, p. 28.

[22] MacNeice, 'Subject in Modern Poetry', *Essays and Studies 1936* [1937], repr. Heuser, p. 69.

[23] Stephen Spender, rev. of George Barker, *Janus*, in the *London Mercury*, 32/92 (Oct. 1935), 601.

way of indulging rather than destabilizing the self. MacNeice's insistence on 'manifest subject' during the decade,[24] intended partly to counter this tendency, necessarily left severely limited room for the dream material itself. Even so, the issues raised by the surrealists, though not the uses to which they were put, continued to be of relevance to the development of MacNeice's dream logic.

With 1940, many of the 1930s touchstones were beginning to seem inadequate, and MacNeice's 'manifest subject' was among them. 'Order to View', written in March of that year, has its subject in dream material and the patterns of parable. The approach to an empty house, known before, is one of the basic motifs in the poet's writing of this kind, and is presented here in a designedly unstable stanza with shifting end- and internal rhymes carried over the stanza-breaks. Stasis, even paralysis, are both associated with the return to the house; its garden suggests death ('a crypt | Of leafmould dreams'), and the scene is full of signs that signify nothing ('a tarnished | Arrow over an empty stable | Shifted a little in the tenuous wind'). Mac-Neice breaks the ominously static scene with other signs:

> A sudden angry tree
> Shook itself like a setter
> Flouncing out of a pond
> And beyond the sombre line
> Of limes a cavalcade
> Of clouds rose like a shout of
> Defiance. Near at hand
> Somewhere in a horse-box
> A horse neighed
> And all the curtains flew out of
> The windows; the world was open.

The movement from a closed to an open world is achieved by essentially the same means as those by which the nightmare stasis itself was depicted, by precisely observed phenomena set down plainly and without any explicit connection with each other. How-ever, this is not the random alignment of dream images of Surrealism; this takes place instead within carefully shaped contexts, both of the return to the home motif and that of the internal organization of the poem itself. The shift from closed to open offers a paradigm of one kind of parable pattern for MacNeice, the transformation of stasis

[24] Heuser, p. 69.

and death into movement and life which takes place in the scene of early memory (here, as so often, the garden). A similar pattern is behind 'The Dowser' and 'The Return' (both of 1940): in the first of these, the Dowser's command to dig produces something other, or more, than expected:

> A well? A mistake somewhere . . .
> More of a tomb . . . Anyhow we backed away
> From the geyser suddenly of light that erupted, sprayed
> Rocketing over the sky azaleas and gladioli.

The poem's ending is itself an eruption of the unexpected: again, the grave-bed of clay is a place also of birth, and the closed is opened by intuition, the 'feel of a lost limb | Cut off in another life'. The opening-up of the earth in 'The Return' is also a matter of recognition, an understanding of 'All the lost interpretations' to bring back Persephone from Hades. The parable content of all these poems is a matter of opening possibilities, and is clearly in a different mode from the ethical or didactic significations of 1930s parable art. It is this which also underlies the rest of MacNeice's parables: the impulse for breadth of signification, beginning in the personal dream rooted in memory, then progressing through myth to the pattern of the writing itself.

In *Varieties of Parable*, MacNeice used T. S. Eliot as an example of a poet who 'has indulged' his images so that 'they think they are there in their own right': quoting from 'The Journey of the Magi', Mac-Neice notes Eliot's admission of 'the almost magical compulsion exercised upon a poet by certain remembered objects or events in his own experience', but goes on to write that, for most readers, 'These images are significant; but why, they cannot say, any more than their author can'—'whatever it is', he concludes, 'it has no place in any category of "parable writing" '.[25] If this is one kind of 'significance' which is alien to parable, another kind is that of factually orientated writing, where, 'as often in the 1930's . . . the sheer limitation of the content is taken to confer significance'. Here, too, MacNeice sees something lacking: 'This significance, unfortunately, is more often than not a label tacked on from outside rather than a light shining from within.'[26] It is possible to hear in this an echo of the debates of the late 1920s on the subject of significant form, which MacNeice

[25] *Varieties of Parable*, pp. 105, 106.
[26] Ibid. 130.

had tackled in his very early poetry by making his symbols often signify only each other, and which the emphasis on 'manifest subject' in his 1930s work had implicitly rejected. Again, if significance as a totem is taken as an extreme development of modernist aesthetics, the idea of parable seems to steer a course between such extremism and its opposite, the elevation of manifest subject into a literary criterion of value. The imagery and detail in MacNeice's parable writing do not signify things outside their immediate context in an allegorical, one-to-one correspondence, but function within the patterns of parable and myth themselves, in the 'special world' represented there. The material of dreams, in other words, is disciplined by the parable shapes or the myths within which it functions, and is thus more than Surrealism's 'pure psychic automatism', extreme Modernism's self-enclosing significance, or the clear-cut references of reportage.

For MacNeice, two shapes in particular dominate his conception of parable: the morality and the quest. Both patterns adapt well to drama, and the poet's post-war writing for radio provided numerous examples of this; but they are essential influences on his poetry also, especially on that of the last two volumes. Many of the poems in *Solstices* and *The Burning Perch* are fragments of either morality or quest, but by the time these poems are written, neither morality nor quest is capable any longer of the clear working-out in MacNeice's hands that the term 'parable' would suggest. The limits of such patterns had been tested partly in dramatic experiments. MacNeice's most ambitious morality, *One for the Grave*, written in 1958, a version of *Everyman* set in a television studio, is complemented by a number of radio plays in broadly the same mode. However, Mac-Neice's first morality comes not from the BBC years, but from 1925/6, when he wrote and abandoned a short play, tentatively entitled *Third Time*. Many of the elements of the later 'psycho-moralities' are present here: the central figure is a child, John, living in 'Paragon Place', whose allegiance is sought by 'Romantic', 'Artistic', and 'Moral Temperaments', along with a 'Kind Old Gentleman' who is in fact the Devil.[27]

This play, which has, strangely enough, a number of the hallmarks of MacNeice's mature radio-writing technique, shows John rejecting all three Temperaments in favour of the presents offered by the Kind

[27] 'Third Time' in 1925/6 notebook, Bod. Lib. (see Chap. 2, n. 25 above).

Old Gentleman, who has declared at the beginning that 'I'll show him up, the selfish good-for-nothing little blighter'. The Romantic Temperament encourages John to climb 'the stairs at the top of your house' which 'end in a cul-de-sac' and 'have no door at the top—only a window'. He promises a transformation familiar from MacNeice's much later parable and dream imagery:

> In an hour's time take this sword by its enamelled hilt and go up those stairs. Carpets of red and yellow will be soft under your feet and canaries will sing perched on the balustrade. So they will seem while you ascend, but when you reach the top darkness will close again, dark noises and dark scents. . . . Open the window to its fullest and step upon the sill. Wave your sword in the air and cling to the hilt. Then will your sword become a hippogryph with yourself in the saddle.

John is tempted away from this transformation of closed to open, just as he is also lured away from the Artistic Temperament's offers. The third of these Temperaments, the Moral, makes its representations while John's mother is dying, but again despite the best efforts of the boy's 'Familiar Spirit' ('Your mother has been very good to you. You must therefore do right by her'), it is the Old Gentleman who wins the day with offers of a motor cycle. As the play ends, the Moral Temperament's call, 'in a great voice', of 'Your mother is dead, John, dead, dead', contrasts with the boy's delighted cry in the distance, 'Hooray! It's a Raleigh two-stroke'. *Third Time* is a parable of testing and loss—lost opportunities, imaginative and otherwise, lost childhood, and a lost, even disowned, mother. The play might well be seen as a remarkably early, if crude, version of *Persons from Porlock* (1963); at all events, it is a decidedly sombre morality for a schoolboy to write.

MacNeice's mature Everyman-figures are often of a particular type: although *One for the Grave* allows its Everyman to shift classes from time to time, the most convincing of MacNeice's characters are akin to the Tom Varney (drawn from Graham Shepard) of *He Had a Date*; 'An uneasy intellectual from the upper classes, he is shown reacting against his own background and upbringing.'[28] The life of his own generation was always the pattern for MacNeice's moralities— even John in *Third Time* represents a rebellious youth of similar stock—and the moralities themselves are as much histories of the time as of individual lives. Essentially, the central figures are seen to

---

[28] MacNeice, 'Portrait of a Modern Man', *Radio Times*, 11 Feb. 1949, p. 7.

exist at the mercy of their contexts, whether family, social, or historical, and are watched fighting against the odds to maintain a degree of individuality. This basic pattern has its effect upon the poetry, as in the sequence 'Notes for a Biography' in *Solstices*, for example, or its more complex partner 'As in Their Time' in *The Burning Perch*. Like a typical figure from MacNeice's moralities, the subject of 'Notes' questions his own actions in the light of his times— 'Had it been strength | Or weakness what he had done and what his rulers had done?' The love-affair of the poem's third section, like other apparently 'personal' elements of his character, is worn away by the impersonal force of time, again symbolized by the sea, 'cruel, spendthrift, endless'. The intrusion of the impersonal and external into the personal life is the common theme of all of MacNeice's moralities, and in 'Notes' it means that the sea moves from being a symbol of the destruction of love to being a possible future reminder of that love ('Things will come back to him that were never gone | And the shifting sea will stand for permanence'). Similarly, the personal is implicated in the public: in the wake of Hiroshima ('A milestone in history, a gravestone in time'), responsibilities have to be faced by the private voice:

> When I first read the news, to my shame I was glad;
> When I next read the news, I thought man had gone mad,
> And every day since the more news that I read
> I too would plead guilty—but where can I plead?

This could be compared with the verdict delivered on Everyman in *One for the Grave*, where the letters of his name spell out 'earth', 'virus', 'evil', 'ruin', 'yellow', 'might', 'anguish', and finally 'nobody'.[29] 'Notes' finishes characteristically with a gesture of defiance against the forces that threaten and reduce individuality, ending with the determination to 'stand as if under fire | With a sweet-smelling bunch in my hand, face to face with Never'. The sequence is typical in its stripping-down of an individual voice to scrutinize its conditioning by background and immediate context, but typical also in defying the idea that identity may thus be stripped down finally to nothing.

MacNeice's fascination with the patterns of the morality could be seen as a development of his interest in the metaphysical problem of the nature of the self and the relation between the self and the other; at the same time, the moralities themselves also show an inclination

---

[29] MacNeice, *One for the Grave: A Modern Morality Play* (1968), 38.

to employ a particular kind of self as an example of the problems faced by men of MacNeice's own background and generation. Inevitably, this example was beginning to date by the time of the poet's later radio moralities. However, the basic pattern used by MacNeice, of reduction, clarification, and final defiance of the self against the forces outside, is related also to another rich form of parable, that of the quest. At school, MacNeice's favoured reading— as he often pointed out later—included prominently quest literature, from Malory to Hans Anderson. It is important that, for MacNeice, the quest as such always begins from personal identification and association. In the quest stories, MacNeice's early tastes did not lead him towards identification with the successful, but with the ill-fated or unlucky. The Icelandic sagas exercised a lifelong fascination in this respect, and even in Malory the young MacNeice tended to identify with Gawain, whose affinities with the saga characters are obvious: 'the furthest from being a paragon' among knights, Gawain, according to MacNeice in 1936, 'makes no attempt to amend himself and, when the hermit tells him to do penance, refuses'.[30] The perfect Galahad, who is successful on the quest, did not attract MacNeice: in a short parable written at Oxford in 1929, 'Garlon and Galahad', the Grail is given throwaway treatment ('Spring always returns, you know, and the hero never dies; that is not what we go to the movies for'). Galahad, 'the Complete Hero', is struck down by Garlon on the very edge of his quest's completion; MacNeice concentrates not on the 'new System, a new Beauty, a new Power, a new Synthesis' of Galahad, but on the things he ignores on his quest, four creatures drawn straight from the poet's own nightmare imagery, the third of which was to feature often in his later writing: 'He came into the slums where there was a cripple swinging himself along on his crutches which were so high that his legs dangled between them as if on a gallows. "Who are you?" asked Galahad. "I," said he, "am the Superman."'[31] In *Out of the Picture*, this same figure has the name of 'Time',[32] and this is one thing Galahad certainly ignores in his transcendental quest. MacNeice's focus on the unsuccessful quest, or at least the quest which brings a bitter reward, like his fascination with the patterns of morality, was present in his writing

---

[30] 'Sir Thomas Malory', Heuser, pp. 52–3 (c.f. MacNeice, *The Strings Are False* (1965), 221).

[31] MacNeice, 'Garlon and Galahad', *Sir Galahad*, 1/1 (21 Feb. 1929), 15.

[32] The same image is used to represent time in MacNeice's 1934 play, *Station Bell*.

from a very early stage. Also, the goal of the quest was determined
for MacNeice not by abstract principles, but in terms of the adventures
met with by the quester—the goal cannot be seen, but is constructed
(or, of course, lost) along the way. Again, this has a strongly personal
application for the poet. In a parable affixed to *The Strings Are False*,
arising out of his experiences in 1940/1, MacNeice wrote of a
'seventh son of a seventh son' who 'lived with his father in a house
where everything was always the same'. This son, equipped with
three coins to grant wishes, sets out from his father's house on a quest
that seems to have no object other than to make things 'different'.
After a series of adventures, and with one wish remaining, he comes
to 'a lake of ice and a figure skating in the middle of the lake'. The last
wish is used to bring the skater closer: 'There was a swish of curtains,
a meter ticking, warmth on his shins. He opened his eyes; the frozen
lake and the skater, the prisms and the fountains were gone; he was
back in his father's house where everything had always been the
same. But now everything was different.'[33] It is likely that the story
refers specifically to MacNeice's feelings for Eleanor Clark in the
context of his return to England in 1941, but the pattern itself is
suggestive: life takes the subject away from his father's home, but
also provides the terms on which he can return to both the house and
the father. The quest, in MacNeice's version, is often based on this
pattern, though its relevance is seldom seen by the poet as only, or
even primarily, familial; what is mapped out functions as a myth
implicit in experience. Here morality (a chronicle of experience) and
quest meet; MacNeice's character Roger, in *One Eye Wild* (1952),
'like many of us today, suffers from the lack of a mythology',[34] and
the poet often uses parable as a way of making good this lack.

However, the 'mythology' supplied by MacNeice through parable
is far from being a way of reducing tensions on the surface of
experience; indeed, it could be argued that it never succeeds com-
pletely as a resolution of the tensions basic to his work, between
individual experience and its social, temporal, or historical contexts.
The Dark Tower (1946), the poet's finest work for radio, occupies a
crucial position; it is fair to say that without the play a good deal of
the later poetry would have been impossible. The quest here has an
apparent object, to confront 'the Dragon' with the challenge-call,
made clear from the beginning; the hero, Roland, does fulfil his

[33] *The Strings Are False*, pp. 204–6.
[34] MacNeice, 'Portrait of a Would-Be Hero', *Radio Times*, 7 Nov. 1952, p. 6.

quest, and in this sense the work has the straightforwardness de-
manded of parable by MacNeice. However, the play's issues are far
from straightforward for the poet, especially as regards the working-
out in action of the familial aspect of its parable. Roland's quest is
again one which takes him away from home in order to bring him
home, from the house without a father to the father's approving gaze
at the scene of trial before 'the Dark Tower'. Yet the purpose of the
quest is partly to fulfil this pattern: 'to bequeath free will to others' is
part of the movement from mother to father which Roland decides to
make. Christopher Holme has placed this play in the category of 'the
uncertain quest' (his two other categories for MacNeice being the
perverted and the false quests), seeing it as 'a probing self-analysis',
and noting the relevance of the poet's loss of his own mother in
childhood.[35] Personal elements are most certainly present in the
play, and cannot be dissociated from the 'meaning' of the parable
itself. However, the form of parable and its breadth of reference
make the private aspects of *The Dark Tower* more than personal in
their application. In this sense, the play offers a good example of how
MacNeice found parable a fertile medium in which private obsessions
could develop into artistic form without becoming autobiographical
intrusions or indulgences.

Clearly, Roland's mother is quite different from the mother Mac-
Neice lost as a child; the traumatic effect of that loss, however, is
relevant to *The Dark Tower*, in so far as it is reflected in the power of
the mother's will over her son on his quest. In fact, this quest is not
fulfilled until the mother's will has been disobeyed and the force of
her memory disregarded in Roland's exercise of 'free will'. The
mother gives birth to a 'child of stone' on her death-bed whom she
wishes to send on the quest in Roland's place: MacNeice's explanation
of this, that she, 'in bearing so many children only to send them to
their death, can be thought of as bearing a series of deaths', so that
'her logical last child is stone—her own death',[36] could be complicated
by reference to one of his own early poems in which 'Time' is
destroyed by a stone child rising from the sea.[37] At any rate, the stone
child's task is performed by Roland instead, under the approving

---

[35] Christopher Holme, 'The Radio Drama of Louis MacNeice', in J. Drakakis
(ed.), *British Radio Drama* (Cambridge, 1981), 61, 60.

[36] MacNeice, *The Dark Tower and Other Radio Scripts* (1947, repr. 1964), 197.

[37] Cf. 'Twilight of the Gods', from MacNeice, *Blind Fireworks* (1929) (quoted
above, Chap. 2, p. 56).

gaze of his fathers and brothers; finally the mother's voice returns, urging her son to 'strike a blow for all dead mothers'.[38] Other personal elements are close to the surface: Roland's brother, and immediate predecessor on the quest, is called Gavin, the same name given later in *Autumn Sequel* to MacNeice's friend Graham Shepard, killed at sea in 1942; Sylvie, Roland's lover from home, recalls MacNeice's first wife Mary in the imagery with which she is associated, so that, before leaving, Roland speaks to her in the voice of MacNeice's early love-poetry:

> Today is a thing in itself—apart from the future.
> Whatever follows, I will remember this tree
> With this dazzle of sun and shadow—and I will remember
> The mayflies jigging above us in the delight
> Of the dying instant—and I'll remember *you*
> With the bronze lights in your hair.[39]

This is also, of course, the characteristic imagery for flux and time in MacNeice's poetry; Roland's quest, which, to be fulfilled, has to leave Sylvie behind, is also one for something over and above 'the dying instant'; furthermore, it is a quest away from the demands made by others, and towards the duties felt by the self. Edna Longley has remarked that in MacNeice's writing, 'No absolute line can be drawn between the quest as search and the quest as self-pursuit':[40] this means both a return to the private roots of art and a more abstract confrontation of the problems of time and the self, Roland's encounters in the desert with 'the Clock' and 'the Parrot'. There is no distinction between 'personal' and 'abstract'; increasingly, each is implicit in the other.

Although the quest in *The Dark Tower* is 'uncertain', it is at least fulfilled, and the play's parable pattern is completed. The sense in which the play is important to MacNeice's later poetry lies partly in this completion, which could not really be repeated. Roland asserts 'free will', but the path that leads to his assertion is one on which the momentum of the quest-parable seems to deny the importance and value of the individual, reducing him to a single figure in a broad pattern: the play ends with Roland's discovery of himself, and the imminent annihilation of that self. However effective this is within the context of the play, it still does not constitute a solution of the

---

[38] *The Dark Tower* (1964), 65.   [39] Ibid. 30.
[40] Longley, *Poetry in the Wars*, p. 238.

problems of individuality which continued to haunt MacNeice's poetry after the war. By the time of *Varieties of Parable*, MacNeice wrote of 'one's everyday discovery that selfhood cuts one off from the rest of the universe', and discussed how Beckett's characters are 'always looking for themselves and so, *ipso facto*, for that which is not themselves'.[41] Put in terms of the quest, a search such as this can never be completed; and perhaps parable, in the light of this, is only partially adequate as a poetic vehicle. Roland's discovery of the self and its duty is achieved almost emblematically by MacNeice, and even here the parable shape is completed not by fate but by the exercise of individual will. In fact, it is only a short step from this to work in which parable fails the individual, or does not provide the expected completion of his quest. The knowledge of the self, like the difficult confrontation with time, resists the endings usually implicit in the very forms of parable.

How unsatisfactory the forms of completion could be for MacNeice may be seen in the quest sections of *Autumn Sequel*, cantos XIV–XVI. Here the poet makes his most ambitious attempt at psychological parable in poetry, a quest with a young man as its protagonist which follows a course back to the womb and away from it again, as a fairground ride. Again, a knowledge of individuality, however costly, is seen as a guarantee of freedom, 'the give and take of humanity': it is also an escape from a nightmare image of motherhood and maternal power. Yet there is a certain flatness to MacNeice's resolution here: although 'The Quest goes on and we must still ask why | We are alive', a provisional solution is offered (canto XVI):

> all we can do
> Is answer it by living and pay the debt

> That none can prove we owe. And yet those debts accrue
> Which we must pay and pay but, what is odd,
> The more you pay the more comes back to you.

The humanist bathos here is MacNeice at his weakest, imposing a meaning on the completion of his parable which seems to devalue whatever vividness that parable possessed. Essentially, what Mac-Neice is doing is allegorizing his own poem; as he was to acknowledge later, parable cannot afford to undergo this kind of process, and his own radio play *The Queen of Air and Darkness* had fallen foul of the demands of allegory. In this connection, MacNeice noted his envy of

---

[41] *Varieties of Parable*, pp. 93, 140.

Spenser's 'knack of making such reflections solid or, putting it more generally, of making his abstractions concrete'.[42] Similarly, the poet also wrote that 'We should read Spenser as we read Kafka, accepting his symbolic world as a *real* one and letting its underlying meanings infiltrate into our consciousness without too much forcing or ferreting on our part.'[43] The failure of MacNeice's psychologically presented quest in *Autumn Sequel* (where the poet allows himself more Spenserian personifications than ever before or after) is due to this 'forcing or ferreting', making the concrete abstract in a world too overtly symbolic to seem real. The completed quest, in these terms, can only be flat and disappointing.

Parable, for MacNeice, came increasingly to imply incompleteness in its execution, and, with this incompleteness, its incorporation into lyric poetry became more feasible. Indeterminate parable is the basis of the poet's achievement in *Solstices* and *The Burning Perch*, but the development towards this late idiom is evident in *Visitations* (1957). In poems such as 'The Burnt Bridge', 'The Tree of Guilt', or 'Figure of Eight', MacNeice makes use of parable as a basic idiom without imposing, or even suggesting, a meaning beyond the form itself: quests are translated here into the simultaneous precision and indeterminacy of dreams. In 'The Burnt Bridge', MacNeice uses bare quatrains and simple diction to embody the parabolic progression from darkness to light, closed to open, sought by the poet in the early 1940s. Here, however, the object of the quest is far from certain: the protagonist knows that 'his long-lost dragon lurked ahead, | Not to be dodged and never napping', but finds instead 'a bridge and a shining lady':

> She stood where the water bubbled bright
> On the near bank, the known bank;
> He took her hand and they struck a light
> And crossed that bridge and burnt it.

The meeting is just as decisive as a climactic encounter with a dragon; the pair come to 'the sea that leads to nowhere' when the final transition from night to day, closed to open, takes place. The poem recalls *The Dark Tower* insistently, not only in the dragon and the sea with its 'ship sunk years before', but in the presentation of psychological aspects of the quest. The hero, who 'the more he

---

[42] Ibid. 113.

[43] MacNeice, 'Spenser's Symbolic World', *Radio Times*, 26 Sept. 1952, p. 15.

dreamt was the more alone | And the future seemed behind him',
with 'the past displayed before him', recalls Roland when he goes
into the wood 'against his will', but with a difference: he does not
confront the object of his quest with defiance, but discovers and
accepts it with love. The lady's dismissal of the original quest is
reminiscent also of Sylvie: ('Dragons? she said, Let dragons be').
Marsack's suggestion that 'some dragon still has to be vanquished,
that the finding of love is only a beginning', is one possible reading:[44]
another, however, might propose the lady as the true object of the
quest, the 'daylight' in contrast to the dragon's darkness which
effects a profound change (MacNeice's draft titles for the poem in
fact included 'Dragon or Princess' and 'Come Dragon, Come Prin-
cess'[45]). The bridge which is burnt is that between night and day, and
the hero finds himself in a parable of acceptance and beginning
rather than confrontation and 'doom'. In this sense, the poem
undoes the determinacy of the quest, but other poems of the period
employ parable techniques to different effect.

  Both 'The Tree of Guilt' and 'Figure of Eight' are written from
darker perspectives, in which the 'dragon' to be faced is the force of
time. The tree in the first of these poems is menacing from the
beginning, but puts on the appearance of kindness and the associations
of love—doves and carved names—only to reassert its true nature
with the passing of time: 'And in those branches, gibbet-bare, | Is that
a noose that dangles there?' As in 'Figure of Eight', the crucial change
takes place while the protagonist is unconscious of it:

> Till he finds later, waking cold,
> The leaves fallen, himself old,
> And his carved heart, though vastly grown,
> Not recognizably his own.

The disjunction between past and present selves is made sinister
here; in 'Figure of Eight', also, the repetition of the bus journey of the
first stanza in the train journey of the second shows a different self
having to complete the pattern laid down by another, whose metaphor
of being 'dead on time' now has to be made literal. Both poems are
rooted in the solitude which 'The Burnt Bridge' leaves behind, and

---

[44] Robyn Marsack, *The Cave of Making: The Poetry of Louis MacNeice* (Oxford,
1982), 118.

[45] A first draft of 'The Burnt Bridge', with these variant titles, is in a 1955 notebook
containing material for *Visitations* (1957), currently among miscellaneous MacNeice
papers deposited in the Bodleian Library.

both anticipate an appointment with the dragon. In a verse fragment dating from this period (immediately following drafts of 'The Burnt Bridge' in a notebook), MacNeice sketched this solitary assignation again, suggesting more clearly the nightmare that underlies the parables of the poems:

> Staring hard at the far mirage, he thought
> I have been caught before but I think this time—
> Look at the reflected faces—this time it must be water,
> But five steps on he knew he had been caught
> Once more, the desert was back in its place, and the Lord
> Repeating the Word of the Lord over and over.[46]

At the core of the parable scene here is the dread of sterility, loss of identity, and infinite repetition which lies beneath much of Mac-Neice's late poetry. The voice of 'the Lord | Repeating the Word of the Lord' is a nightmare manifestation of the father's house where everything is always the same, one important co-ordinate of parable's 'special world' for MacNeice.

'The Truisms', from *Solstices*, is one of MacNeice's most intense parable poems using the pattern of departure from, and return to, the paternal home; elements of this motif are also strong in 'Selva Oscura' in the same volume. Both poems, however, are developments of the image presented more bleakly in the 1955 poem 'House on a Cliff'. The house in this poem is described starkly in terms of interior and exterior, with its setting equally simple and threatening: 'The empty bowl of heaven, the empty deep'. Tom Paulin has remarked on the poem's 'terrible stoic isolation', and identified 'a mysterious openness within or beyond the poem's mirror-like reflections of a dead closed universe'.[47] Certainly, 'House on a Cliff' is a powerful juxtaposition of the open and closed poles which are characteristic of the 'special world' of MacNeice's parables, drawn towards the nightmare of 'the locked heart and the lost key'. The house itself is the scene in which time follows its course, with 'The strong man pained to find his red blood cools, | While the blind clock grows louder, faster'. In these surroundings, the idea of the self is necessarily confused and contradictory—'a purposeful man who talks at cross | Purposes, to himself, in a broken sleep'—and not the self to be found at the end of the quest which leads back to the familial house. The

---

[46] 1955 notebook. Abbreviations have been silently expanded.
[47] Tom Paulin, *Ireland and the English Crisis* (Newcastle upon Tyne, 1984), 78.

isolation so powerful in the poem, which seems to deny the assertion of *Autumn Sequel* xiv that 'Outside and inside shift | Into each other continually', is the block against which 'Selva Oscura' and 'The Truisms' later work. The first of these places particular emphasis on the 'I' within the poem, the 'inside' relating to the 'outside':

> And yet for good can also be where I am,
> Stumbling among dark treetrunks, should I meet
> One sudden shaft of light from the hidden sky
> Or, finding bluebells bathe my feet,
> Know that the world, though more, is also I.

This realization turns the poem towards the parable conclusion, in which 'Some unknown house' becomes the home to which 'I' can return. In 'The Truisms', 'a house | He could not remember seeing before' also proves to be home, and to offer, explicitly this time, a return to the father. Just as 'Selva Oscura' depends on the knowledge that 'the world, though more, is also I', 'The Truisms' turns on its climactic line, 'He raised his hand and blessed his home'. Both poems take the parable elements of identity and familial home (between which, in *The Dark Tower*, there was considerable tension), and fuse them in new patterns. The isolation contained inside 'House on a Cliff' is in both cases banished from the house on finding an open identity, open both to the world and to the familiar voices of truism.

The victories won in poems like these still have to be set against the darker productions of MacNeice's later years, in which parable seems to be approached sometimes rather ironically as a framework. In his radio work, MacNeice tended to rewrite the themes of his earlier plays in this way. *The Mad Islands* (1962) is a quest which revises the terms of *The Dark Tower*, while *Persons from Porlock* (1963) is a dark revision of the poet's 'psycho-moralities'. In the first play, the hero, Muldoon, decides to frustrate the vengeful purpose of his quest, and allows his embittered mother to die; in the second, Hank, an artist, lives through his own life and that of his time beset by interruptions and frustrations, with his achievement an honourable second-best. Both Muldoon and Hank have a certain purity of motive, but both find that such purity is not necessarily enough; MacNeice wrote of Hank that 'As a painter my hero believes—to use a stock distinction—in making images rather than gestures and, after the war at least, tries to go his own way, undeterred by changes in fashion',[48] but the 'Persons from Porlock' attend on his integrity just as they would on the makers of gestures. Muldoon, in *The Mad Islands*, meets parable representations of forces in the contemporary world, but finds that he himself has no role to play in the parable, deciding to leave his quest unfulfilled. The plays do not suggest that 'parable' as such is to be abandoned; they suggest rather that the shapes of parable, its movement towards neat completions, are of less importance than the details met along the way. Again, MacNeice seems to be returning to ideas implicit in some of his 1930s writing, disowning determinism or limitation in favour of more open-ended frameworks. With this openness, the problem of the limits of the self is raised again—is Hank right, for example, in thinking that his art can exist in isolation from its contents? The Persons from Porlock seem to represent the revenge of the external world on the 'pure' artist, so that the whole play becomes a much more sombre and mature version of the process enacted in *Out of the Picture*. Mac-Neice's conception of parable in his later years, then, makes room for this problematic openness and indeterminacy.

If parable and dream are the idioms basic to the late poetry, it is important to note that, for MacNeice, the indeterminacy of the latter tended to qualify the former's completed shapes. 'Dream logic' is itself an amalgam of the two idioms, and its workings in the poetry will be examined in the next chapter. However, the late preoccupation with parable in this sense was a development of ideas long present; ultimately, it was an intensification of a basic anxiety which Mac-Neice sometimes expressed in more abstract terms, that involving time and identity, and the nature of the self. Here, in fact, MacNeice's parable, though it departs considerably from the nature and purpose of 1930s parable art, comes close to Auden's post-war interpretation of the term in his reading of Kafka (later to figure in MacNeice's own *Varieties of Parable* as an important modern parable-writer): Auden wrote of 'the simplest brute fact that the "I" which feels and knows and acts can never be defined by what it feels and knows and acts', going on to observe that 'Man, therefore, can never know the whole truth, because as the subject who knows, he has to remain outside the truth, and the truth is therefore incomplete.'[49] Parable offered MacNeice a way of entering the subjective perspectives of the 'I' by

---

[48] MacNeice, *Radio Times*, 22 Aug. 1963, p. 44.

[49] W. H. Auden, 'K's Quest', in A. Flores (ed.), *The Kafka Problem* (New York, 1946), 52.

way of a larger 'myth', one free from the factual demands of
'reportage', in order to present more clearly the 'special world',
internal and external at once, which the self has to inhabit. In his
introductory note to *The Dark Tower*, written in the same year as
Auden's observations, MacNeice remarked that 'The fact that there
is method in madness and the fact that there is fact in fantasy (and
equally fantasy in "fact") have been brought home to us not only by
Freud and other psychologists but by events themselves.'[50] It is this
realization which keeps MacNeice's parable mostly distinct from
allegory, forming an essential link between the material of parable
and the events outside the immediate scope of the individual's
experience. This subjective range, beginning from the basic point of
'I', is continually opened and expanded; indeed, the impulse towards
this expansion sometimes comes into conflict with the limits imposed
by the parable frameworks themselves. Auden's perception of how,
in Kafka, the truth is always necessarily incomplete, fits exactly
MacNeice's parable idiom in which easy completion of patterns is
also impossible. Rather like Spenser's *Faerie Queene*, MacNeice's
parable is both an unfinished idiom and one which is of itself
unfinishable: 'The questions . . . admit of no answer: the nearest one
gets to an answer is in the sheer phrasing of the question.'[51]

[50] *The Dark Tower* (1964), 21.
[51] *Varieties of Parable*, p. 124.

7

Nightmare and Cinders: The Late Poetry

MacNeice's last two volumes of poetry, *Solstices* (1961) and *The Burning Perch* (1963), mark the climax of his career, containing much of his best and most enduringly influential work. Coming after his sometimes heavy and laboured writing of the late 1940s and mid-1950s, these books, along with their immediate predecessor, *Visitations* (1957), have seemed to critics to represent a surprising late flowering, a 'lyric return' for which to be grateful. Indeed, this poetry does seem to have taken MacNeice himself by surprise: writing on *Visitations*, he noted that 'When the lyrical impulse did return, this interval of abstention, it seems to me, had caused certain changes in my lyric writing—I naturally hope for the better.' These changes ('more concentrated and better organized . . . relying more on syntax and bony feature'[1]) stem partly from an application to the lyric medium of the principles tested in the longer poems, but partly also from a deliberate disciplining of his material on MacNeice's part which owed much to his ideas of 'parable' and 'dream logic'. Another decisive influence on this late poetry is the poet's increasing tendency to examine his own life and the life of his time retrospectively, so that the 'dream logic' of the poems is a kind of Last Judgement on the poetry written in the 1930s and after. The late poems share the matrix of metaphysical preoccupations of many of their predecessors—the problematic understanding of the self, time's subversion of history and the individual—but tackle these difficulties in what is, for MacNeice, a new idiom. At this stage in his career, one of the most important contexts for the poetry is MacNeice's own *œuvre*; in this sense, at least, the late flowering might be seen as Yeatsian in character.[2]

---

[1] MacNeice, *Poetry Book Society Bulletin*, 14 (May 1957), [1] (repr. Heuser, p. 211).
[2] C.f. MacNeice's note on *The Burning Perch*, in *Poetry Book Society Bulletin*, 38 (Sept. 1963), [1] (repr. Heuser, p. 247): 'Fear and resentment seem here to be serving me in the same way as Yeats in his old age claimed to be served by "lust and rage" '.

Visitations may be read in the light of the late poetry as an important transitional volume, developing from the structural experiments of *Ten Burnt Offerings* towards a lyric element less fettered by the demands of discursive form. The full benefits of the metaphysical wrestling MacNeice attempted in the early 1950s begin to become apparent here, and the one crux which recurred time and again in that writing, the nature of the self, starts to be absorbed, operating implicitly within, rather than explicitly upon, the poetry. Two more factors distinguish this poetry from that of the previous volumes, those of parable and dream material, and with these comes an increasingly personal voice. It is at this point in MacNeice's career that the description 'middle-aged' begins to be useful. The old MacNeicean preoccupation with time now takes on a sharper edge: as at the beginning of 'Beni Hassan', 'It came to me on the Nile my passport lied | Calling me dark who am grey', so in 'Dreams in Middle Age' the passing of time exerts a dull, unromantic pressure on the imagination instead of producing the dramatic confrontations and transformations expected by the younger man:

> The debris of the day before; the faces
> Come stuttering back while we ourselves remain
> Ourselves or less, who, totting up in vain
> The nightlong figures of the daylong ledger,
> Stick at a point.

The prosaic course of everyday experience, which MacNeice had tried to transform, or at least circumvent, in *Autumn Sequel,* is beginning to be represented more starkly here, as a way of becoming 'Ourselves or less' while the self contracts into the scope of its immediate concerns. This contraction happens even in dreams, but dreams are also the element in which it can be countered—albeit through nightmare:

> No, sooner let the dark engulf us. Sooner
> Let the black horses, spluttering fire, stampede
> Through home and office, let the fierce hands feed
> Our dying values to the undying furnace.

The route towards being 'ourselves or more' is a grim one, but preferable to the restrictive normality of everyday experience. This poem sets both the tone and the terms for MacNeice's late work, for which one of the principal idioms is that of nightmare, of 'dying values', public and private, being fed to the 'undying furnace' of' time. The threatening background to this ('The watch will stop and mark the red cross on the door | And cry "Bring out your dead!" at any and every moment'—where the 'watch' is on the wrist as well as at the door) functions in much of MacNeice's late poetry as an exhumation of the past to provide fuel for the 'undying furnace'. This poetry is, to use the terminology of the dedicatory lines to *The Burning Perch*, 'nightmare and cinders': the elements of dream and retrospection are the agents of transformation into a new idiom for the poet, but one with the familiar aim of expanding the self into something 'more' rather than allowing it to contract further into isolation and routine.

There are two areas of past experience in particular which Mac-Neice feeds into the furnace of his late poetry: the private memories of childhood in Ireland, and the more public recollections of life in the 1930s and 1940s. If the former provides the material for some of the most important poems in *The Burning Perch* (notably 'Soap Suds'), the more 'public' past is also significant in the late poetry. *Solstices* contains three such retrospective poems: 'The Messiah', 'The Atlantic Tunnel', and 'Homage to Wren', all referring back to 1940–1, a crucial period in MacNeice's own life and career, private memoirs of a very public phase of life. The new light in which events from these years are presented shows how MacNeice's lyric medium is beginning to blend private and public into a dreamlike amalgam. 'The Messiah' demonstrates how the poet's memory of his time in hospital in New Hampshire in 1940 recovering from peritonitis is in fact one of confusion between inner and outer, other and self, in which a cryptic vision is witnessed by a divided and uncertain 'I'. The same period had been the subject of section IV of the 'Jigsaws' sequence in *Visitations*, involving similar distortion of the self; here a double, 'some nameless stranger', comes between the self and its possible extinction. Uncovering this *doppelgänger* is less easy, however:

> Who is this, ramifying.through
> My veins, who wears me like a mask—
> Or is it I wear him? One week
> Later I found that I could spare
> The strength to ask, but could not speak.
> The stranger was no longer there.

The puzzle of identity remains unsolved: the whole section (like the rest of the sequence) is something of a riddle. The 'stranger' is both inside and outside the self at once, part of the 'I' and something separate from it. 'The Messiah' relates to this riddle also: the poem externalizes the 'nameless stranger' to make him the 'New Surgeon' seen through the ward windows. This figure, too, is nameless, observed by the poet's split self ('I split in two, one naïve, one know-all') as a refugee from Europe (like MacNeice) without an identity, and having simply to hiccough when asked his name. Even so, the Surgeon is of enormous importance:

> But he's also the New Messiah.
> (*Longer pause*) The what?
> A new mutation of man,
> He knows the answers to everything.
> Everything?
> Yes, except
> He cannot cure himself. It's very sad, you know.

This vision is of a distinctively 1930s character, and the Surgeon is strongly reminiscent of Auden's 'Healer'. Remembering 1940, with the 1930s dead and buried, MacNeice recalls a potent image of the hopes and ideals of that time as a figure publicly powerful but privately crippled, the brilliant skills of a disabled self.[3] The whole poem embodies a complex image of the disjunction between inside and outside: a split self trying to comprehend the other, while the other is mutilated, deprived of a self. 'The Messiah' answers the riddle of 'Jigsaws' with a further complication in the relation between inside and outside, its medium of delirious vision serving to clarify the split in the perceiving self just as dreams, for MacNeice, are responsible for resolving aspects of the external world into distinct entities.

The effects achieved in 'The Messiah' by the confusion of inner and outer, self and other, are important for MacNeice's late work as a whole. Again, *Visitations* may be seen as preparing the ground in this respect, complicating perspectives while simplifying the forms of the poetry itself. Instead of the discursive voice, it is the lyric unit which must embody the structural discipline needed for MacNeice's purposes. In 'Visitations' itself, the poet's use of discursive principles in a lyric medium produces a new kind of sequence, in which all eight

[3] Cf. the account in MacNeice, *The Strings Are False* (1965), 28–9.

sections, each with its own internal structure, present differently realized versions of the same theme, each one broadening and complicating the other's scope. The 'visitations' in question take place against a bleak background, whether for the integrity of the individual or the more immediate threat of 'A genie that grew like a mushroom, deleting the words of creation' (VII). Each section relies on a clearly defined syntactic and metrical structure based on patterns of repetition; yet the sections also share the theme of making repetition 'redeemable'. In fact, the transcendence of darkness in 'that dark day | Which means your own' (I), is effected, however briefly, by making use of the structures of repetition, as in the closely textured, liturgical exercises in fixing 'the indefinable | Moment' of sections II and IV. It is in section VI that this resolution of self and time, repeating a pattern established at the beginning, has its widest application:

> The world one millimetre beyond him—
>   Is it the Muse?
> The soul untold light years inside him—
>   Is it the Muse?
> The python of the past with coils unending,
> The lion of the present, roaring, rending,
> The grey dove of the future still descending—
>   Are they the Muse? Or no?

Again, this seems to set the terms for MacNeice's late work: the self's boundaries of inside and outside are implicated vitally with the boundaries presented by time, the co-ordinates of past, present, and future. The 'Muse', which appears in one form or another in every section of 'Visitations', is the possibility of transcending, or at least making sense of, the limitations encompassing the self; it may, or may not, in fact be present. The whole sequence makes its structure integral to meaning, suggesting the possibilities of playing off repetition against variation. The self makes a virtue of displacement against the background of an undermining (and potentially destructive) every-day life, from the atom bomb to a new version of Plato's cave, where 'he sat in his office with in-tray and out-tray | While nobody, nothing came in but typed memoranda' (VII). As well as the flashes of hope in the sequence, the scenarios of later nightmares are already present.

Another sequence in *Visitations*, 'Donegal Triptych', though structurally closer to the earlier poems (especially in its rather forced third section), confuses further the line that is often preserved in MacNeice's work between the self and its observations. The poem's first section brings the prosaic experience of routine and age up against instincts which upset the usual co-ordinates of the self:

> But arrival? Go your furthest,
> The Muse unpacks herself in prose;
> Once arrived, the clocks disclose
> That each arrival means returning.
>
> Returning where? To speak of cycles
> Rings as false as moving straight
> Since the gimlet of our fate
> Makes all life, all love, a spiral.

This 'spiral' looks forward to MacNeice's observation on *The Burning Perch* that 'most of these poems are two-way affairs or at least spiral ones: here again, as in poems I was writing thirty years ago (I myself can see both the continuity and the difference), there are dialectic, oxymoron, irony'.[4] In 'Donegal Triptych', the prosaic nature of the surface of experience is undercut by the spirals revealed by time, so that the self's perceptions, too, must change—'All our ends once more begin, | All our depth usurps our surface'. The result of this, that 'Surface takes a glossier polish, | Depth a richer gloom', is apparent in the characteristic perspectives of the late work, where depth and surface, inside and outside, are present simultaneously, often under the revealing lights of dream or nightmare. The worst problem, however, is not nightmare but straightforward routine and the passing of time:

> Yet the cold voice chops and sniggers,
> Prosing on, maintains the thread
> Is broken and the phoenix fled,
> Youth and poetry departed.

This is the blind alley which the late poetry converts into a spiral, a two-way affair. The past is more important than ever, a 'thread' in which the poet's imagination works with 'continuity and difference'.

Important themes from MacNeice's earlier work are reassembled in his late poetry with a new intensity and sense of urgency. In particular, the work of the 1930s returns in this new context, and old preoccupations take on new power. The dominant themes centre on

---

[4] Note on *The Burning Perch* (see n. 2).

the concern with time as flux undermining the stability of identity, and the difficulty of bringing the self to its 'home'. In the last two volumes, the whole imagery of 'home' is exploited extensively by MacNeice, who incorporates the metaphysical tensions of the self in vividly realized domestic structures. 'House on a Cliff' had been a major precursor of these late domestic poems, but they take its stark conflict between interior and exterior as a starting-point for their mixed perspectives of depth and surface. Two important examples from *Solstices* are 'Variation on Heraclitus' and 'Reflections', both of which also display the intensified awareness of form as a vehicle of meaning which marks much of the late poetry. Heraclitus, whose 'everything flows' tag is behind the very early MacNeice, is injected into a domestic interior, so that even the writer's pen and paper, and the chair on which he sits, are caught up in the irresistible flux:

> No, whatever you say,
> Reappearance presumes disappearance, it may not be nice
> Or proper or easily analysed not to be static
> But none of your slide snide rules can catch what is sliding so fast

The poem's argument, in fact, is not all that far removed from those of MacNeice's poems of the late 1920s and the early 1930s, but what has changed significantly is its element: the speaking voice rides its long (and faintly classical) lines, using enjambement liberally, in a way mimetic of the loss of the stability of fixed limits. The resultant momentum comes to an abrupt and decisive halt:

> I just do not want your advice
> Nor need you be troubled to pin me down in my room
> Since the room and I will escape for I tell you flat:
> One cannot live in the same room twice.

The cold, secure closure of this last line caps MacNeice's argument, but its deliberate flatness raises, or helps to bring to the surface, other issues. Edna Longley has written of the poem's 'maximising another habitual imagery, flux',[5] and of how it 'celebrates another positive, flux':[6] yet the cold comfort of the last line, like that concluding 'Charon', is a curious mode of celebration. If flux ever really represents a positive value for MacNeice, it does so with the significant qualification that it makes the concept of the self finally

---

[5] Edna Longley, 'Louis MacNeice: 'The Walls Are Flowing', in G. Dawe and E. Longley (eds.), *Across a Roaring Hill: The Protestant Imagination in Modern Ireland* (Belfast, 1985), 100.

[6] Edna Longley, *Poetry in the Wars* (Newcastle upon Tyne, 1986), 220.

untenable—'I will escape', perhaps, but, in escaping, 'I' will no longer remain 'I'. Capping the argument means closing down the verse, flattening its rapid flow with the dead hand of the actual variation on Heraclitus, 'one cannot step in the same river twice'. Compared with 'River in Spate', the poem tempers its vitality with an unremittingly bleak perspective, the depth that both brightens and usurps its surface.

'Reflections', too, launches the self into a chaos of perspectives, deconstructing its identity in multiplied mirror images. The features of a room repeat themselves in repeating syntactic shapes; the self, at the centre of its 'home', is thereby transformed into something other than itself, with the familiar patterns of its everyday environment now pressing in dangerously:

> My actual room stands sandwiched between confections
> Of night and lights and glass and in both directions
> I can see beyond and through the reflections the street lamps
> At home outdoors where my indoors rooms lie stranded . . .

The whole disruption and displacement of the 'I' in this process is a matter of seeing 'beyond and through', refracting both the domestic interior into the external scene, and the external scene into the 'home', so that in the end the 'I' itself is seen 'beyond and through' by the poem's perspectives. Again, there is a resonant pacing and timing to the closure:

> Where a taxi perhaps will drive in through the bookcase
> Whose books are not for reading and past the fire
> Which gives no warmth and pull up by my desk
> At which I cannot write since I am not lefthanded.

The self is in focus again at the end of 'Reflections', but it is a different self, reflected into otherness, over which the 'I' is powerless. Inside and outside have shifted into each other, a nightmare transformation of 'home' into the scene of the self's disintegration. Formally, the poem is an exceptional achievement, matching the dazzling surfaces of MacNeice's visual imagination with a controlled rush of versification; the poem's sheer speed is part of its relentless drive away from the stability of the self and its surroundings. It is not enough to say that 'Reflections' inhabits the nightmare world common in MacNeice's late poetry: in important respects, the poem's movement, its internal mirroring and repetition, and the transformation it effects *are* the nightmare, one in which 'home' is deeply implicated.

It is tempting to approach MacNeice's later work and its dominant concerns from a psychological, and indeed biographical, point of view, but there is something to be gained from resisting the temptation, especially as regards the increasing prominence of 'home' as a thematic and imagistic crux in the poetry. 'Home' certainly had more than a purely personal significance in 'Ode' (1934), and while MacNeice's terms of reference do change considerably, the continuity between this and the recurrent imagery of houses and domestic interiors of the late poetry cannot be ignored. MacNeice's poetry of the early 1930s was determinedly 'homeless', making use of displacement as a means of testing and opening the self in poetry to elements outside which it had found difficulty in incorporating itself. In this late writing, too, the self is implicated closely in all questions of 'home', but the homelessness is now far from being a deliberate strategy: as in 'Reflections', it tends to operate more as a powerful centre of tension, even fear. If the poetry written by MacNeice in the early 1930s sets out to leave home behind, his late work is perhaps an attempt to return, though it is one resigned in advance to its ultimate frustration. Both continuity and difference are of great importance here, and MacNeice's frequent retrospective gestures serve to emphasize this, implicitly aligning the internal dramas of *Solstices* and *The Burning Perch* with the external panoramas of *Poems* (1935).

Of course, MacNeice put considerable stress on the imagery and ideas of 'home' in his parable writing, and it is this parable aspect which effects the most important change on the image's symbolic weight between the 1930s and the late 1950s. The father's house is a scene which has to be escaped and returned to on the son's own terms; the return at the conclusion of 'Selva Oscura' is a return also to the 'I', reconciled to that which it had once to leave behind. It is the return of the prodigal son, but he is a son with no reason for repentance:

> Perhaps suddenly too I strike a clearing and see
> Some unknown house—or was it mine?—but now
> It welcomes whom I miss in welcoming me;
> The door swings open and a hand
> Beckons to all the life my days allow.

The poem's realization that 'the world, though more, is also I', is paralleled by its image of the house that 'welcomes whom I miss in welcoming me'. Home becomes a site for reconciliation between the self and the other, a place which the self, once open to 'the world', can approach again. 'The Truisms' presents a similar scene, again expressed in terms of a parable departure and return, but takes further the suggestion of morality at the end of 'Selva Oscura', setting out what is certainly a darker version of the parable motif. The 'box of truisms | Shaped like a coffin' is no use until its material has been lived through:

> Then he left home, left the truisms behind him,
> Still on the mantelpiece, met love, met war,
> Sordor, disappointment, defeat, betrayal,
> Till through disbeliefs he arrived at a house
> He could not remember seeing before,

Only after this process can the 'box | Shaped like a coffin', and the house in which it has been left, disclose their relevance. If these experiences have to be lived through, the truisms have to be died into—'The truisms flew and perched on his shoulders | And a tall tree sprouted from his father's grave'. The shape of the parable is completed in the poem, but the completion means death as well as reconciliation with the father. As in all of the late poetry, an awareness of mortality, like that of the passing of time, is inescapable; there is a dark irony for MacNeice in the fact that, while the son leaves the house 'to clear the air', it is 'through disbeliefs' that he returns to the house he left. MacNeice's own 'escape' from the family (and, in particular, from his father) was one from belief into disbelief; in the nightmares of the late poems, the belief to which he can return is one in the certainty of death. It is death, also, which settles the boundaries of the self once and for all.

'The Wall', also from *Solstices*, is MacNeice's most convincing attempt to force a way through the barriers of both personal memory and the unavoidable irony of death. The poem's setting is again linked to 'my father's lush garden with a cemetery beyond the hawthorn hedge'.[7] Confronting the fact of death, 'The Wall' does not attempt re-entry into the father's house, but faces the house's wall in order to force an exit. The writing is stark and its personal associations intense:

> The bed had known birth and death;
> Where was a wall had once been a window.

[7] MacNeice, 'Experiences with Images', *Orpheus*, 2 (1949), 126 (repr. Heuser, p. 159).

> Now all the light is behind him.
> The wall is a blind end.

This combines the basic parable opposition of closed and open, light and dark, with an amalgam of child- and death-bed (again, biographical elements suggest themselves in view of MacNeice's early suspicion that his birth had been in some way responsible for his mother's death[8]). The transformation is achieved just as starkly, with wall changing to window, darkness to light:

> And there was light
> Before him as through a window
> That opens on to a garden.
> The first garden. The last.

However, it is still worth asking how complete this transformation can be: the 'garden', both 'first' and 'last', is perhaps still the father's, the scene of a coming full circle of birth and mortality, like the grave-bed of 'The Introduction'. The repetition, or the completion of a circular parable pattern, is the paradigm for both dream and nightmare in MacNeice's work. Again, even in 'The Wall', escape turns out to lead to a place that has never really been left behind, the 'first garden' of the father's religion.

On the whole, it is darkness rather than light which is pervasive in MacNeice's late poetry, and nightmare rather than dream which is its dominant element. In 'The Riddle', the house is approached in terms of the inside/outside distinction, but the poem is less slight than it seems at first. The riddle itself (recalled in *The Strings Are False* with the answer, 'the wind') asks what is waiting outside—'What is it that goes round and round the house?'—as the cold, dark elements make their way in through 'the chink in the kitchen shutter'. The security evoked in the poem's first quatrain—'The range made our small scared faces warm as toast'—seems to make the threat from outside all the more real. In his second quatrain, MacNeice changes scene, but, once again, this is not enough to leave the first house behind, nor to leave behind the indefinable threat from outside:

> But now the cook is dead and the cooking, no doubt, electric,
> No room for draught or dream, for child or mouse,
> Though we, in another place, still put ourselves the question:
> What *is* it that goes round and round the house?

[8] See MacNeice to John Hilton, autumn 1929, Hilton papers, Bod. Lib., fos. 34–6.

The answer here is no longer 'the wind', and the contemporary scene no less than the remembered kitchen with its range is an interior threatened and questioned by that which it cannot encompass. In this sense, the poem itself is a riddle without an answer, communicating instead an intense foreboding. The house, and what is outside the house, are two poles which begin to exert pressure on MacNeice's late poetry in ways other than just the parable patterns of the 'home' poems discussed above. Rather than the completed circles of 'Selva Oscura' or 'The Truisms', the poetry often gravitates towards the open-ended nightmare of usurpation of the known by the unknown, of the inside by the outside, of 'Reflections' or of the empty spaces pressing in upon 'The Riddle'.

This tension gives more weight to MacNeice's continuing interest in the possibilities of travel in poetry—he did in fact single out his travel poems in his note on *Solstices*, and, also in the early 1960s, he made detailed proposals to Faber and Faber for a collection of his 'Poems of Place', as well as planning, and in part executing, his *Countries in the Air* project.[9] In this late phase of his career, MacNeice saw travel as a symbol for the opening of the self to the other, a way of leaving the home for the empty spaces outside. Some of the travel poems—especially 'Solitary Travel' or 'Half Truth from Cape Town'—easily achieve the resonance for which MacNeice hoped. Both of these are miniature dramas of the self, travel poems in which the necessity for travel is in excess of the ground actually covered. In the latter, the personal baggage of memory and perspective carried by the self, as the Indian poems of the late 1940s had proved, is a limitation for the self, setting the terms on which it can travel. In strange surroundings, 'Between the goldmines and the padded cell', MacNeice evokes memories of the Irish troubles, where problems lie in wait 'Till Prod should tumble Papish in the river'. There, as in Cape Town, the self is stranded between two poles, 'Between a smoking fire and a tolling bell'; now, travel brings the self only 'Between here and you', and the last stanza repeats this 'Between . . .' trope:

> So here I rest, with Devil's Peak above,
> Between a smoking fire and a calling dove,
> Its voice like a crazy clock that every ten
> Minutes runs down, so must be wound again;

[9] MacNeice's proposal for a volume to be called *Poems of Place* is found in a letter to Charles Monteith of Faber and Faber dated 15 Sept. 1961.

> And who is all but come or all but gone
> I cannot tell. The dove goes on, goes on.

The lightness of touch here in fact brings together two of MacNeice's symbols for time and the self, one a threat and the other a religiously tinged promise. The 'crazy clock' is a habitual image for time's threat to the self, but it is used here as a representation of the dove's voice (which recalls 'The grey dove of the future still descending' of 'Visitations'). The future, in effect, has taken the place of the 'tolling bell', but is now, like that bell, associated partly with sinister aspects of time. The self is left between one thing and another, with any note of promise once implicit in the dove's call now muted, made part of the world of repetition in which Ireland in memory and Cape Town in actual observation are both caught up. 'Solitary Travel' also senses 'the futility of moving on' as mere continent-hopping:

> Time and the will lie sidestepped. If I could only
> Escape into icebox or oven, escape among people
> Before tomorrow from this neutral zone
> Where all tomorrows must be faced alone . . .

Here the act of travelling does nothing to allow the self to open, leaving it in fact more severely alone, caught again in a repetitive pattern, in 'what, though not a conclusion, stays foregone'. Time is not really side-stepped at all, as the sequence of 'tomorrows' suggested by the final couplet imply. Travel, as is evident from these and other poems in *Solstices*, will not necessarily bring the self out of the solitude imposed by memory and repetition; MacNeice's fascination with the 'outside' entails a different kind of travel from that of the globe-trotting reporter.

'Country Week-End' III in *Solstices* looks outside the domestic surroundings to 'Wild grass in spate in a rainy wind', and evokes memories of watching funerals outside the rectory in Carrickfergus, or of a stay 'on an Irish island' where, outside 'the whitewashed room', 'One small ark | Was casting off to find Atlantis | But I did not dare embark'. Finally, MacNeice speaks of both the 'stone' of houses and the 'skin' of the body as seeming 'weak to hold this peace inside | Four walls', and contrasts this weakness with the persistence of the outside elements:

> Worth what compared with that
> First element, those fluent spears?

Spearmen or not, ourselves, in dreams,
This element, once ours, though lost,

In dreams may still be fought and wooed;
So let this rain keep falling, let
The wind from the west be backed by waves
On which the mind can embark anew.

This is a suggestive starting-point for an analysis of the travelling in MacNeice's late poetry; far from being another foray into the sources of good copy for journalistic writing, it is a venture into a dangerous outside element which has to be carried out partly in terms of 'dream'. In fact, the embarkation suggested by the poet is itself heavily dependent on the dream element, and carries mythic overtones: MacNeice's imaginative travels are all now towards the West, and the venture towards the 'outside' is in the nature of the *immram*. Like those of his own Muldoon in *The Mad Islands*, MacNeice's travels mix depth with surface, inside with outside; the presence of mortality as another concern leads such travels even further. In Alwyn and Brinley Rees's book *Celtic Heritage*, which MacNeice admired, he found the *immram* described in terms which chimed with his own concerns in the late poetry:

In the 'Voyages', we submit, have been preserved the tattered remnants of an oral Celtic 'book' of the dead, which proclaimed that the mysteries of the world beyond death had been at least partially explored and the stations of the soul's pilgrimage charted. . . . Thus . . . the *immram* has its own function. It is to teach the 'craft' of dying and to pilot the departing spirit on a sea of perils and wonders.[10]

The *immrama* from inside to outside, surface to depth, are frequent in *Solstices* and *The Burning Perch*, and are themselves parts of a highly individual and distinctive 'book of the dead' in which the 'perils and wonders' emerge from the routine of everyday existence.

MacNeice's most urgent poetry, then, travels in dream and nightmare. If this constitutes the 'depth' of the late work (sometimes, in its obsession with tunnelling and the underground world, literally so), there is also a 'surface' beneath which it runs. This could perhaps be identified with the late intensity of MacNeice's rather over-vaunted 'Horatian' tones, but should certainly be associated also with the personal recollections and retrospections which begin in *Solstices*

---

[10] Alwyn and Brinley Rees, *Celtic Heritage: Ancient Tradition in Ireland and Wales* (1961), 325.

and are carried over into *The Burning Perch*. As MacNeice's work makes its involvement with the self more dangerous, allowing it to open on to the other as nightmare, the personal, speaking voice and its coherence become more important also. Again, the process seems to begin at the time of *Visitations*, when the poet composed and abandoned an autobiographical piece, 'Tipperary', later repeating the attempt, more successfully, with 'The Blasphemies' in *Solstices*.[11] 'Tipperary', however, in which the imaginative reshaping of the poet's life is still only half-complete, is a revealing poem, taking each stage of MacNeice's development as a step on the way to an undefined goal. Like 'The Blasphemies', this is in some ways a circular course, in which each step forward leads back eventually to the nursery—even the stanza given to the thirties reveals a perspective-haunted concern:

> From the maze of love & guilt, from the attempt to be public minded,
>   There was yet a way to go
> From the spyglass on Madrid or Addis Ababa or Munich
> From the gradual dissolution of the mockery kings of snow
> From 30 years of faulty vision & then revision & then being blinded
>   A long way to go.

Vision and revision, and their eventual obliteration by the changing circumstances of time, typify the progression and retrospection of the poem: the fifth line (above) was later altered by MacNeice to 'From thirty years of staring into the sun & being blinded', already simplifying matters somewhat.[12] The self in 'Tipperary', which is openly Louis MacNeice, voyages away from home, but looking backwards—'40 years of watching the world in a seat back to the engine | With both the world & himself crying "I told you so" '. This backwards perspective means that the poem can end only by looking back to its beginning, 'While he waits for his old nurse to finish papering the nursery'. The whole process is a scrutiny of the self in its time, and is incomplete—'his self-examination has been both contrived and cursory'. The poem waits for, though it cannot see, the future—'He has come a long way | (Maybe yet a way to go)'.

---

[11] Two drafts of 'Tipperary' are extant: the first is in a notebook for 1955, along with other poems for *Visitations*, currently deposited among miscellaneous MacNeice papers in the Bod. Lib.; a later version is found in the MacNeice collection of the Humanities Research Center, Texas, and is transcribed in Robyn Marsack, *The Cave of Making* (Oxford, 1982), 124–7. The main quotations here are from the first version.   [12] See Marsack, *The Cave of Making*, p. 125.

'The Blasphemies' replaces this concern for perspective and direction
with different co-ordinates, those of the unanswerable question or
riddle: 'The sin against the Holy . . . though what | He wondered was
it?' In fact, the poem could be seen as an amalgamation of the
autobiographical mode with MacNeice's more familiar attempts to
put questions to the self; here, however, the starkness and directness
with which both the self is presented and the questions are put makes
'The Blasphemies' a more disturbed, even nightmarish, poem than
'Tipperary'. The frame of reference now is primarily religious, and
begins with the self in childhood trying to suppress its own thoughts,
in particular the unthinkable 'Damn God', the sin against the Holy
Ghost:

> Damn anyone else, but once I—No,
> Here lies the unforgivable blasphemy.
> So pulling the cold sheets over his head
> He swore to himself he had not thought
> Those words he knew but never admitted.

This crucial effort at self-censorship becomes the measure for the
future development of the self through its time (though external
circumstances impinge less directly here than in 'Tipperary'). The
substitutes for, and variations on, God each bring the self up against
its unanswerable riddle, a point beyond which the mind cannot pass.
In effect, it is this which forces each stage of the development; in his
forties, for example, the poet brings back the images of religious faith
as imaginative symbols, but cannot answer the questions this raises:

> Have we not all of us been in a war
> So have we not carried call it a cross
> Which was never our fault? Yet how can a cross
> Be never your fault?

Again, the self is questioned out of its acceptance of one perspective,
so that 'The words of the myth, | Now merely that and no longer
faith, | Melt in his hands'. The final phase brings the self back to the
initial question, making it in fact 'a walking | Question but no more
cheap than any | Question or quest is cheap'. 'The Blasphemies' is a
meditation on the way in which the self is shaped not only by
experience, but by its interpretations and doubts of its own status.
The surface, in each phase, is usurped by the doubts beneath, which
themselves come ultimately from the child's fear of a God who will
punish the self for its thoughts, perhaps for its very existence.

Personal development, then, is seen as a series of evasions which never succeed in answering the initial riddle. The effort to 'prove one's freedom', like the quest which takes its hero away from home only to return him there, may finally be impossible, an evasion of an inevitable repetition.

MacNeice's autobiographical self of 'The Blasphemies' is subverted by something other; in much the same way, his 'morality'-type biographies are broken up into fragments in the late poetry. The 'Jigsaws' sequence in *Visitations* splits up into what is essentially a series of riddles; 'Notes for a Biography', in *Solstices*, allows its central figure to be undermined by his times, leaving him alone and defiant—'I will stand as if under fire | With a sweet-smelling bunch in my hand, face to face with Never'. Here, as also in 'The Slow Starter', it is time which undermines the self, and mortality which forces it into a corner. In this latter poem, the 'watched clock' speaks for death's irony:

> Oh you have had your chance, It said;
> Left it alone and it was one.
> Who said a watched clock never moves?
> Look at it now. Your chance was I.

The pressures behind this comparatively straightforward poem are complex: is a life lived in defiance of time, or in conjunction with it? Like the question that seems to return at the end of 'The Blasphemies' only because it has never really been away, time riddles the integrity of the self which affects to defy it. The most thoroughgoing, and difficult, treatment of this problem comes in *The Burning Perch*, with the sequence 'As in Their Time'. This is made up of twelve five-line biographies, all of them syntactically self-involved and reflexive, having no overt connection other than their self-mirroring structures. In fact, the sequence is the logical extreme of the disjunctions in 'Jigsaws' or 'Notes for a Biography', isolating and compressing various 'selves' caught by their times. The thinking member of MacNeice's own generation, for example, is now seen in his essentials, trapped in a half-justification (VIII):

> For what it was worth he had to
> Make a recurring protest:
> Which was at least a gesture
> Which was a vindication
> Or excuse for what it was worth.

Again, this has the circularity of a riddle, questioning and qualifying the terms 'gesture', 'vindication', and 'excuse'; the 'recurring protest' of a life is 'for what it was worth'—'it' being finally the life itself as well as the protest. Time, in this sequence, strips down identity: in section x, the 'Citizen of an ever-expanding | Universe' lives 'among plastic gear so long' that 'When they decided to fingerprint him | He left no fingerprints at all'. This nightmare of modernity is one way of presenting the more radical instability which prevents the self and its 'home' from being fixed or stable (IV):

> He was the man you thought
> And I thought too was me
> That never was on land
> Or sea but in fact was at home
> On both and never was.

The self will not stand still, even for the 'I' in the poetic voice who attempts to hold it; as a result, the sequence allows time to outrun the coherences of biography. Perhaps these poems turn a cruelly cold eye on a generation, but in this respect they are in tune with many other pieces in *The Burning Perch*, where the depth usurps the surface, often disturbingly, and the surfaces themselves suggest a drop under the feet. The self in this volume is fractured radically in the element of nightmare.

'Memoranda to Horace' is the most polished attempt at articulating a personal voice in *The Burning Perch*, and is a considerable success: even so, what the voice articulates leads back to those forces from which it anticipates defeat. Horatianism itself is seen as having little to offer to lessen the nightmare of contemporary life and the passing of time. In his note on *The Burning Perch*, MacNeice mentioned 'something of a Horatian resignation', but qualified this immediately: 'my resignation, as I was not brought up a pagan, is more of a fraud than Horace's'.[13] The sequence does indeed ensure the removal of any pretension to a Horatian resignation, making as much of differences between the two poets as of similarities; it is the nature and the pitch of the voice itself which seems to be the main point of contact. MacNeice's account of what affinity there is, in section II, is revealing— 'It looks as if both of us | Met in the uniqueness of history a premise | That keeps us apart yet parallel, | The gap reducible only by language'. The 'premise' is time again, and attempts to cope with

[13] Note on *The Burning Perch*.

this, for both Horace and MacNeice, are attempts to fill a 'gap' with language, to construct a self, in poetry at least, which acts as 'an antidote | To the poison of time' (iv). Here of course the materials available to the two poets differ: where Horace's culture is 'pagan', MacNeice has to work with the ingredients of a differently conditioned imagination. The 'for you over-Gothic' elements of fantasy and nightmare become important in this respect:

> With whom to hobnob is a mortification
> Of self-respect, one's precious identity
> Filtered away through what one had fancied
> Till now were one's fingers, shadows to shadows.

This nightmare subversion of identity is MacNeice's only choice ('a mortification | Of self-respect' was one of the necessities associated with his own escape from family values in the 1920s[14]), and its conversion of aspects of the self into 'shadows' is set against the absolute obliteration offered by contemporary, time-bound life:

> Which yet means relief from the false identity
> Assumed in the day and the city, the pompous
> Cold stereotype that you in your period
> Tried to escape in your Sabine farmhouse.

Effectively, this Horatian poem is a determination to avoid urbanity, setting itself the choice between the world of 'shadows' and the prosaic prospect of 'a blank posterity | One's life reduced to standing room only'. The poem's conversational and lapidary surface is again made to consider the unclassical 'shadows' which the self will have to enter. The interior, with 'standing room only', is to be quitted in favour of an external element in which 'the sky was dirty | All day, there is snow to come, there are monsters | To come and corrupt me'.

The Burning Perch is MacNeice's most concerted and sustained exploration of the idioms of this 'outside' of the self, which is also the idiom of nightmare. The poems may perhaps be seen as a series of *immrama*, and parts of a 'craft of dying' in which memory and imagination fuse in an examination of both the self and its time, transforming the poet's earlier considerations of the place of the self into a new, and much more urgent, kind of material. Pure nightmare had of course been present in *Solstices* too: in 'Bad Dream', MacNeice laid his scene in another house, though 'one with none of the

---

[14] See *The Strings Are False*, p. 103.

consolations offered by parable. Here the world outside is as cheap and sinister as ever, one of sex, violence, and a mockery of religion:

> Outside there were no other houses, only bedizened hoardings
>   With panties prancing on them
> And an endless file of chromium-plated lamp posts
>   With corpses dangling from them
> And one gaunt ruined church with a burglar alarm filibustering
>   High and dry in the steeple.

Yet the house in fact offers no refuge from the outside; instead, the external elements find their expressions inside, and catch the young man who has entered, 'who wanted to eat and drink | To play, pray, make love'. The drama which is enacted here is a parable of loss and guilt—a girl's arm appears from the floor, but the man is paralysed and unable to respond to the cries for help. The arm vanishes again into the floor, from the surface to the depths. Outside and inside finally become indistinguishable in a cruel surrealist circus, where 'The chaps outside on the lamp posts | Hooted, broke wind and wept' as the decisive loss is made certain:

> Men the size of flies dropped down his neck while the mansized
>   Flies gave just three cheers
> And he could not move. The darkness under the floor gave just
>   One shriek. The arm was gone.

Although the poem is complemented by 'Good Dream', in which a female figure, 'Her, no other', is actually discovered rather than lost, 'Bad Dream' functions more for the sake of its nightmare imagery's intensity than to put over a specific 'parable' meaning. The loss is important (and perhaps the girl ultimately represents a lost mother as well as a lost love), but the mechanics of nightmare have become more important still: the house is no refuge, the external world is on the attack, and the self is paralysed.

Paralysis is particularly prominent in *The Burning Perch*, and is built in, in a modified form, to the structures of the poems themselves, where syntax repeats itself, halts, and changes, working with or against the flow of the verse. In 'After the Crash', nightmare takes the form of stasis, where the self is frozen as it looks on where 'life seemed still going on'; the scene is set for Judgement Day, but, as in other poems in the volume, the apocalyptic hints turn out to be red herrings—the 'gigantic scales in the sky' in fact balance emptiness with emptiness. For the self, not even death will bring a revelation; it is 'too late to die', too late, perhaps, for any gesture to break the cycle of repetition and meaninglessness. Similarly, MacNeice sees history as moving not towards a culmination but into bathos and futility. In 'Greyness Is All', the only possible course is to wait 'Until the final switch is thrown | To black out all the worlds of men | And demons too'. 'Spring Cleaning' also shows the surface of the contemporary world crumbling, and brings MacNeice's old image of the stylite to sound his warning:

> While on a pillar in the sands
> A gaunt man scours his plinth and hauls
> His empty basket up and cries:
> Repent! It is time to round things off.

Yet even this last image is compromised by its context in the poem, where 'Towers of pennies for spastic children | Wobble and crash'; differentiating between the signs of imminent catastrophe and prosaic accident is not made easy, and the saint on his pillar may be just as 'mechanical' as the poem's other images.

One crucially important element in these poems is MacNeice's nightmare logic, which now influences the structure as well as the imagery. Just as it is a characteristic of dreams that they operate logically in detail although the details follow each other illogically, the poems often exploit a tightly structured syntax and verse shape in their disorganization of images. Often, too, the logic of repetition within poems is what fuels the nightmare. 'Château Jackson' is an extreme example of this, but more subtle uses are to be found in 'Another Cold May' or 'Réchauffé'. In the first of these, the shape of the phrase 'the move | Is the wind's, not theirs', is repeated, often keeping the enjambement, until finally the phrase fills a line of its own, setting the seal on another image of paralysis, where

> the square
> Ahead remains ahead, their petals
> Will merely fall and choke the drains
> Which will be all; this month remains
> False animation of failed levitation,
> The move is time's, the loss is ours.

The tulips, like chess-men, function in the poem as images of 'false animation', for which any progress or even independence is illusory

(compare 'Hold-Up' in *Solstices*), and finally the connection between
the wind and time, tulips and the self, is insistent. The final filling-out
of the syntactic motif means that the poem achieves a closure which
is akin to the Yeatsian clicking-shut of a box; yet, as in other poems,
this very finality carries ominous overtones of repetition and paralysis.
In 'Réchauffé', the last line of each stanza mirrors the first in every
respect except that it omits the last word—'The food on the walls of
the dark tombs' becomes 'The food on the walls of the dark'. The
effect of this near-repetition is again an unsettling one; deep in the
Egyptian tombs, and in the history and geography of the land itself,
the possibility of catastrophe lies only a small variation on normality
away. In the final stanza, where 'The dams on the breast of the mad
Nile | Secure both budget and mind', the repetition with variation
opens up another vista:

> And yet who knows what sudden thrust
> In the guts, what gripe in the mind, might burst
> The dams on the breast of the mad?

Nightmare is not brought under control by the poem's structure
here; rather, the nightmare is implicit in that structure, removing one
word to change everything, so that the picturesque 'hands on the
ends of the sun's rays', become the threatening 'hands on the end of
the sun'. Catastrophe and madness in the poem cannot be dissociated
from the structures of words.

Nightmare logic operates most interestingly in *The Burning Perch*
when applied to the routine of the contemporary world. MacNeice
returns partially to the mode particularly characteristic of his 1930s
work, with long galleries of vividly descriptive and heavily visual
images, but the difference now is that these function within a tightly
controlled framework of nightmare logic in which the observing self
is put under pressure. 'Flower Show' uses this technique, with its
monstrous flowers forcing their observer under:

> these blooms, ogling or baneful, all
> Keep him in their blind sights; he tries to stare them down
> But they are too many, too unreal, their aims are one, the controlled
> Aim of a firing party.

The world observed now observes, and prepares to strike back;
similarly, syntax enforces a sinister reflexivity on the self that tries to
manipulate it—in 'In Lieu', finally 'in lieu of a flag | The orator hangs

himself from the flagpost'. The self is threatened both by the external world on which it spectates and by words, the very medium in which, as poetry, it must exist.

In 'The Pale Panther', this nightmare logic creates a particularly difficult poem, partly owing to the suppression of links between constituent images. In fact, this is crucial to the poem's effect, its own 'Runways in rut, control | Towers out of touch': there is no control over the external world here, and the agents of possible action, the airman and the milkman, are themselves belated and powerless (the airman, of course, being a hardy 1930s stage-property, now helplessly out of his time). 'The Pale Panther' is certainly haunted by war and imminent destruction, but also merges the apparently symbolic with the stubbornly prosaic, the 'shards | Of caddis'. Like the self in 'After the Crash' for whom 'It was too late to die', the agents in 'The Pale Panther' are too late to act; the sun has 'stopped play'. It may be useful to see the poem as something of an anti-parable; that is, it employs the methods of MacNeice's parable poetry, but denies them any final coherence. The stasis of nightmare spreads eventually into the reader's resources for reading the poem; in this, 'The Pale Panther' represents perhaps the extreme point of nightmare logic in *The Burning Perch*.

Finally, however, MacNeice's particular variety of *immram*, his own book of the dead, is at its sharpest when personal tensions are powerful. Three of the volume's finest poems, 'The Taxis', 'Charon', and 'The Introduction', are voyages into the element outside the self in which mortality comes to the surface as a concern. 'The Taxis' is a highly concentrated version of the autobiographical development of 'The Blasphemies', but deepens the dark side of that poem still further by its device of undermining the self's singleness or stability of identity. The accompanying ghosts, visible to the cabby but not to the self, increase in number with each stanza; what appears to the self to have been left behind is in fact what still remains in attendance, 'an odd | Scent that reminded him of a trip to Cannes'. To ask why these others remain invisible only to the self is to ask how the self can ever have been deluded into believing in a single 'I'. Finally, the company is too numerous for the cabby to accommodate it:

> As for the fourth taxi, he was alone
> Tra-la when he hailed it but the cabby looked
> Through him and said: 'I can't tra-la well take
> So many people, not to speak of the dog.'

'Alone' or not, there will be no more rides here. The crowd which time has added to the self even includes 'the dog' now; as in other poems of this period, this dog can be both an actual creature and the dog at the gates of the underworld. The strength of 'The Taxis' is that the fluency of its medium achieves such a close blend of the literal with nightmare that any distinction between literal and symbolic functions of the images is finally impossible.

In 'Charon', of course, the dog is less ambiguous, and the poem as a whole is more obviously a voyage into the other world. Again, however, the literal details of London are preserved intact, and the poem's bus journey leads to both the Thames and the Styx at once. The structure of 'Charon', its carefully controlled forward momentum, is punctuated with repetition, 'we just jogged on', 'black with money/suspicion/obols', but the repetitions are not, as elsewhere, ways of accentuating an intuition of stasis; instead, they make even more shocking the impact of the ferryman's dead-pan demand, 'If you want to die you will have to pay for it'. The other world makes a demand drawn from the commerce of the living, and the surface usurps depth. At the same time, religious overtones are half-felt—'the inspector's | Mind is black with suspicion', or the conflation of Cerberus with a cock crowing:

> we could see
> The lost dog barking but never knew
> That his bark was as shrill as a cock crowing,
> We just jogged on.

It is worth comparing a recollection in 'Tipperary' of 'the doubts and denials and the cock about to crow'. As MacNeice admits in 'Memoranda to Horace', the poet's imagination cannot be a pagan one, and this tinges even the cold encounter with Charon with the suspicion that experience—the journey itself—might possibly, as in parable, have been a kind of test: either Cerberus at the gates of the underworld or the cock accusing Peter could be present here. The nightmare is still a species of riddle.

The road to the underworld had been charted long before in MacNeice's poetry: in 'Eclogue between the Motherless', however, it is one leading to a family hell:

> The night marked time, the dog at the lodge kept barking
> And as he barked the big cave opened of hell
> Where all their voices were one and stuck at a point

Like a gramophone needle stuck on a notched record.
I thought 'Can I find a love beyond the family
And feed her to the bed my mother died in
Between the tallboys and the vase of honesty
On which I was born and groped my way from the cave
With a half-eaten fruit in my hand, a passport meaning
Enforced return for periods to that country?

Here the element of repetition, although it does not enter the structures of the writing itself, is what makes the family world 'hell'; the self, with its original sin of 'a half-eaten fruit', has to appease the mother, even through sexuality. The bed on which the mother died and the son was born is the centre of the scene of repetition, hell. By the time of writing 'The Introduction', MacNeice's underworld had lost this obviously familial tinge, but it was still the scene of a strange romance. The poem's repetition and variations, with and against the grain of the verse, transform the scene from 'grave glade' to 'green grave', from the surface to the depths. As so often, the surface is tortured by an awareness of what is underneath—'beneath | The grass beneath their feet the larvae | Split themselves laughing'. The laughable irony is that of time as well as death; the mirroring lines of 'she frightened him because she was young | And thus too late', and 'he frightened her because he was old | And thus too early', do not quite cancel each other out—time has cheated the romance. Perhaps the 'green grave' is indeed a grave-bed, and death a curiously literal consummation here: certainly, for MacNeice, this grave is connected with 'the bed my mother died in' through the very element of dream or nightmare in which it exists, one which always leads back to 'home' and all that 'home' represents.

This is not to say that the bleakness of the late poetry is unrelieved—MacNeice insisted upon 'the good things . . . still there round the corner'[15]—and several of the poems in *The Burning Perch* hint at the possibilities of memory as well as its liabilities. Yet the volume is a stern one, unsparing in its scrutiny of the self, as in the vivid nightmare of the 'I twitter Am' of 'Budgie'. The self is both Louis MacNeice and any individual living and working in the contemporary world, and this self is usurped time and again by what it may attempt to ignore or is powerless to change. Finally, though, riding the nightmare or treading down the cinders is possible, if at a price. Two

---

[15]   Note on *The Burning Perch*, repr. Heuser, p. 248.

courses, neither of them an 'escape', are implicit in the late poetry:
one is setting out on the *immram* into the unknown, the outside;
while the other is tunnelling down into the world under the self, the
depths which include the darkest of personal memories. In this sense,
both 'Thalassa' (which may have its roots as early as the 1940s[16])
and 'Coda' begin to look beyond the 'nightmare and cinders' of *The
Burning Perch*. In *Persons from Porlock* (1963), the hero, Hank,
insists that there is 'No time under ground, you know':[17] he is
overcome by time in his life above the ground, but in the caves he
finally beats the clock by dying—death in the plays transcends the
mundane and destructive progression of time. A similar evasion of
time is perhaps present in 'Coda', where the movement from past to
present to future is downwards, through the repetitions of time and
experience, towards something other:

> Maybe we knew each other better
> When the night was young and unrepeated
> And the moon stood still over Jericho.
>
> So much for the past; in the present
> There are moments caught between heart-beats
> When maybe we know each other better.
>
> But what is that clinking in the darkness?
> Maybe we shall know each other better
> When the tunnels meet beneath the mountain.

The self's movement downwards, even if it is ultimately to be
associated with death, is also a movement towards these others
which, in the repetition and routine of time, it can recognize only
'between heart-beats'. The two obsessions present throughout
MacNeice's writing, with time and with the limitations of the self,
work in conjunction here so that the poem does not close, but hints at
a reopening of something lost, a return of the self to the other which
it had known all along, when the tunnels meet. Like 'Thalassa' 's *ne
plus ultra* of 'every adverse force', the process points to continuations
beyond the ending of the poem. The nightmare and cinders, in the
light of this, are perhaps more in the nature of a new start.

---

[16] See Marsack, *The Cave of Making*, p. 158.
[17] MacNeice, *Persons from Porlock and Other Plays for Radio* (1969), 128.

8
The 'Ould Antinomies': Ireland

ALTHOUGH MacNeice is now read increasingly as a major Anglo-Irish writer rather than as an adjunct to the Auden group, a change in labels should not be mistaken for a leap in critical insight. 'Anglo-Irish' is in itself of little use in this context, perhaps aligning MacNeice with the class to which Yeats laid claim which embodied, for the younger poet, 'nothing but an obsolete bravado, an insidious bon-homie and a way with horses'.[1] Even so, 'Anglo-Irish' does at least bring to the fore the inevitable connection between MacNeice's and Yeats's poetry; this primarily literary issue in fact leads into the broader implications of the poet's relation to Ireland generally, and the role that the country played in his work. In one sense, Ireland was necessarily crucial in the poet's imaginative world as the scene of a difficult childhood in which periods of happiness were contrasted with those of melancholy and fear. In a memoir, MacNeice's sister recalled an underlying sense of displacement in even the earlier years:

My father occasionally told us stories of Connemara, but my mother spoke of it so constantly and with such love and such longing that I think it was she who really made it come alive for Louis and myself. It became for us both a 'many-coloured land', a kind of lost Atlantis where we thought that by rights we should be living, and it came to be a point of honour that we did not belong to the North of Ireland. We were in our minds a West of Ireland family exiled from our homeland.[2]

It is important that, from the beginning, 'home' for MacNeice was always somewhere else. Exile of one kind or another is the condition of a great deal of MacNeice's poetry: in the fragmentary 'Landscapes of Childhood and Youth' of about 1957, he remembered that in his childhood 'for many years I lived in nostalgia for somewhere I had never been'.[3] This differs from the young Yeats's more concrete

---

[1] MacNeice, *The Poetry of W. B. Yeats* (1941, repr. 1967), 97.
[2] Elizabeth Nicholson, 'Trees Were Green', in T. Brown and A. Reid (eds.), *Time Was Away* (Dublin, 1974), 14.
[3] MacNeice, *The Strings Are False: An Unfinished Autobiography* (1965), 217.

nostalgia to the same degree that MacNeice himself differs from the Anglo-Irish stereotype: here it is Ireland, or one part of it at least, that provokes the longing for another better (and even more 'Irish') place. For the young MacNeice, the emotional conflict is not between Ireland and England but between Connemara and Carrickfergus, one way of being 'Irish' and another. Transposed into an English context, MacNeice's feelings for Ireland were sufficiently complicated to prevent him taking up the Anglo-Irish pose which he called 'playing the Wild Irish Boy'—'my background was pathetically suburban'.[4] It is for reasons such as these that the mature MacNeice, whether a Northern- or an Anglo-Irish poet, has to be considered as something of a special case; but special cases may also be the most revealing.

In his brief but intensely perceptive essay, 'The Man from No Part', Tom Paulin has provided the best analysis of MacNeice's sense of displacement, of being 'a visitor everywhere', and its corollary: 'For the English reader he appears to be Irish, while for certain Irish readers he doesn't really belong to Ireland.'[5] Yet the parallel between the poet's determined homelessness and his visitor's standing for Irish and English critics alike, need not imply that MacNeice's poetry exists in some kind of national limbo, or, if it does, that such a place is without its own significance; as Edna Longley has observed: ' "a painful no man's land" can become an imaginative country'.[6] Clearly, MacNeice's imaginative engagement with Ireland may be distinguished from that of, say, Patrick Kavanagh, but the difference between the two should not be simplified into that between 'exile' and 'belonging'. MacNeice's work corresponds with neither of these extremes; Ireland was really too close to the poet's imagination to be the focus for 'nostalgia'. If images from childhood formed a matrix for much of the persistent imagery of his poetry, Ireland itself became for MacNeice an embodiment of the kinds of tension involved in writing, and of the problems posed by the projection of the self in the public otherness of a literary medium. On the level of events, Ireland tended to confront MacNeice with the problems that he encountered in the act of writing itself, concentrating for him 'the light and shade

---

[4] MacNeice, *The Strings Are False: An Unfinished Autobiography* (1965), 217.

[5] Tom Paulin, *Ireland and the English Crisis* (Newcastle upon Tyne, 1984), 75.

[6] Edna Longley, 'Louis MacNeice: "The Walls Are Flowing"', in G. Dawe and E. Longley (eds.), *Across a Roaring Hill: The Protestant Imagination in Modern Ireland* (Belfast, 1985), 99 (quoting Terence Brown).

of my own experience, the corroborations and refutals of my myths, the frustrations and illuminations I have found in various travels'.[7] In accusing MacNeice of being 'a tourist in his own country', it is easy to forget that 'travels' were at the very heart of his work, taking the self out of its accustomed context to face difficult otherness, testing the known against the unknown. For MacNeice, Ireland was effectively the epitome of this process, a 'home' in some senses, but always unstable, shifting, a matter of changing light and shade. Writing to E. R. Dodds in 1948 that 'I wish one could either *live* in Ireland or *feel oneself* in England', MacNeice summed up the difficulty as 'one of them ould antinomies'.[8] The ironic use of the Yeatsian term is appropriate: Ireland represented for MacNeice a vitally contradictory concentration of impulses, like the older poet both germane and alien to his imaginative instincts. To be displaced from a force this powerful is perhaps the only way of maintaining a degree of independence, but it does not mean that the force can be left behind, nor that it is anything less than crucial in the shaping of the imaginative instincts themselves.

MacNeice's relation to Ireland is often seen in the light of the idea of division or 'spiritual hyphenation', the dilemma of being neither one thing nor the other. 'Oh this division of allegiance!'[9] is a cry which does indeed reverberate through the poet's work, but it has left him open to misinterpretation, its tone being less final and certain than the *odi atque amo* formula into which it can harden. When such a division is noted in MacNeice nowadays, it is inevitably tinged with other contemporary Irish divisions, especially that of the identity of the Protestants of Northern Ireland. This particular division of allegiance is seldom acknowledged as a cliché, but it does effectively function as such, even in the field of literary criticism. The stereotypes are long-established; 'An Ulster Protestant' (probably W. R. Rodgers) writing in *The Bell* in 1941 was saying nothing new when he described his countrymen in these terms:

For the Northern Protestant's feelings are deep because they are not extensive and have not been dissipated in words. He would *like* to have eloquence. But he suspects and hates eloquence that has no bone of logic in

---

[7] MacNeice's proposal for a book, *Countries in the Air*, quoted by E. R. Dodds in his preface to *The Strings Are False*, p. 14.
[8] MacNeice to Dodds, July 1948, Dodds fo. 88[r].
[9] *The Strings Are False*, p. 78.

it. . . . We are really a 'split' people, we Protestant Ulstermen. Our eyes and thoughts are turned towards England, but our hearts and feet are in Ulster.[10]

MacNeice's work exists in the context of these ideas, but it does not conform to them. His eloquence has perhaps proved costly to the poet's reputation, but it does relate back in some ways to this desire for the 'bone of logic', while in others it flies determinedly in the face of logical principles. The paradox of this particular echo of the stereotype is reflected on a broader scale, where the divisions in MacNeice's poetry are less those of a 'split' people than of a permanently displaced self. 'Carrick Revisited' seems to show this in its declaration of 'division':

> Torn before birth from where my fathers dwelt,
> Schooled from the age of ten to a foreign voice,
> Yet neither western Ireland nor southern England
> Cancels this interlude; what chance misspelt
> May never now be righted by my choice.

This kind of division is almost assertive, echoing Yeatsian principles of chance and choice to present an attitude that is reluctant to concede loss. These lines are not 'split' between Ireland and England; rather, they allow those places to become poles or co-ordinates of an independent voice. There is no head and heart dichotomy here such as is central to the cliché of division, though there is a degree of anxiety as to the conditions of the voice's independence. The self's freedom from the constraints of place or tradition may be seen from another angle as loneliness, and 'Carrick Revisited' is one of Mac-Neice's poems in which 'time and place' undermine fixed certainties of perspective. The self is divided, not so much between England and Ireland as between 'the Particular' and 'All other possible bird's-eye views'; if this very realization means that the self is profoundly displaced, the displacement is also a condition of its freedom.

While MacNeice's poetry both inhabits and subverts the cliché of division, the ways in which it carries out this subversion are remarkably Yeatsian. When dealing with Ireland, the poet constantly manipulates strongly stressed ideas of perspective, and makes use of contradiction and paradox in both structure and imagery; furthermore, the presence of the older poet is often felt in more immediately obvious areas of MacNeice's work. In fact, the 'literary' and the

---

[10] 'An Ulster Protestant' [W. R. Rodgers], 'Conversation Piece', in the *Bell*, 4/5 (Aug. 1942), 309–10.

'personal' aspects of MacNeice's relation to Ireland cannot really be dissociated, since the question of his debt to Yeats, for example, finally involves his feelings towards Ireland as a whole; the 'ould antinomies' operate even in the ways in which MacNeice represents his own childhood. Similarly, the more technical aspects of his poems do not exist in a formal vacuum, but involve elements of broader attitudes from which they cannot really be separated. This chapter will argue that aspects of MacNeice's early experience, in particular the death of his mother when he was 7 years old, influenced significantly his later literary dealings with Ireland, and that even the particular kinds of 'division' encountered in his poetry have important personal resonances, making absolute distinctions between 'private' and 'public' contexts almost meaningless.

It is remarkable that almost all of MacNeice's poems with specifically Irish subjects concern themselves to a great degree explicitly with the perspectives from which they work. This concern is clearly to be seen in 'Carrick Revisited', with its 'particular' and 'possible bird's-eye views', but it can also be observed in MacNeice's earlier work. In the poem which effectively marks MacNeice's transition from juvenilia to mature writing, 'Belfast' (1931), there is a heavy reliance on visual images; much of his early work had been similarly visually orientated, but was often overcrowded and rapidly intercut so as to achieve a kaleidoscopic effect. In 'Belfast', the cutting is more measured, each stanza (and sentence) centred upon a single strong visual image, or group of closely related images. The insistent suggestion of cruelty and death (the gantries 'like crucifixes', the factory woman 'shipwrecked' while wealth comes from 'the salt carrion water') culminates in the controlled finalities of the last stanza:

> Over which country of cowled and haunted faces
> The sun goes down with a banging of Orange drums
> While the male kind murders each its woman
> To whose prayer for oblivion answers no Madonna.

The poem's visual perspectives deepen here into a bleak sense of closure, the inevitability of the familial 'murder' which extinguishes the saving aspects of the feminine in this male-centred culture. The setting of the sun, which puts an end to the poem's visual aspect, ushers in this denial of escape to the accompaniment of 'the banging of Orange drums'. Although MacNeice shows the masculine aspect of the North as profiting from 'the salt carrion water', the effect of this image is not, as Paulin claims, to 'look out towards the open sea and England',[11] but rather to keep the gaze fixed on the shipyards; the poem's perspective is directed firmly 'Down there at the end of the melancholy Lough', and follows this darkening course into its final murderous obscurity. The poem is not an imaginative escape from, or exorcism of, the North, but an attempted entry which is frustrated, its resources of perspective disabled.

Perspective itself is crucial in MacNeice's 'Irish' poems of the 1930s. 'Belfast' is the most uncompromising of these, pushing the visual line to the point where it is overcome by darkness in which man destroys woman. 'Valediction', on the other hand, manipulates the tourist's eye-view to a rather different end, in effect attempting to enact a murder in which the first-person voice is itself implicated. The violence in 'Valediction' is carried on in full view (the poet is determined that he will 'merely look on | At each new fantasy of badge and gun'), and it is directed against another, different, feminine figure, that of Ireland herself. Belfast figures here again, acknowledged now as 'my mother city', with its surrounding mountains seen as 'my paps', and is just one aspect of a larger motherhood that has to be repudiated. The repudiation itself is powerfully visual, but is over-ridden again by aural elements:

> Cursèd be he that curses his mother. I cannot be
> Anyone else than what this land engendered me:
> In the back of my mind are snips of white, the sails
> Of the Lough's fishing-boats, the bellropes lash their tails
> When I would peal my thoughts, the bells pull free—
> Memory in apostasy.

The bells—a habitual nightmare image for MacNeice—like the Orange drums of 'Belfast', take over from the visual perspective which in 'Valediction' is dwelt on obsessively as that of the 'tourist'. Derek Mahon has written that 'This "tourist in his own country" enjoyed, as a tourist should, the sensuous qualities of light and landscape, for both of which he had a painter's eye',[12] but that enjoyment, the 'painter's eye' itself, serves something of a loaded purpose:

---

[11] Paulin, *Ireland and the English Crisis*, p. 77.
[12] Mahon, 'MacNeice in England and Ireland', in T. Brown and A. Reid (eds.), *Time Was Away: The World of Louis MacNeice* (Dublin, 1974), 119.

I will exorcise my blood
And not to have my baby-clothes my shroud
I will acquire an attitude not yours
And become as one of your holiday visitors,
And however often I may come
Farewell, my country, and in perpetuum . . .

To determine to become a tourist while at the same time, as Edna
Longley has pointed out, continuing to attach the possessive pro-
noun to Ireland,[13] is to force rather than discover a division of
allegiance within the self. This forcing is the forcing of independence
from the mother, 'not to have my baby-clothes my shroud'. In
'Valediction' perspective becomes an instrument with which to curse
the mother, objectivity with a vengeance.

'Train to Dublin' (1934) offers an ideal framework within which
MacNeice's perspective can operate. This poem, like 'Rugby Football
Excursion' in *The Earth Compels*, comes close to the language of the
tourist brochure, where some of the images are presented with a
startling clarity, again in terms of shifting light and shade ('the
trough of dark | Golden water for the cart-horses, the brass | Belt of
serene sun upon the lough'). However, 'Train to Dublin' is concerned as
much with the experience of perception itself, the flux of the passing
moment, as with what is actually perceived; it is an exercise of the
freedom won more bitterly in 'Valediction'. 'Rugby Football Excur-
sion' merges its perspectives with strong non-visual sense-impressions
—smell is predominant—to portray Dublin and its 'Endurance of
one-way thinking':

Inkshops, the smell of poverty, pubs at the corner,
A chimney on fire and street on street of broken
Fanlights over the doors of tenement houses—
Token of the days of Reason.[14]

The poem anticipates the later, more fully realized, 'Dublin' in its
scrutiny of the 'Augustan capital | Of a Gaelic nation'. The final
image, though, is still one of departure ('a sapphire pinhead | Sirius
marks Dun Laoghaire'), and again the perspective is explicitly that of
a visitor, going 'Back to my adolescence, back to Ireland', but
returning again from his trip. However warm the tones of poems like
these may sometimes appear, both are written from the apostate

[13] Longley, 'The Walls Are Flowing', p. 105.
[14] MacNeice, 'Rugby Football Excursion', in *The Earth Compels* (1937), 61.

perspective, and carry out the promise, or the threat, to 'merely look on'.

Where MacNeice goes beyond this attitude to perspective in the treatment of Ireland is in 'Carrickfergus', a complex poem in which memory and sense-impressions lead to something deeper than the vivid surface. If one aspect of the poem has its context securely in the mid-1930s—the fear that the 'puppet world of sons' may prove to be puppets indeed, and follow, like Roland later in *The Dark Tower*, their fathers and brothers to death—another is located in the private landscape of the rectory ('my father's medium-sized lush garden with a cemetery beyond the hawthorn hedge').[15] The First World War marked the beginning of division in MacNeice's experience: not only the division between the home garden and the England to which the boy is sent, but also (which remains outside the frame of the poem) the final separation from the mother brought about by her early (and, for her son, distressingly mysterious) death. 'Carrickfergus' is a poem much concerned with fathers and sons, and covers a period in which the world of the father encroaches steadily upon that of the child, when the presence of the soldiers nearby marks out the garden as 'my father's'. The masculine values of the Norman, and of more recent industry, are also passed on to the child, cutting him off from 'the Irish Quarter':

> I was the rector's son, born to the anglican order,
>   Banned for ever from the candles of the Irish poor;
> The Chichesters knelt in marble at the end of a transept
>   With ruffs about their necks, their portion sure.

There is a deep connection in 'Carrickfergus' between losing a mother and losing access to Ireland's feminine aspect, joining instead the ranks of the threateningly stony Chichesters and their modern successors, with a 'portion' to make secure. Memory in this poem is not 'in apostasy' (which suggests a deliberate withdrawal) but in displacement; along with this, the emphasis on the purely visual diminishes, giving way to a more complex description of a remembered landscape. The very sounds of the poem are a mixture of the rough and consonantal with the ghost of classical metre, the indigenous Ulster noise with the smooth patterns of verse learned in an English

---

[15] MacNeice, 'Experiences with Images', *Orpheus*, 2 (1949), 128 (repr. Heuser, p. 159).

public school.[16] 'Carrickfergus', then, embodies division on a number
of different levels, from parent and child to Ireland and England.

Whatever the depths suggested in 'Carrickfergus', perspective'
remained crucial in MacNeice's specifically 'Irish' poetry. An im-
portant shift in emphasis is to be seen after the war, however, in a
series of poems written during a protracted stay in Ireland over the
spring and summer of 1945. MacNeice's poetry of the war years led
him towards the parable mode, and it was in 1945, in Ireland, that
the poet wrote one of his longest and most fully realized parables,
The Dark Tower. The 'Irish' poems of the same period have a
similarly decisive status in his work as a whole. One such poem is
'Under the Mountain', with its play of perspective between what is
'Seen from above' and the view 'when you get down'. House, field,
and sea (suggesting again the co-ordinates of a childhood described
in 'Experiences with Images') are regarded from both perspectives,
and the mundane angle forces a decisive close:

> And when you get down
> The house is a maelstrom of loves and hates where you—
> Having got down—belong.

'The house' here is one of MacNeice's many similar parable proper-
ties. That the perspective of 'belonging' should focus on the harsh
and the unlovely, the human rather than the picturesque ('The field
is a failed or a worth-while crop, the source | Of back-ache if not
heartache'), is a significant switch from the tourist's eye-view which
MacNeice had made register most acutely in the 1939 sequence, 'The
Closing Album'. In this, MacNeice's perspectives were not quite
'tourist' enough to satisfy the sense of intellectual and moral decisive-
ness which the war was beginning to encourage: descriptive lines
here were spliced abruptly with bald statements of fact ('The war
came down on us here', 'What a place to talk of war'), prefiguring the
poet's disapproval of Eire's neutrality, a national application of the
uncommitted tourist's detachment to international affairs. The per-
spectives of 'Neutrality' in 1942 are centred on the heart, perhaps a
bitter joke at the expense of heart-centred Irish sentiment in exile,
but, with the war over, MacNeice returns to the particular as a focal
point. In 'Littoral', for example, there is a conflict between the

---

[16] On the vestiges of classical metre, see David Z. Crooks, 'MacNeice's "Carrick-
fergus" ', the *Explicator*, 42/4 (Summer 1984), 45–6 (an article which does, however,
rather overstate the case).

perspective of description, the poem's angle of approach, and that of interpretation, the poem's destination as 'meaning', returning to the old MacNeicean image of the sea as an area where neither particulars nor abstractions are able to impose stability:

> Indigo, mottle of purple and amber, ink,
> Damson whipped with cream, improbable colours of the sea
> And unanalysable rhythms—fingering foam
> Tracing, erasing its runes, regardless
> Of you and me
> And whether we think it escape or the straight way home.

While this is part of the post-war shift of emphasis in MacNeice's writing from 'reportage' to the underlying concerns of parable, it has relevance also to his changing orientation towards Ireland. Along with the observer's perspective on his subject, the poem offers the subject's perspective (or rather the lack of it) on the observer (compare the double take of 'Under the Mountain'). This awareness of alternative possibilities is what modifies MacNeice's approach to Ireland from one centred upon the gestures of contradiction and repudiation, to one relying instead on paradox and 'antinomies' with their admission of multiple perspectives.

In *The Poetry of W. B. Yeats*, MacNeice gives his own version of the Yeatsian 'antinomies' with regard to Ireland, in terms which have a clear relevance to his own situation: 'The Irish dialectic is best, perhaps, resolved by a paradox: Ireland, like other countries, has obvious limitations; these limitations, if rightly treated, become assets. I would suggest therefore as a final antinomy this: *It is easy to be Irish: it is difficult to be Irish.*'[17] This provides the link between the violently contradictory rhetoric of *Autumn Journal* XVI and MacNeice's post-war approach to Ireland in terms of 'paradox'. In the late 1930s, MacNeice's increasing fascination with Yeats was already forcing this development, but another touchstone was provided by the Irish figure who had been given a distinctly Yeatsian celebration in 'Eclogue from Iceland', Stephen MacKenna. For MacNeice, MacKenna occupied a significant position in the development of Ireland's image of herself, mediating between a self-destructive culture of contradiction and a culture of vital antinomies. E. R. Dodds claimed that 'MacKenna's function in Dublin was to be a missionary of Europeanism', offering a third choice to the alternatives

---

[17] *The Poetry of W. B. Yeats*, p. 51.

of having 'to become a cultural dependency of England or to exist as an isolated and therefore stagnant community on the fringe of civilization'.[18] MacNeice saw this in terms of MacKenna's Hellenism, writing in 1936 that 'MacKenna's two loves were Ireland and Greece. The former was possibly fanatical but it was tempered by the good sense of his Hellenism.'[19] Again, in 1937, the poet considered how Hellenism itself might be tempered by Irishness: 'For my own part, though my job is lecturing about the Greeks, I have two traditions behind me which encourage me to rush into very un-Greek extremes or excesses. First of all, I am an Irishman, and the Irish are notorious for not knowing where to stop, either in conversation or in action.'[20] The second reason given here by MacNeice is that of the English language itself, with 'its lack of classical shape, its controlled imbalances'. Ireland as a matter of 'extremes or excesses' is exactly what MacNeice makes the country in *Autumn Journal* xvi, but 'Hellenism' (itself given somewhat ironic treatment in that poem) was to modify the picture, just as MacKenna himself modified the Yeatsian quality of 'bitterness' into an evil rather than a good in Ireland:

There is in Ireland, in politics, in criticism, in the treatment of differences in religion, a bitterness, very striking at first sight both in talk and writing, which alone is enough to show that we are a backward people, paying by our lack of wisdom for the waste of force to which our history and our temper acting together have led us.[21]

In absorbing this, MacNeice took a deeper interest in the element of difference within both Ireland and his own relation to the country, to the point where 'limitations, if rightly treated, become assets'. After the war, paradox in the matter of Ireland became for the poet a source of strength; the development is akin to one from *odi atque amo* to the Yeatsian 'My hatred tortures me with love, my love with hate'.[22] If 'Irish' had been a useful label for publishers in the 1930s in making MacNeice an attractive commodity for the English poetry market, by the 1940s the issue went much deeper: *Holes in the Sky*

---

[18] *Journal and Letters of Stephen MacKenna*, ed. E. R. Dodds (1936), 38.
[19] MacNeice, rev. of *Journal and Letters of Stephen MacKenna*, ed. E. R. Dodds, in *Morning Post*, 4 Dec. 1936, p. 19.
[20] MacNeice, 'In Defence of Vulgarity', the *Listener*, 29 Dec. 1937, p. 1407.
[21] *Journal and Letters of Stephen MacKenna*, pp. 121–2.
[22] W. B. Yeats, 'A General Introduction for My Work', in *Essays and Introductions* (1961), 519.

(1947) confirmed the poet's status as, to use Francis Scarfe's description of 1940, 'damnably Irish'[23] in a way far removed from the advocacy of the Faber blurb to *Poems* (1935) which launched 'a genius representative of the spirit of his Northern Ireland'.

Autumn Journal XVI, like 'Valediction', looks as though it might be its author's last word on Ireland; in some senses, though, it is closer to a beginning, and represents a crucial point in the development from contradiction and denial towards paradox and guarded affirmation. Its style, that of oxymoron writ large, plays extremes off against one another ('And one read black where the other read white, his hope | The other man's damnation'); perspective throughout the section is split into two polar opposites. Both North and South are given the same treatment, with the South's post-Independence history, like the loyalist pieties of the North, being denied the immunity of their own images of themselves. The positive side of this mutual undercutting is more difficult to see; *Autumn Journal* is still a long way from claiming that 'The slums of Dublin are deplorable but they are also vital', as MacNeice wrote much later, showing how 'O'Casey's work as a consequence is one great example of oxymoron'.[24] However, 'family feeling' is still far from absent in MacNeice's poem. An image from both 'Belfast' and the last, powerful line of 'Valediction' ('your dolled-up virgins') resurfaces and is expanded here:

> The shawled woman weeping at the garish altar.
> Kathaleen ni Houlihan! Why
>   Must a country, like a ship or a car, be always female,
> Mother or sweetheart? A woman passing by,
>   We did but see her passing.
> Passing like a patch of sun on the rainy hill
>   And yet we love her for ever and hate our neighbour
> And each one in his will
>   Binds his heirs to continuance of hatred.

MacNeice's Ireland in *Autumn Journal* enacts a drama of 'family feeling', with North and South, male and female, engaged in a destructive struggle over, amongst other things, the poet's own independent voice. Attitudes themselves are a trick of the light here, and the shifting light and shade of Ireland is an important theme for

---

[23] Francis Scarfe, *Auden and After: The Liberation of Poetry 1930–1941* (1942), 62.

[24] MacNeice, rev. of *Sean O'Casey: The Man and His Work* by David Krause, in the *Observer*, 27 Nov. 1960, p. 23.

MacNeice,[25] never wholly negative in its implications. It is interesting that Kathaleen ni Houlihan should dominate the section to such a degree; although 'both a bore and a bitch', she is clearly at the heart of the drama constructed by MacNeice here, just as the female aspect is always present, above or below the surface, in his other 'Irish' poems of the 1930s. The voice that goes through the motions of independence in *Autumn Journal* XVI sums up its attitude in the most un-Irish of mediums, a Latin tag—'*odi atque amo*'—the language whose rudiments MacNeice learned at his father's knee, and which, among other things, the boy in 'Carrickfergus' leaves Ireland to learn.[26] Just as in 'Valediction' MacNeice confesses that 'I cannot deny my past to which my self is wed', so here there can be no complete denial of the female, 'Mother or sweetheart', who offers such a cruelly mixed legacy. Even Yeats's Muse-figure of Maud Gonne comes within MacNeice's range, herself broken down into familial components, 'a jumble of opposites'; division in this poem may indicate freedom from one standpoint, but, from other perspectives, it may be seen as a sign of bondage to Kathaleen ni Houlihan, the spirit of divisiveness. What forces the issue finally is an awareness of the presence of an immediate context, the rest of *Autumn Journal*, 'a world of bursting mortar', allowing the poet to question 'Your assumption that everyone cares | Who is the king of your castle' (continuing the poem's running image of the threatened castle). Just as Ireland functions within the context of the whole poem to compromise easy, abstract political perspectives, those very international issues come back to compromise the matter of Ireland.

All of this has certain important implications for MacNeice's work. Essentially, the degree of freedom won by the poetic voice in *Autumn Journal* XVI is conditioned by the appeal it makes to its own context (compare the earlier use of perspective itself as a weapon). In terms of 'belonging' to Ireland, MacNeice is relying upon displacement not just for his own independence, but in order to clarify, or

[25] See *The Poetry of W. B. Yeats*, p. 50: 'An Irish landscape is capable of pantomimic transformation scenes; one moment it will be desolate, dead, unrelieved monotone, the next it will be an indescribably shifting pattern of prismatic light.'

[26] *The Strings Are False*, p. 59: 'While I was nine my father began to teach Elizabeth and me Latin. This was a great adventure but my father's impatience upset me, he thought I was very illogical . . . "*Ducibus ducibus*" I said, and this private pattern in my mind fitted in somehow with the stripes on the tigers and knowledge was power and a wind blew down the vistas.' This is followed immediately by material relating to the wartime setting of 'Carrickfergus'.

read deeply into, the Irish condition. Displacement, in other words, has become in some ways exemplary as well as a matter of personal fact, offering the means of viewing clearly the Irish impulse towards division, 'sheep and goats, patriots and traitors'. Already, the contradictions of the surface are starting to be resolved, through the perspective of displacement, into paradox. Again, it is worth comparing an approach to the apparently contradictory from MacNeice's later career; in the radio play *They Met on Good Friday* (1959), Gormlai, the Queen of Ireland, asks: 'Who are the foreigners?', and goes on to describe her country: 'In this land of mists and cattle-raids and bickerings, this land that is pinned together with thorn trees and still keeps falling apart, this land where you take one step and you sink in a bog or you take one glance at the sky and get lost in the clouds, was it not time for new blood, for men from the north and the east?'[27] This description is antinomical, between the bog and the clouds, and reliant on both, even though the speaker regards the country with disdain; at the same time, it is clearly more than 'a jumble of opposites'. Similarly, in his 'Prologue' to the ill-fated book *The Character of Ireland*, MacNeice returned to the tricks of light as those of a prism that 'retains identity' (compare 'the trick beauty of a prism' that enters 'Valediction' at the price of 'drug-dull fatalism'):

> Inheritors of paradox and prism
> And stigmatised to the good by the Angry Dove,
> As through our soft and rain-shot air the sun
> Can alchemise our granite or boulder clay,
> So we, marooned between two continents,
> And having missed half of their revolutions
> And more than half their perquisites can still,
> Sophisticated primitives, aspire
> In spite of all their slogans and our own
> To take this accident of time and place
> And somehow, even now, to make it happy.[28]

The ways in which the Irish are 'Inheritors of paradox' for MacNeice are double-edged but vital; it is as though Ireland as a whole is seen as displaced from Europe and America, 'marooned between two continents', but the tricks of light are signs also of the positive potential

---

[27] MacNeice, *They Met on Good Friday* (1959), in *Persons from Porlock and Other Plays for Radio* (1969), 77.

[28] MacNeice, 'Prologue' (to unpubl. *The Character of Ireland*), *Time Was Away*, p. 3.

of such displacement. By this stage, paradox is regarded as a strength, and division as a resource as well as a debility.

The year 1945 was an important one in MacNeice's development towards this attitude. The poet had been unsparing in his criticism of Irish insularity as reflected in wartime neutrality; the poem 'Neutrality' is another contextualization of Ireland using inner and outer perspectives, seeing inside the 'fermenting rivers, | Intricacies of gloom and glint', of the Yeatsian West as well as MacNeice's own light-and-shade imagery, while outside both the country and the heart are surrounded by destruction. With the war over, MacNeice holidayed in the West, and the poems written during this time are themselves situated under 'the shadow and sheen of a moleskin mountain | And a litter of chronicles and bones', as well as, like 'Neutrality', accepting the full implications of the oxymoron 'bitterly soft' which Edna Longley has read as a 'sense of some logical and moral missing link'.[29] 'Last Before America' is much concerned with the sense of something missing, 'a defeated | Music that yearns and abdicates', and converts the map of the West into an image of incompleteness and desire, as 'certain long low islets snouting towards the West | Like cubs that have lost their mother'. To some extent, this image (and the poem as a whole) revises the terms of 'Neutrality' by suggesting that Ireland is not deliberately sealed off from its context, and that the nature of its relation to what lies outside makes the island itself displaced with regard to 'emigrant uncle and son'. America functions in this poem as myth:

> A land of a better because an impossible promise
> Which split these families; it was to be a journey
> Away from death—yet the travellers died the same
> As those who stayed in Ireland.

In symbolic terms, the desire for the lost mother comes from a split in the family, 'a journey | Away from death' which cannot in fact succeed. Comparing this poem with 'Carrick Revisited' (also 1945) suggests another way of approaching the problem of division: identity depends upon displacement here, and the situation of Southern Ireland may resemble that of MacNeice's North in this respect. *The Dark Tower*, written during this period, is relevant to such questions in its treatment of the individual's identity and his displacement from, or proximity to, familial tradition or duty. MacNeice referred

[29] Longley, 'The Walls Are Flowing', p. 108.

to his extended stay in Ireland, during which he wrote the play in 1945, as part of an 'allergy to England',[30] and the play does share with his poetry of the time a number of suggestive themes carried over from earlier, more explicitly 'Irish' work. Roland is sent on his quest by a powerful mother, following his brothers and father; the crucially important imperative of completing the quest of his own free will means that he cannot finally obey even his mother's decision to relent (on the point of turning back, Roland's thought is 'All right, Mother dear, I'm coming'[31]). In the end, the voice of Roland's mother, who has died giving birth to a 'child of stone', returns to urge her son, now free of everything but his own free will, to 'strike a blow for all dead mothers'.[32] In fact, this is a paradoxical freedom, which entails thwarting the mother's will in order to give freedom to one's own; yet the result accords with her first wish all the same—Roland fulfils his quest. These elements are very close to those active in MacNeice's 'Irish' writing of the time, poetry which approaches, or rather reapproaches, the country 'with a family feeling'. Independence had previously been a matter of attack for the poet, of actively thwarting the 'mother', but the perspectives of the 1945 poems clearly go beyond this stage of involvement in their acceptance and coming to terms with displacement, even perhaps preparing to strike a blow for, rather than against, 'all dead mothers'.

If a dead mother had always been linked with Ireland in MacNeice's imagination, in 1945 a more recently deceased father was also to the fore. 'The Strand' takes the Western coast as its setting, and re-approaches the poet's father in terms of the West, finding 'something in him solitary and wild'. Even so, the father's Ireland was not the same as the lost mother's; where the country names themselves are associated for MacNeice with memories of women (in the later 'Country Weekend', for example, there are 'Bustling dead women with steady hands | One from Tyrone and one from Cavan | And one my mother'), the father's provenance was rather the sea. This may be seen in a passage from *I Crossed the Minch*: 'The first time I went to the West of Ireland I drove in a saloon car with my father, and as we came over a hill, still some miles from the coast, my father, who had not been back there for many years, leaped in his seat under the constricting roof and cried like Xenophon's troops "The Sea! The

---

[30] Barbara Coulton, *Louis MacNeice in the BBC* (1980), 78, quotes MacNeice's reference to this stay in Ireland as being part of an 'allergy to England'.
[31] MacNeice, *The Dark Tower* (1967), 61.   [32] Ibid. 65.

Sea!" [33] Memories like this seem in themselves to temper Ireland
with Hellenism for MacNeice, escaping from the dark interior of the
North into the father's freedom and that of the father's culture. 'The
Strand', similarly, recalls Bishop MacNeice out of his immediate
Northern context, 'Carrying his boots and paddling like a child'. In
part, the poem is a way of returning to 'his father's house where
everything had always been the same' with the knowledge that now
'everything was different'.[34] This aspect of Ireland completes the
Northern churchman by restoring him to his Western (and, for
MacNeice, ultimately feminine) origins:

> My father. Who for all his responsibly compiled
> Account books of a devout, precise routine
> Kept something in him solitary and wild,
>
> So loved the western sea and no tree's green
> Fulfilled him like these contours of Slievemore
> Menaun and Croaghaun and the bogs between.

The names here carry the force of incantation, their own 'contours'
serving to level out the roughness of the bishop's 'devout' North.
However, MacNeice complicates this by allowing the 'mirror of wet
sand' to be obscured by the sea, and both his father's image and his
own to vanish, into the past as into the foam, with the lines 'No sign |
Remains of face or feet when visitors have gone home'. The resolution
is momentary only, and the poem ends with an acceptance of
displacement and disjunction as inescapable. Even so, this division is
itself 'the same but different' for having glimpsed the resolution of
identity in the sand's mirror. In conveying this through the medium
of 'family feeling', 'The Strand' seems to be much more successful
than the more explicit and extravagant 'Western Landscape', with its
figure of Brandan, 'a part of a not to be parted whole', set against that
of the poet, 'neither Brandan | Free of all roots nor yet a rooted
peasant'. Here too, however, identification with the Western land-
scape is followed by an awareness of the self as 'the visitor', still in
part displaced in this environment.

'Woods' (1946) also employs MacNeice's father as an important
figure, but comes from the opposite direction to the poems of 1945;
here the poet uses England to test the limits of characteristically
'Irish' ways of perception. In this sense, the poem might be seen as a

[33] MacNeice, *I Crossed the Minch* (1938), 22.
[34] *The Strings Are False*, p. 206.

defence of the kind of division implied in the idea of spiritual hyphenation, but there are other elements present, notably that of testing the limits of the English wood with its romantic associations, 'a dark | But gentle ambush', against the Irish forest with its 'neolithic night'. The romance world associated with the poet's later childhood offers a sweetheart-figure here—'a love | Also out of the picture-book'—but the family is elsewhere:

> Thus from a city when my father would frame
> Escape, he thought, as I do, of bog or rock
> But I have also this other, this English, choice
> Into what yet is foreign; whatever its name
> Each wood is the mystery and the recurring shock
> Of its dark coolness is a foreign voice.

However well 'Woods' celebrates a facet of the English landscape, the poem is emphatic on the subject of its foreignness, returning implicitly to the family as opposed to the sweetheart. At the same time, the poem offers a glimpse into landscape that is associated with the characteristic shapes of MacNeice's writing—'An ordered open air long ruled by fence and dyke'. Just as the romantic imagination of his teens was far removed from his father's 'True and Good | With their interleaving half-truths and not-quites', so the imaginative possibilities, the open and yet defined spaces of poetry, are perhaps alien privileges, 'inconsequent' from a sterner perspective. Again, poetry's independent voice exists for MacNeice partly in contrast to familial values, not now as a contradiction, negating them, but as an antinomy, imparting to them greater force.

It has been suggested here that MacNeice's attitudes to Ireland are in some senses analogous to his attitudes towards his own family and past, but this is not necessarily a reductive, overly biographical reading: for MacNeice, those 'private' areas of experience shaded into the much more 'public' areas of ideas, poetics, and (indirectly) politics. Texts and contexts here seem to mirror each other; Ireland influences MacNeice's poetry as a whole, just as the poet's writing itself influences his view of Ireland. Terms such as 'division', there-fore, must be used with some caution: it is worth asking how many poets, Irish or otherwise, have managed completely to embody 'unity' in their writing. From the 1950s onwards, MacNeice's appar-ently warmer attitude towards Ireland (which involved also more actual contact with the country) went together with a tendency to regard Ireland as embodying in microcosm those tensions and divisions which are characteristic of the modern world in general. 'Half Truth from Cape Town', for example, remembers childhood and the hatreds of Belfast that 'Waited like vultures in their gantried nest | Till Prod should tumble Papish in the river'. The divisions perceived here by MacNeice (as in India) are fundamental, but they do perhaps lose a vital degree of particularity in proving a general point. An important sequence of poems from 1954, 'A Hand of Snapshots', represents the closest point reached by MacNeice in his approach to the elements of Irish life that had always been alien to him, a tentative edging around the imaginative country of Kavanagh. At the close of 'The Left-Behind', the 'home' (which, of course, is a word that resonates through a great many MacNeice poems, notably 'The Strand') is the scene only of isolated existence: 'And the night is old and a nightbird calls me away | To what now is merely mine, and soon will be no one's home'. Yet the sequence is much concerned with the meaning of 'home', balancing various alternatives against this bleak perspective: in 'The Back-Again', a return to Ireland from the wider world is also a rediscovery—a brother who has stayed behind is now 'An oaf, but an oaf with dignity and the sense | That it is a fine day if it rains only a little'. The problem is that 'home', whether one stays or leaves, cannot be a stable place of belonging, as the ideal requires it to be; again, displacement is inevitable, and more radically troubling in its implications than 'exile' could ever be. 'The Once-in-Passing' is an attempt to catch the moment of belonging, but, like other attempts to snatch permanent values from volatile flux, it can be provisional and temporary only; once more, the pose of a 'tourist in his own country' is one which is assumed deliberately:

> Here for a month to spend but not to earn,
> How could I even imagine
> Such a life here that my plain days could earn
> The life my dreams imagine?
> For what takes root or grows that owns no root?

Like Brandan in 'Western Landscape', the voice here speaks out of an ordinary displacement: if the life that dreams imagine is to be found anywhere, it is in the ideal rather than in the actual place that is 'home'. Even within the poem, 'The permanence of what passes' is imagined, and the final clearing of vistas—'As though the window opened | And the ancient cross on the hillside meant myself'—is also an effort of the imagination, a provisional answer to the poem's unanswerable riddle. 'The Here-and-Never', too, is largely a riddling poem, structured to resemble the double perspective of 'home', but in effect repeating the warning of 'Carrick Revisited' on 'Time and place—our bridgeheads into reality | But also its concealment!':

> So now, which here should mean for ever,
> And here which now is the Now of men,
> They come and go, they live and die,
> Ruins to rock but rock to houses,
> And here means now to the opened eye
> And both mean ever, though never again.

There are no answers to this riddle either, or rather the answers are apparently contradictory. However, MacNeice clearly regards Ireland as a country where the different uses of time, place, and belonging can come into something of an antinomical relationship, and thereby may be exemplary. Ireland is both a remembered place of extreme loneliness and a scene of palpable community; more and more, it comes to represent for MacNeice the 'halfway house between sky and sea' of 'Donegal Triptych':

So now from this heathered and weathered perch I watch the grey
    waves pucker
And feel the hand of the wind on my throat again,
Once more having entered solitude once more to find communion
With other solitary beings, with the whole race of men.

Hedged around with ambitions such as these, MacNeice's Ireland resembles in its exemplary importance the Ireland constructed by Yeats, concentrating the obsessions of his whole work into one physical location.

The question of Yeats's influence upon MacNeice is inevitably relevant to understanding the nature of MacNeice's Ireland; the question also has a bearing upon the issue of Yeats's influence upon Irish poetry and culture as a whole. In 1949 Austin Clarke compared Yeats to 'an enormous oak tree which, of course, kept us in the shade, but did exclude a great number of the rays of, say, friendly sun', going on to remark that 'we always hoped that in the end we could reach the sun, but the shadow of that great oak tree is still there'.[35] This collective belatedness implicitly includes MacNeice, or

---

[35] Austin Clarke, quoted in W. R. Rodgers, 'W. B. Yeats: A Dublin Portrait' (1949), in *BBC Features*, ed. L. Gilliam (1950), 186.

at least has been taken to include him: Dillon Johnston has written that Yeats's influence 'hindered and even thwarted the developmet of his immediate successors', numbering among these not just obviously weak writers like F. R. Higgins, but also Rodgers, Hewitt, Clarke, Kavanagh, and MacNeice.[36] Johnston seems to be proposing a classic case of precursor anxiety as an inhibition in poetic development after Yeats; certainly, there are few poets so insistent on the subject of their own strength as Yeats, and few cultures as sensitive as post-Independence Ireland towards which such strength has been directed. MacNeice's relation to Yeats is the most direct of any Irish poet of his generation, but the 'anxiety of influence' here, if it is present at all, would be misleadingly described as an inhibition on development.

Yeats's importance to the poets of the 1930s has been remarked upon by Samuel Hynes, who has written on the role played by the recently-deceased poet in Auden's personal and poetic reorientations of 1939.[37] Hynes has proposed that 'the younger poets did share one crucial belief with Yeats—what we might call faith in the momentum of history'.[38] Indeed, for Day-Lewis in 1934, Yeats was 'the most admired of living writers', and 'a lesson to us in integrity, demanding from us a complete subjection to the poetry that occupies us, yet never asking of poetry more than lies within its proper jurisdiction'.[39] The 'faith in the momentum of history', and the 'lesson to us in integrity' could not be reconciled for long, and these two aspects of Yeats are to be found at loggerheads in Auden's 1939 'The Public v. the Late Mr. William Butler Yeats'. Yet Hynes implies that MacNeice's relation to Yeats developed rather differently, as an 'instinctive intimacy' owing partly to his being Irish and partly to being 'less dogmatically political than his fellow Thirties poets'.[40] Whether MacNeice was quite so far outside the 1930s circle as Hynes suggests, is open to debate, but it is true that his relation to Yeats was different in kind and intensity from that of Auden, for example, and that it went beyond its immediate 1930s political context. In fact, what MacNeice distilled from 1930s political enthusiasms was, on a theoretical level,

---

[36] Dillon Johnston, *Irish Poetry after Joyce* (Notre Dame, 1985), p. ix.

[37] Samuel Hynes, *The Auden Generation: Literature and Politics in England in the 1930s* (1976), chap. X.

[38] Samuel Hynes, 'Yeats and the Poets of the Thirties', in R. J. Porter and J. D. Brophy (eds.), *Modern Irish Literature: Essays in Honor of William York Tindall* (New York, 1971), 10.

[39] Cecil Day-Lewis, *A Hope for Poetry* (Oxford, 1934), 3.

[40] Hynes, 'Yeats and the Poets of the Thirties', p. 9.

analogous to Yeats's ideas: his 1935 assertion that 'there are no hard and fast, no private minds',[41] was part of a more general playing-up to the 'Anima Mundi' at the expense of individualism, but how far this implies the abandonment of Yeatsian 'personality' as a value is unclear. MacNeice's 'Ode' (1934) sets itself in a complex relation to 'A Prayer for My Daughter', pushing one aspect of the older poet's work through to its contemporary implications, in which 'the self as an indestructible substrate' is made obsolete by the pressure of events. In bringing the 'Anima Mundi' into contact with what are distinctively 1930s preoccupations, MacNeice revises the 'flourishing hidden tree' of Yeats's poem into the wider metaphor of 'human society as an organism'. As with other poems in which MacNeice makes reference back to Yeats, the Yeatsian procedure is employed to produce results that are almost as distant as possible from Yeats's own ideas.

Yet the refusal, in a poem like 'Ode', to admit to the stability of any 'home' offends more than Yeatsian proprieties: in terms of 1930s alignments, political certainties are undermined at the same time as bourgeois liberalism. 'Ode', like much of *Poems*, anticipates disaster rather than detecting a revolutionary impulse for renewal. That MacNeice was lacking in revolutionary *bonhomie* was noticed by Yeats himself, and was a commonplace in the 1930s reaction to his work. Yet in 1936, reviewing *Dramatis Personae*, MacNeice asserted what he saw as a central Yeatsian value above those of the conventionally 'committed' writing of the time:

Furious impartiality—a phrase which must sound like nonsense among all our party shirts—is an ideal implicit in some of Yeats's own writing. The idle woman, the defiant beggar are the incarnation of Yeats's desire to flout the go-getting world that is concerned with means towards ends. 'Come then and sing about the dung of swine.' The dung of swine is Yeats's answer to the politicians and to the politician in himself.[42]

'Furious impartiality' comes very close to what critics found in *Poems*, a book that seemed both insistently contemporary and curiously apolitical in its day. All of MacNeice's 1930s work is determinedly open to the paraphernalia of modernity, however, and dismissive of the chances of survival for the isolated individual: in

[41] MacNeice, rev. of *The Destructive Element* by Stephen Spender, in the *Listener*, 8 May 1935, suppl. p. xiv (repr. Heuser, p. 6).

[42] MacNeice, rev. of *Dramatis Personae* by W. B. Yeats, in the *Criterion*, 16/42 (Oct. 1936), 121.

this respect, it is the precise opposite of what Elizabeth Cullingford has seen as Yeats's prescription for the Irish, 'discipline of self and hatred of the age'.[43] For MacNeice, the discipline of the age, accepted in all of its manifestations as a part of poetry's legitimate subject, came in the 1930s to entail a distrust of the self as an independent unit. As with 'Ode''s reversal of 'A Prayer for My Daughter', MacNeice's uses of Yeats in the 1930s provided mirror images of his own concerns: the differences between the two poets' ideas here are of less significance than the fact of direct reversal—as MacNeice realized, writing later that the 'discrepancy between our views is not of cardinal importance'.[44]

In *The Poetry of W. B. Yeats*, MacNeice attempted to explain 'the Auden school', 'nominally affiliated to Communism' in Yeatsian terms, seeing in their work 'more the gloom of tragedy than of defeatism', with in the background 'a code of values, a belief in system, and—behind their utterances of warning—a belief in life'.[45] Elsewhere in the book, MacNeice remarks that 'Yeats's determinist cyclic philosophy seems to my generation defeatist, but I would suggest that this determination is a bluff, perhaps an unconscious one.'[46] In other words, Yeatsian myth is not final and binding, but in fact undermines its own finalities. The implied transformation of 'a belief in system', as exemplified in Yeats's philosophy, into a 'belief in life' was made explicit by MacNeice when he discussed Auden's 'Spain' in 1939, claiming that although 'At first sight this may look defeatist', 'The point is, however, that this verse, like the whole poem, recognises the necessity of conflict', stressing Auden's belief in 'free will, the power of choice' as underpinning his poem's apparently Marxist system.[47] With both Auden's and Yeats's philosophies of conflict MacNeice tends to focus on humanistic implications; whether in the seeming Communism of 'committed' writing, or in the apparent determinism of Yeats's system, MacNeice concentrates often on those points at which the values of 'free will, the power of choice' surface, while at the same time accepting the downgrading of individualism which both tendencies of thought entail. There is a basic ambivalence with regard to the status of the self here, unresolved

---

[43] Elizabeth Cullingford, *Yeats, Ireland and Fascism* (1981), 127.
[44] *The Poetry of W. B. Yeats*, p. 27.
[45] Ibid. 120–1.   [46] Ibid. 197.
[47] MacNeice, 'Tendencies in Modern Poetry' (discussion with F. R. Higgins), the *Listener*, 27 July 1939, p. 185.

in all of MacNeice's 1930s work (and crucially so in *Autumn Journal*), but it is important to remember that the poet's ambivalences were as important to his actual achievement during the decade as the 'antinomies' of conflicting assertion were to Yeats. Here, too, Mac-Neice seems to provide a mirror image of the older poet.

MacNeice's understanding of the self in poetry was always conditioned by that of the flux against which it was set, and even here Yeats might be seen as providing a kind of model. Edna Longley's schematization of the 'generation-gap between MacNeice and Yeats' as 'democracy, linguistic as well as social, *versus* aristocracy', or 'relativism *versus* absolutism',[48] like any statement involving Yeats, does not hold completely: even Yeats's absolutism was not absolute, and he was not always oblivious to what MacNeice called 'the hailstorm of data'—rather, as MacNeice saw, he refused to accept it as binding. The world which, for Yeats, Berkeley could be seen to refute, 'that only exists because it shines and sounds',[49] is not unreal for him, but only an incomplete perception of the whole. Similarly, Yeats approved of Croce's contention that philosophy is necessarily idealist, that even materialism relies upon an idea of matter. The early MacNeice had been considerably indebted to Idealism, even if sometimes negatively so, and Croce and Gentile were important formative influences upon his ideas of the self. Like Yeats, MacNeice was aware that to assert a coherent self was in some way to deny the absolute validity of the 'hailstorm of data'. In his copy of Croce's *Logic*, Yeats marked a passage which claimed that perception itself is 'commemorative and historical, because the present, in the very act by which we hold it before our spirit, becomes a past, that is to say an object of memory and history'.[50] These ideas could well be said to lie behind much of MacNeice's writing, particularly in its often heightened concentration on the present tense; even in 'The Stygian Banks':

> We have no word for bridges between our present
> Selves and our past selves or between ourselves and others
> Or between one part of our selves and another part,
> Yet we must take it as spoken, the bridge is there . . .

Memory, and poetry as the articulation of memory, are 'bridges' for MacNeice, as they were for Yeats, but both poets are intensely aware

---

[48] Longley, 'The Walls Are Flowing', p. 119.
[49] W. B. Yeats, *Explorations* (1962), 325.
[50] See Donald T. Torchiana, 'Yeats and Croce', in W. Gould (ed.), *Yeats Annual*, 4 (1986), 9.

of the extent to which such bridges are fabricated and imposed upon the flux of time. If Yeats needed an awareness of the 'hailstorm of data' in order to reject it, MacNeice for his part required the possibility of absolutes against which to register the flux and momentum of the present moment. In the post-war years, this background to MacNeice's characteristic perspectives becomes steadily more important: here again, to borrow Edna Longley's phrase, the differences between Yeats and MacNeice do indeed reveal 'greater kinship than even the polarities of reaction allow'.[51]

Issues such as these are in no sense remote from those involved in MacNeice's relation to Ireland. The principal difficulty that Ireland posed for the poet was that it both formed a fundamental level of the self and threatened to stifle other levels. MacNeice's nightmares of time are Irish nightmares, taking place in the imaginative domain of the rectory garden at Carrickfergus; any coherence of the self was achieved in the face of a disruptive chaos, an acute sense of loss located in Northern Ireland. The previous chapters have contained comparisons of poems by MacNeice and by Yeats, but clearly this kind of direct indebtedness is much less than the whole of the 'influence' involved. Yeats was the most successful creator of a poetic self among modern poets; he also used his Irish identity as an important component of that self. MacNeice, on the other hand, seems always to have been haunted by the liabilities presented by the idea of the self in the modern world. W. J. McCormack has included MacNeice (along with Beckett) in a group of Irish writers 'in whose very different *œuvres* the whole metaphysics of identity, the self and so forth, is subject to an intensely sceptical scrutiny'.[52] Certainly, MacNeice's 'Neutrality' seems in itself enough to confirm Mc-Cormack's contention that 'behind the interrogation of the idea of the self lies a broader involvement in the issue of Ireland's identity and integrity *vis à vis* Europe at war'. However, the question of the self has more than this specific application for MacNeice: the uncertainties over the status of the self, which the poet developed in England in the 1930s, made him come back to the literary influence of Yeats in the light of the divisions in both Ireland and his own relation to the country. If Yeats used Ireland to construct a dominant myth of the self, MacNeice undermined the self to complicate and

---

[51] Longley, 'The Walls Are Flowing', p. 119.
[52] W. J. McCormack, *The Battle of the Books* (Mullingar, 1986), 66.

qualify the myth of 'Ireland', just as he could see the experience of travel as a way of breaking down 'myths' of his own.

Ultimately, MacNeice's personal myths lead back to Carrickfergus, the early disappearance and death of a mother, and a lonely and frightened boy prone to nightmares. Ireland always functions to some extent as a parental presence in his work, in one way lost (the mother), and in another partially rejected (the father and his North). For MacNeice, the West is a myth to counter the denials of the North, but Ireland as a whole remains open to refutal from other areas of experience. In 1938 the poet was able to qualify his attitude to Northern Ireland in this way, writing that 'even if I had adequate grounds for hating them [the people of Belfast] I still ought to make sure that I am not hating them mainly because I identify them with the nightmares of my childhood'.[53] Of course, the separation of myth from experience could never prove so easy as this, especially in a country where history and myth go hand in hand. The mother-figure of MacNeice's 1930s poems has to be rejected, however; much later, in *The Mad Islands*, her life is up for auction:

Lot 100, ladies and gentlemen, is dying at this moment in the centre of Ireland. She is of advanced years but has been well preserved in hatred. She has not one grey hair on her head nor, even on her deathbed, one tear in her eye. She has caused in her time a great deal of trouble. . . . She has plenty of venom in her yet—prolong her life and add a chapter to the annals of Ireland.[54]

Muldoon, her son in the play, does not make a bid. The laying-to-rest of Kathaleen ni Houlihan is the necessary destruction of one myth, but at another level it must also be an acceptance of the fact of loss: MacNeice associates Ireland with a real mother as much as with a figure of Nationalist sentiment, and private loss underlies much of his public myth in this respect. The poet's answer to the imperative of unity of identity and self was to undermine both concepts, but implicitly this undermines national identity as well, for the charge of 'division' can be levelled, in MacNeice's terms, only from a perspective which is itself disunited. Again, Yeats is casting a long shadow here. As Denis Donoghue has claimed: 'The man to beat is Yeats', since 'while an argument can be refuted, and a thesis undermined, a vision

[53] MacNeice, 'Recantation' (an earlier version of 'A Personal Digression', in *Zoo* (1938)), *The Honest Ulsterman*, 73 (Sept. 1983), 8.

[54] MacNeice, *The Mad Islands* (1963), in *The Mad Islands and The Administrator* (1964), 47.

can only be answered by another one'.[55] MacNeice's Ireland, as simultaneously private and public as that of Yeats, undercuts any stable 'vision', but it is still an 'answer' to Yeats, one of the most formidable to have come from Ireland since his death, the implications of which continue to make themselves felt.

MacNeice's uses for Ireland, and Ireland's for MacNeice, are both complex topics.[56] Both involve questions of perspective, of understanding 'division' (and devisiveness), and of coming to terms with the awkward legacy of Yeats. It has been suggested here that MacNeice's Irish context inevitably involves both highly personal and drily metaphysical aspects; yet it is in modern Ireland, and in Northern Ireland in particular, that those metaphysics—of the self and the other, the unity or division of identity, freedom and the forced conditioning of the voice—have been translated into real, and immediately pressing, issues. In this sense, it looks as though Ireland may well prove to be the most important of all the contexts for MacNeice's work, one in which his texts have a significant and continuing life.

---

[55] Denis Donoghue, 'Afterword', in *Ireland's Field Day* (1985), 120.

[56] On MacNeice's influence on Irish culture North and South, see Edna Longley, 'Progressive Bookmen: Politics and Northern Protestant Writers since the 1930s', the *Irish Review*, 1 (1986), and Peter McDonald, 'Ireland's MacNeice: A *Caveat*', the *Irish Review*, 2 (1987).

Bibliography

Books by Louis MacNeice (arranged chronologically)

Blind Fireworks (1929).
Roundabout Way (pseud. Louis Malone) (1932).
Poems (1935).
The Agamemnon of Aeschylus (1936).
Out of the Picture (1937).
Letters from Iceland (with W. H. Auden) (1937).
Poems (New York, 1937).
The Earth Compels (1938).
I Crossed the Minch (1938).
Modern Poetry: A Personal Essay (Oxford, 1938; 2nd edn. 1968).
Zoo (1938).
Autumn Journal (1939).
Selected Poems (1940).
The Last Ditch (Dublin, 1940).
Poems 1925–1940 (New York, 1941).
The Poetry of W. B. Yeats (1941).
Plant and Phantom (1941).
Christopher Columbus (1944).
Springboard (1944).
The Dark Tower and Other Radio Scripts (1947; *The Dark Tower* repr. 1964).
Holes in the Sky (1948).
Collected Poems 1925–1948 (1949).
Goethe's Faust (1951).
Ten Burnt Offerings (1952).
Autumn Sequel: A Rhetorical Poem in XXVI Cantos (1954).
Visitations (1957).
Eighty-five Poems (selected by MacNeice) (1959).
Solstices (1961).
The Burning Perch (1963).
The Mad Islands and The Administrator (1964).
Astrology (1964).
Selected Poems (ed. W. H. Auden) (1964).
The Strings Are False: An Unfinished Autobiography (ed. E. R. Dodds) (1965).

Varieties of Parable (Cambridge, 1965).
Collected Poems of Louis MacNeice (ed. E. R. Dodds) (1966).
One for the Grave: A Modern Morality Play (1968).
Persons from Porlock and Other Plays for Radio (1969).
The Revenant: A Song Cycle (Dublin, 1975).
Selected Literary Criticism of Louis MacNeice, ed. A. Heuser (Oxford, 1987).
Louis MacNeice: Selected Poems, ed. M. Longley (1988).
Selected Prose of Louis MacNeice, ed. A. Heuser (Oxford, 1990).

Articles and Reviews by Louis MacNeice (arranged chronologically)

C. M. Armitage and Neil Clark's *A Bibliography of the Works of Louis MacNeice* (1973; 2nd edn. 1974) is often unreliable, and should be consulted with caution. As far as MacNeice's prose is concerned, the bibliography supplied by Alan Heuser in his *Selected Prose of Louis MacNeice* (Oxford, 1987) is comprehensive and accurate, and should be used in preference to Armitage and Clark.

Rev. of *Autobiographies* by W. B. Yeats, in *Cherwell*, 19/1 (19 Jan. 1927), 28.
Rev. of *The Enormous Room* by E. E. Cummings, in *Oxford Outlook*, 10/47 (Nov. 1928), 184–5.
'Garlon and Galahad', *Sir Galahad*, 1/1 (21 Feb. 1929), 15.
'Our God Bogus', *Sir Galahad*, 1/2 (14 May 1929), 3–4.
Rev. of *The Life of the Dead* by Laura Riding, *New Verse*, 6 (Dec. 1933), 18–20.
Reply to 'An Enquiry', *New Verse*, 11 (Oct. 1934), 2, 7.
Rev. of *The Destructive Element* by Stephen Spender, the *Listener*, 8 May 1935, supp. p. xiv.
'Poetry To-Day', in G. Grigson (ed.), *The Arts To-Day* (1935), 25–67.
'Sir Thomas Malory', in D. Verschoyle (ed.), *The English Novelists* (1936), 17–28.
Rev. of *Dramatis Personae* by W. B. Yeats, in the *Criterion*, 16/62 (Oct. 1936), 120–2.
Rev. of *Journal and Letters of Stephen MacKenna*, ed. E. R. Dodds, in *Morning Post*, 4 Dec. 1936, p. 19.
'Subject in Modern Poetry', *Essays and Studies 1936* (1937), 144–58.
Rev. of *The Note-Books and Papers of Gerard Manley Hopkins*, ed. H. House, in the *Criterion*, 16/65 (July 1937), 698–700.
'Letter to W. H. Auden', *New Verse*, 26–7 (Nov. 1937), 11–13.
'In Defence of Vulgarity', the *Listener*, 29 Dec. 1937, pp. 1407–8.

'The Play and the Audience', in R. D. Charques (ed.), *Footnotes to the Theatre* (1938), 32–43.

'A Statement', *New Verse*, 31–2 (Autumn 1938), 7.

'Today in Barcelona', the *Spectator*, 20 Jan. 1939, pp. 84–5.

'Tendencies in Modern Poetry' (discussion with F. R. Higgins), the *Listener*, 27 July 1939, pp. 185–6.

'The Poet in England Today', *The New Republic*, 25 Mar. 1940, pp. 412–13.

'Yeats's Epitaph', *The New Republic*, 24 June 1940, pp. 862–3.

'American Letter', *Horizon*, 1/7 (July 1940), pp. 462, 464.

'John Keats', in *Fifteen Poets* (Oxford, 1941), 351–4.

'Traveller's Return', *Horizon*, 3/14 (Feb. 1941), 110–17.

'Touching America', *Horizon*, 3/15 (Mar. 1941), 207–12.

'The Way We Live Now', *Penguin New Writing*, 5 (Apr. 1941), 9–14.

'The Tower that Once', *Folios of New Writing*, 3 (Spring 1941), 37–41.

'The Morning after the Blitz', *Picture Post*, 3 May 1941, pp. 9–12, 14.

'L'Écrivain brittanique et la guerre', *La France libre*, 11/62 (15 Dec. 1945), pp. 103–9.

'The Traditional Aspect of Modern English Poetry', *La Cultura nel mondo* (Rome), Dec. 1946, pp. 220–4.

'An Alphabet of Literary Prejudices', *Windmill*, 3/9 (Mar. 1948), 38–42.

'India at First Sight', in *BBC Features*, ed. L. Gilliam (1950), 60–4 (broadcast Mar. 1948).

'Psycho-Moralities and Pseudo-Moralities', *Radio Times*, 17 Sept. 1948, p. 7.

'Eliot and the Adolescent', in T. Tambimuttu and R. Marsh (eds.), *T. S. Eliot: A Symposium* (1948), 146–51.

'Experiences with Images', *Orpheus*, 2 (1949), 124–32.

'The Crash Landing', *Botteghe Oscure*, 4 (1949), 378–85.

'Poets Conditioned by Their Times', *London Calling*, 10 Feb. 1949, pp. 12, 19.

'Poetry, the Public and the Critic', *New Statesman and Nation*, 8 Oct. 1949, pp. 380–1.

'Notes on the Way', *Time and Tide*, 28 June 1952, pp. 709–10; 13 July 1952, pp. 779–80.

Rev. of *A Reading of George Herbert* by Rosamund Tuve, in *New Statesman and Nation*, 13 Sept. 1952, pp. 293–4.

'Spenser's Symbolic World', *Radio Times*, 26 Sept. 1952, p. 15.

Rev. of *Edward Lear's Indian Journal*, in *New Statesman and Nation*, 4 Apr. 1953, p. 402.

Rev. of *The English Epic and its Background* by E. M. W. Tillyard, in *New Statesman and Nation*, 19 June 1954, p. 804.

Rev. of *Poetry and the Age* by Randall Jarrell, and *Inspiration and Poetry* by C. M. Bowra, in *London Magazine*, 2/9 (Sept. 1955), 71–4.

Rev. of *Poetry Now*, ed. G. S. Fraser, and *Mavericks*, ed. H. Sergeant, in *London Magazine*, 4/4 (Apr. 1957), 52–5.

Note on *Visitations*, in *Poetry Book Society Bulletin*, 14 (May 1957), [1].

Rev. of *Over the Bridge* by Sam Thompson, in the *Observer*, 31 Jan. 1960, p. 23.

Rev. of *Sean O'Casey: The Man and His Work* by David Krause, in the *Observer*, 27 Mar. 1960, p. 23.

Rev. of *Poems* by George Seferis, trans. R. Warner, in *New Statesman*, 17 Dec. 1960, pp. 978–9.

'When I Was Twenty-One', in J. Hadfield (ed.), *The Saturday Book 21* (1961), 230–9.

Note on *Solstices*, in *Poetry Book Society Bulletin*, 28 (Feb. 1961), [2].

'Under the Sugar-Loaf', *New Statesman*, 29 June 1962, pp. 948–9.

Rev. of *The Poetry of Robert Frost* by Reuben Brower, in *New Statesman*, 12 July 1963, p. 46.

Note on *The Burning Perch*, in *Poetry Book Society Bulletin*, 38 (Sept. 1963), [1].

'Childhood Memories', the *Listener*, 12 Dec. 1963, p. 990.

Books and articles containing material on Louis MacNeice

AIKEN, CONRAD, 'MacNeice, Louis' (1941), in *A Reviewer's ABC* (New York, 1958).

ALLEN, WALTER, Introduction to 2nd edn. of *Modern Poetry* (Oxford, 1968).

ALVAREZ, A., rev. of *Autumn Sequel*, in *New Statesman and Nation*, 11 Dec. 1944.

ARMITAGE, C. M., 'MacNeice's Prose Fiction', *The Honest Ulsterman*, 73 (Sept. 1983).

BERGONZI, BERNARD, *Reading the Thirties: Texts and Contexts* (1978).

BROWN, TERENCE, *Louis MacNeice: Sceptical Vision* (Dublin, 1975).

—— 'Louis MacNeice's Ireland', in T. Brown and N. Grene (eds.), *Tradition and Influence in Anglo-Irish Poetry* (1989).

—— and REID, ALEC (eds.), *Time Was Away: The World of Louis MacNeice* (Dublin, 1974).

CHAPMAN, F., rev. of *Poems*, in *Scrutiny*, 4/3 (Dec. 1935).

CONNOLLY, CYRIL, 'Louis MacNeice', in *Previous Convictions* (1963).

COULTON, BARBARA, *Louis MacNeice in the BBC* (1980).

CUNNINGHAM, VALENTINE, *British Writers of the Thirties* (Oxford, 1988).

DAICHES, DAVID, rev. of *The Last Ditch*, in *Poetry* (Chicago), 57/2 (Nov. 1940).

DAVIN, DAN, 'Louis MacNeice', in *Closing Times* (1975).

DAY-LEWIS, CECIL, *A Hope for Poetry* (Oxford, 1934; 2nd edn. with 'Postscript', 1936).

DODDS, E. R., *Missing Persons: An Autobiography* (Oxford, 1977).

GARDINER, MARGARET, 'Louis MacNeice Remembered', *Quarto*, May 1980.

GENET, JACQUELINE (ed.), *Studies on Louis MacNeice* (Caen, 1988) (includes essays by Hedli MacNeice, Terence Brown, Peter McDonald, Edna Longley, Derek Mahon, and Adolphe Haberer).

GRIGSON, GEOFFREY, 'Louis MacNeice', in *Recollections: Mainly of Writers and Artists* (1984).

HABERER, ADOLPHE, *Louis MacNeice 1907–1963: L'Homme et la poésie* (Bordeaux, 1986).

—— 'Louis MacNeice: Poète des années trente, cinquante ans après', *Études Anglaises*, 61/1 (1988).

HEINEMANN, MARGOT, 'Louis MacNeice, John Cornford and Clive Branson: Three Left-Wing Poets', in J. Clark, M. Heinemann *et al.*, *Culture and Crisis in Britain in the Thirties* (1979).

HEPPENSTALL, RAYNER, rev. of *Poems*, in *New English Weekly*, 3 Oct. 1935.

HEWISON, ROBERT, *Under Siege: Literary Life in London 1939–1945* (1977).

HOLME, CHRISTOPHER, 'The Radio Drama of Louis MacNeice', in J. Drakakis (ed.), *British Radio Drama* (Cambridge, 1981).

HOUGH, GRAHAM, 'MacNeice and Auden', *Critical Quarterly*, 9/1 (Spring 1967).

HYNES, SAMUEL, 'Yeats and the Poets of the Thirties', in R. J. Porter and J. D. Brophy (eds.), *Modern Irish Literature: Essays in Honor of William York Tindall* (New York, 1971).

—— 'Auden and MacNeice', *Contemporary Literature*, 14/3 (Summer 1973).

—— *The Auden Generation: Literature and Politics in England in the 1930s* (1976).

—— 'Like the Trees on Primrose Hill', *London Review of Books*, 2 Mar. 1989.

JOHNSTON, DILLON, *Irish Poetry after Joyce* (Dublin and Notre Dame, 1985).

KENNELLY, BRENDAN, 'Louis MacNeice: An Irish Outsider', in M. Seskine (ed.), *Irish Writers and Society at Large* (Gerrards Cross, 1985).

KERMODE, FRANK, *History and Value: The Clarendon Lectures and the Northcliffe Lectures 1987* (Oxford, 1988).

KIRKHAM, MICHAEL, 'Louis MacNeice's Poetry of Ambivalence', *University of Toronto Quarterly*, 56/4 (Summer 1987).

LONGLEY, EDNA, 'Louis MacNeice: "The Walls are Flowing" ', in G. Dawe and E. Longley (eds.), *Across a Roaring Hill: The Protestant Imagination in Modern Ireland* (Belfast, 1985).

—— 'Louis MacNeice: *Autumn Journal*', and 'Varieties of Parable: Louis MacNeice and Paul Muldoon', in *Poetry in the Wars* (Newcastle upon Tyne, 1986).

—— 'Protestant Bookmen: Politics and Northern Protestant Writers since the 1930s', the *Irish Review*, 1 (Cork, 1986).

—— 'MacNeice and After', *Poetry Review*, 78/2 (Summer 1988).

—— *Louis MacNeice: A Study* (1988).

LONGLEY, MICHAEL, 'A Misrepresented Poet', the *Dublin Magazine*, 6/1 (Spring 1967).

—— 'The Neolithic Night: A Note on the Irishness of Louis MacNeice', in D. Dunn (ed.), *Two Decades of Irish Writing: A Critical Survey* (Manchester, 1975).

—— Introduction to *Louis MacNeice: Selected Poems* (1988).

McDONALD, PETER, 'Ireland's MacNeice: A *Caveat*', the *Irish Review*, 2 (1987).

McKINNON, WILLIAM T., *Apollo's Blended Dream: A Study of the Poetry of Louis MacNeice* (1971).

—— 'The Rector's Son', *The Honest Ulsterman*, 73 (Sept. 1983).

MARSACK, ROBYN, *The Cave of Making: The Poetry of Louis MacNeice* (Oxford, 1982).

MATTHIESSEN, F. O., 'Yeats: The Crooked Road', and 'Louis MacNeice', in J. Rackcliffe (ed.), *The Responsibilities of the Critic: Essays and Reviews* (New York, 1952).

MAXWELL, D. E. S., *Poets of the Thirties* (1969).

MENDELSON, EDWARD, *Early Auden* (1981).

MOORE, D. B., *The Poetry of Louis MacNeice* (Leicester, 1972).

MURPHY, DANIEL, *Imagination and Religion in Anglo-Irish Literature* (Blackrock, 1987).

PAULIN, TOM, 'Letters from Iceland: Going North', *Renaissance and Modern Studies*, 20 (1976).

—— 'The Man from No Part: Louis MacNeice', and 'In the Salt Mines', in *Ireland and the English Crisis* (Newcastle upon Tyne, 1984).

POWELL, DILYS, rev. of *Poems*, in the *London Mercury*, 32/192 (Oct. 1935).

REBETSKY, WOLFGANG, *Die Antike in der Dichtung von Louis MacNeice* (European University Studies Series 14, vol. 90) (Frankfurt, 1981).

ROBERTS, MICHAEL, 'Aspects of English Poetry: 1932–1937', *Poetry* (Chicago), 49/4 (Jan. 1937).

ROCHE, TONY, 'A Reading of *Autumn Journal*: The Question of Louis MacNeice's Irishness', *Text and Context*, 3 (1988).

RODGER, IAN, *Radio Drama* (1982).

SCARFE, FRANCIS, *Auden and After: The Liberation of Poetry 1930–1941* (1942).

SCHWARTZ, DELMORE, 'Adroitly Naive', *Poetry* (Chicago), 47/2 (May 1936).

SIDNELL, MICHAEL J., *Dances of Death: The Group Theatre of London in the Thirties* (1984).

SOUTHWORTH, JAMES G., 'Louis MacNeice', in *Sowing the Spring: Studies in British Poets from Hopkins to MacNeice* (Oxford, 1940).

SPENDER, STEPHEN, *The Thirties and After: Poetry, Politics, People 1933–1975* (1978).

STODDARD, EVE WALSH, 'The Poetics of Parable in the Later Poems of Louis MacNeice', *Concerning Poetry*, 18/1 (1985).

SYMONS, JULIAN, 'The Artist as Everyman', *Poetry* (Chicago) 56/2 (May 1940).

——— *The Thirties: A Dream Revolved* (1960).

THWAITE, ANTHONY, 'Memories of Rothwell House', *Poetry Review*, 78/2 (Summer 1988).

TOLLEY, A. T., *The Poetry of the Thirties* (1975).

WHITEHEAD, JOHN, 'MacNeice's *Autumn Journal*', *Stand Magazine*, 20/1 (Winter 1987–8).

WHITEHEAD, KATE, *The Third Programme: A Literary History* (Oxford, 1989).

Index